DARNELL-JAMAL LISBY

art direction
LUCA STOPPINI

design
LucaStoppiniStudio

with contributions by
Dr. MATTEO AUGELLO
ALESSANDRA AREZZI BOZA
MASSIMILIANO CAPELLA
LUKE MEAGHER
STEFANIA RICCI

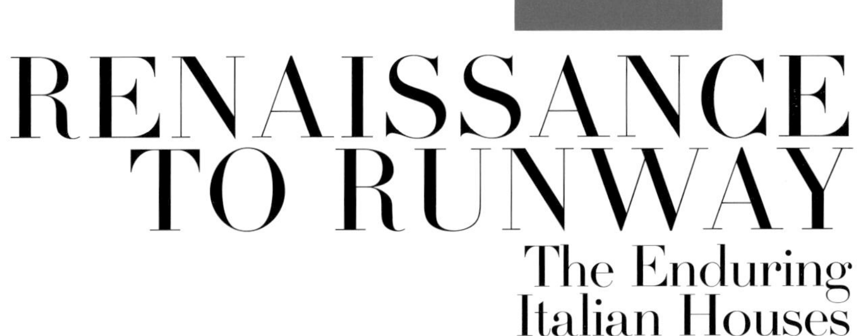

RENAISSANCE TO RUNWAY
The Enduring Italian Houses

THE CLEVELAND MUSEUM OF ART
distributed by Yale University Press, New Haven and London

This publication is made possible in part by the Andrew W. Mellon Foundation.

Published on the occasion of the exhibition *Renaissance to Runway: The Enduring Italian Houses*, on view at the Cleveland Museum of Art from November 9, 2025, to February 1, 2026.

All photos by Luca Stoppini, cover, pages 91, 94–95, 99, 102–4, 107–9, 111–13, 116–17, 120–21, 124–25, 128–29, 130–31, 134, 137, 139–40, 145, 149–152, 155–56, 159–60, 162–63, 167–68, 173, 176–77, 179. © 2025 LucaStoppiniStudio

Set design by Abet Laminati

Images of the works of art in the exhibition were provided by the lenders, unless otherwise noted.

Objects in the collection of the Cleveland Museum of Art were photographed by museum photographers Howard Agriesti, Nathan Ian Anderson, David Brichford, and Gary Kirchenbauer. James Kohler prepared the digital files. The museum holds copyright to its images. When known, other copyright holders and photographers are acknowledged in the credits.

Library of Congress Control Number: 2025946146

Authorized Representative in the EU: Easy Access System Europe, Mustamäe tee 50, 10621 Tallinn, Estonia, gpsr.requests@easproject.com

ISBN: 978-0-300-28428-7

NOTES TO THE READER
All measurements are in centimeters; height precedes width precedes depth.

Tom Barnard, Director of Publications
Emily Mears, Director of Exhibitions
Rachel Beamer, Senior Publications Project Manager

Edited by Jane Friedman
Proofread by Nick Geller
Color management by Maurizio Brivio
Printed in Italy by Conti Tipocolor S.p.A.

The Cleveland Museum of Art
11150 East Boulevard
Cleveland, OH 44106-1797
www.clevelandart.org

Distributed by
Yale University Press
302 Temple Street
P.O. Box 209040
New Haven, CT 06520-9040
www.yalebooks.com/art

This exhibition is presented by the John P. Murphy Foundation.

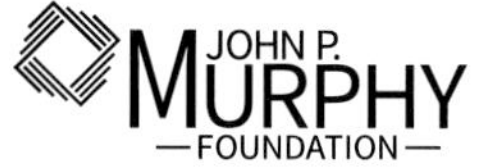

Major support is provided by Courtney and Michael Novak. Generous support is provided by Sandra and the late Richey Smith and the Carol Yellig Family Fund. Additional support is provided by Dr. Russell A. Trusso.

All exhibitions at the Cleveland Museum of Art are underwritten by the CMA Fund for Exhibitions. Principal annual support is provided by Michael Frank and the late Pat Snyder, the Kelvin and Eleanor Smith Foundation, the John and Jeanette Walton Exhibition Fund, and Margaret and Loyal Wilson. Major annual support is provided by the late Dick Blum and Harriet Warm and the Frankino-Dodero Family Fund for Exhibitions Endowment. Generous annual support is provided by two anonymous donors, Gini and Randy Barbato, Cynthia and Dale Brogan, Dr. Ben and Julia Brouhard, Brenda and Marshall Brown, Gail and Bill Calfee, the Leigh H. Carter family, Dr. William A. Chilcote Jr. and Dr. Barbara S. Kaplan, Joseph and Susan Corsaro, Ron and Cheryl Davis, Richard and Dian Disantis, the Jeffery Wallace Ellis Trust in memory of Lloyd H. Ellis Jr., Leigh and Andy Fabens, Florence Kahane Goodman, Martha H. and Steven M. Hale, Janice Hammond and Edward Hemmelgarn, Linda Harper, Robin Heiser, the late Marta and the late Donald M. Jack Jr., the estate of Walter and Jean Kalberer, Mrs. Nancy M. Lavelle, Eva and Rudolf Linnebach, William S. Lipscomb, Bill and Joyce Litzler, Lu Anne and the late Carl Morrison, Jeffrey Mostade and Eric Nilson and Varun Shetty, Sarah Nash, Courtney and Michael Novak, Tim O'Brien and Breck Platner, Dr. Nicholas and Anne Ogan, William J. and Katherine T. O'Neill, Henry Ott-Hansen, the Pickering Foundation, Christine Fae Powell, Peter and Julie Raskind, Michael and Cindy Resch, Marguerite and James Rigby, William Roj and Mary Lynn Durham, in memory of Dee Schafer, Betty T. and David M. Schneider, Elizabeth and Tim Sheeler, Saundra K. Stemen, Paula and Eugene Stevens, the Womens Council of the Cleveland Museum of Art, and Claudia Woods and David Osage.

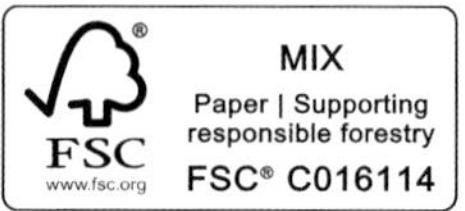

TABLE OF CONTENTS

DIRECTOR'S FOREWORD

Renaissance to Runway: The Enduring Italian Houses is the largest, most ambitious fashion exhibition ever held at the Cleveland Museum of Art (CMA). Featuring approximately 120 fashions and accessories from many of the leading Italian houses, this exhibition showcases the ways in which contemporary expressions are closely intertwined with the historical past. In particular, *Renaissance to Runway* examines Italian fashion's engagement with the fine and decorative arts and the wider cultural milieu of the Italian Renaissance and the early modern era, an engagement that has expanded the purview of Italian design and broader global fashion developments.

In the wake of the country's unification in 1861, the Italian fashion industry began to remobilize in the early 1900s. Around this time, design luminaries such as Fortuny and Maria Monaci Gallenga drew on aspects of early modern Italian culture as a means to establish an identity for Italian fashion. This process continued throughout the twentieth century and up to the present, as manifest in the work of the Italian designers and "enduring" fashion houses featured in this exhibition and catalogue. *Renaissance to Runway* investigates such topics as early modern material culture, textiles, the ways in which dress history may be reconstructed through Renaissance paintings, and the incorporation of Catholic imagery into design experimentation. Ultimately, this project highlights how contemporary fashion may be viewed through the lens of early modern history.

Renaissance to Runway provides a unique opportunity to revisit the CMA's encyclopedic holdings in conjunction with the narratives and themes explored in the exhibition. This publication builds on the exhibition's premises, addressing critical aspects of Renaissance textiles, sociohistorical influences on Italian fashion, the framing of contemporary fashion's references to the Renaissance and early modern era, Italian fashion curation, and the role of fashion archives in celebrating and perpetuating Italian fashion.

For conceiving and bringing this major exhibition to fruition, I thank our inaugural fashion curator, Darnell-Jamal Lisby, and laud his commitment to developing the CMA's future endeavors in fashion education. I extend my gratitude to Alessandra Arezzi Boza for her consultation over the course of the project's realization and for her contribution to this publication. I am also grateful to Luca Stoppini for serving as art director of this catalogue and rounding out its conclusion with a majestic series of photographic highlights of fashion presented in the show. I thank Francesco Carrozzini and Henry Hargreaves for their development of the exhibition's dynamic digital installation and am very appreciative to all the fashion houses and institutional lenders, from New York City to Paris and throughout the Italian peninsula, for allowing us to highlight stunning designs and other related objects from their respective archives and collections. Above all, I thank all those who financially supported and promoted this project, as well as our wonderful, dedicated CMA staff, particularly Eric and Jane Nord Chief Conservator Sarah Scaturro, who worked alongside Darnell-Jamal Lisby to bring *Renaissance to Runway* to life.

William M. Griswold
Sarah S. and Alexander M. Cutler Director
The Cleveland Museum of Art

ACKNOWLEDGMENTS

Renaissance to Runway: The Enduring Italian Houses is an undertaking I could not have realized without the incredible support of many individuals and organizations. I dedicate this publication to my mother, Sheila Bayne, who has always been a guiding light.

I want to thank the Heavenly Father for allowing me this opportunity, giving me the strength to embark on this endeavor, and placing outstanding people around me to help bring it to fruition. Additionally, I thank William Griswold, director of the Cleveland Museum of Art (CMA), and Andria Derstine, deputy director and chief curator, for supporting me throughout the evolution of this project. I also want to extend my gratitude to the museum's Board of Trustees and community of supporters. Without the kindness of individuals like Virginia "Gini" Nord Barbato, Ellen and Bruce Mavec, Michael and Courtney Novak, Sandra Smith, Harriet Warm, and many others in this community, *Renaissance to Runway* would not have been possible.

I am grateful for the deeply rewarding collaboration of the exhibition's consultant, Alessandra Arezzi Boza, who played a major role in helping us assemble objects from so many fashion houses, and who also contributed an illuminating essay to this catalogue. I am very grateful to Luca Stoppini for his art direction on the catalogue and for providing his priceless mentorship. We would like to thank Abet Laminati for their valuable collaboration in creating the sets for Luca Stoppini's photos. I also want to thank all the Elenas of the Interlude Project—Elena Ivaldi, Elena Mereu, and Elena Cimarosti—for supporting me throughout the development of this book. I thank the contributors to the catalogue for graciously lending their voices to the CMA's first-ever fashion publication. In addition to Alessandra's contribution, I am honored that this publication includes insightful essays by Stefania Ricci, director of the Museo Ferragamo, and Massimiliano Capella, director of the House Museum of the Paolo and Carolina Zani Foundation for Art and Culture; I am also very thankful to my dear friend of many years, Luke Meagher, and my new friend, Dr. Matteo Augello, for participating in rich discussions, featured herein. Within the exhibition, I am deeply gratified that my hope for a digital installation was realized thanks to the partnership with Francesco Carrozzini, Henry Hargreaves, and Happy Place, Inc.

Without the participation and generosity of numerous fashion houses, research centers, and institutions, *Renaissance to Runway* would have remained a thought on paper. I would like to thank Antonio Masciariello and his team at Versace, including Eugenia Ioppolo and Cristina Bergonzi. At the house of Giorgio Armani, I owe my thanks to Michi Prendin, Cecilia Dessalles, and Nicole Rubano. At Ferragamo, I give thanks to Stefania Ricci, Paola Gusella, and Tommaso Pieri, not only for lending their beautiful treasures but also, as mentioned above, for Stefania's contribution to this catalogue. I thank Camille Miceli, another remarkable collaborator, alongside her Pucci communications associates—Norman Lemary, Nicola Quadri, and Margaux Balland. The collaboration with Buccellati would not have been possible without Gabriella Lo Iacono, Giorgio Gazzaniga Spairani, and Karlee Crowley. At Bvlgari, I am grateful to have worked with Gislain Aucremanne and Monica Brannetti. In addition to Antonio Marras, I appreciate Patrizia and Efisio Rocco Marras for their support and enthusiasm. Guided by Marilena Antonini, we were able to feature Blumarine's ethereal designs. To illuminate Giambattista Valli's prowess, I am grateful for his willingness to join the project and the collaboration with his team, led by Alejandra Güell Domínguez. I also extend my thanks to Alessandro Michele and the Valentino Heritage team, led by Violante Valdettaro. At Diesel, I am grateful for the collaboration of Alice

Lavetti, Liam Evans, Elena Piccini, and Giulia Sebastiano. At Moncler, the diligence of Anna Zampiga, Olga Scivoletto, and Laura Marra added immeasurably to this exhibition and its catalogue. I thank Diana Papili, Gabriele Giorgini, and Irene Buchetti at Gucci for their willingness to participate in this project. I am grateful for the collegiality of the Alberta Ferretti team, especially Antonella Lamanuzzi, Alessia Imbriani, and Brigitta Sabbioneda. ETRO representatives Elena Cappelletti and Marco Cacchione were a joy to work with. I extend my gratitude to the gracious Max Mara team—Federica Fornaciari, Giulia Francesca De Lisi, and Moncia Sangermano. With equal gratitude, I am privileged to have partnered with Luca Missoni and Sara Crosta at the Missoni Archives; Luca's perspectives played a key role in shaping the exhibition's narratives. I am appreciative of Andrea Caravita's assistance and Moschino's participation. I am also grateful to Silvia Bertocchi of the Sozzani Foundation for her liaising. I am indebted to Enrico Minio Capucci and Paolo Alvise Minio at the Roberto Capucci Foundation, as well as the dynamic Gianfranco Ferré Research Center team—Paola Bertola, Federica Vacca, Emanuela Di Stefano, and Ilaria Trame.

I want to recognize the institutions that were so gracious in allowing us to borrow from their storied collections, including the Palazzo Pitti's Museum of Costume and Fashion, the Uffizi Gallery, the Rossimoda Museum of the Shoe, the Metropolitan Museum of Art's Costume Institute, the Museum at FIT (Fashion Institute of Technology), and the Museum of the City of New York.

Everything that happens at the CMA is made possible by a mighty cohort that is able to shift and pivot at a moment's notice, accommodating the twists and turns that arise in the course of developing a fashion exhibition. The leadership and diligence of Emily Mears and Sarah Scaturro, both of whom I greatly admire, have been crucial to the planning and realization of *Renaissance to Runway*. Even though Tae Smith is not a CMA employee, she is CMA family, and I am indebted to her for her expert mannequin dressing for the exhibition. I am also appreciative of Emily, Sarah, and Tae for uplifting me through the ebbs and flows of making this exhibition a reality. I am grateful to Aleksia Taci for being a phenomenal research assistant during her tenure as intern. I am also thankful to Laura Ziewitz and Rachel Arzuaga for their remarkable organizational skills. I appreciate Alyssa Arend and Jim Engelmann for their creativity in the exhibition's design, Mary Thomas for the exhibition's witty graphics, Aumaine Smith for her editorial precision, and Stephanie Foster for weaving her interpretive skills into the tapestry of this undertaking. I also want to give my thanks to my collections colleagues, including Heather Lemonedes Brown, Mark Cole, Beth Edelstein, Beverly Essinger, Carla Fontecchio, Matthew Gengler, Kerry Gnandt, Robin Hanson, Heather Hodges, Alex Kavalec, Robin Koch, Cory Korkow, Emily Liebert, Gerhard Lutz, Julianna Ly, Marsha Morrow, Alexander Noelle, Beth Owens, Emily Peters, David Piurek, Britany Salsbury, Colleen Snyder, Moyna Stanton, Rebecca Tousley, Deirdre Vodanoff, Ada de Wit, and Dean Yoder. I thank Tom Barnard, Rachel Beamer, Jane Friedman, and Nick Geller, whose professionalism helped bring this publication to life. Last, and certainly not least, I thank the digital team including Jane Alexander, Jeff Judge, and Tessa Shlonsky for executing the audio and video components of the exhibition. To all my colleagues, I truly appreciate you.

Darnell-Jamal Lisby
Associate Curator of Fashion
The Cleveland Museum of Art

SPREZZATURA FOR LIFE

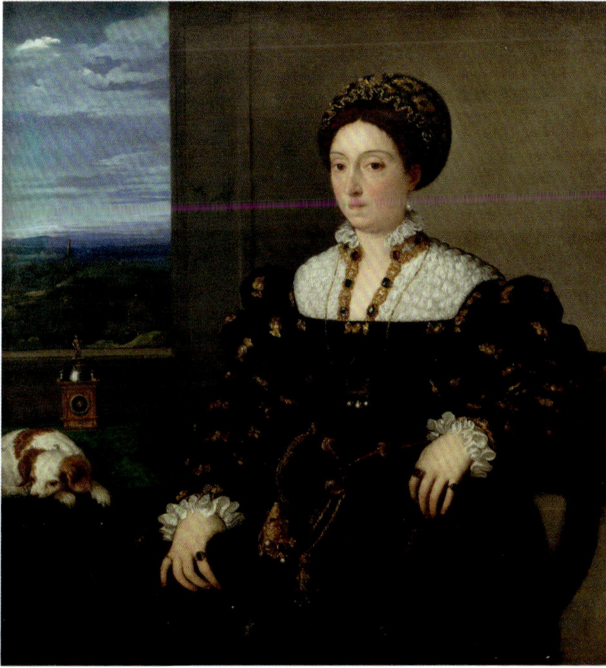

fig. 1 *Portrait of Eleonora Gonzaga*, c. 1537. Titian (Tiziano Vecellio; Italian, 1488/90–1576). Oil on canvas; 114 x 103 cm. Le Gallerie degli Uffizi, 1890 n. 919. Photo: © Gabinetto Fotografico delle Gallerie degli Uffizi

In *The Book of the Courtier*, Baldassare Castiglione (1478–1529), Count of Casatico, sets forth his thoughts on refinement, describing the facets of elegance one should exude in order to be seen as embodying the highest level of taste and sophistication.[1] Published in 1528, the book is set in the palace of his political patron, Guidobaldo da Montefeltro (1472–1508), the Duke of Urbino. The text takes the form of several fictional conversations on sophistication between fictive courtiers with topics that range from one's inner attitude to one's outward appearance and mannerisms. In his status as a count, which he assumed around 1499, Castiglione's ambassadorial duties were closely intertwined with two mighty clans: the Milanese Sforza family, led by Duke Ludovico Sforza (1452–1508), and the Mantua-based Gonzaga, headed by Marquis Francesco II Gonzaga (1466–1519). As such, Castiglione would have had direct interaction with Ludovico and Francesco and their respective wives, Beatrice and Isabella d'Este (1475–1497; 1474–1539) — High Renaissance queens of fashion. When Castiglione relocated to Urbino in 1504 to serve in Montefeltro's court, this was by no means a downgrade, as the Urbino court was among Italy's finest. There, Castiglione would have been in close contact with Elisabetta Gonzaga (1471–1526), Duchess of Urbino, the sister of his first patron, Francesco II, and the marquis's daughter, Eleonora Gonzaga (1598–1655), who would become the Duchess of Urbino directly after her aunt (**fig. 1**). As a firsthand observer of the decadence of the Italian Renaissance, who better to write a book on courtier etiquette?

Defining *Sprezzatura*

Castiglione's characters in the book's first conversation include the cheeky Count Ludovico da Canossa, who opines:

> But having before now often considered whence this grace springs, laying aside those men who have it by nature, I find one universal rule concerning it, which seems to me worth more in this matter than any other in all things human that are done or said: and that is to avoid affectation to the uttermost and as it were a very sharp and dangerous rock; and, to use possibly a new word, to practise in everything a certain nonchalance that shall conceal design and show that what is done and said is done without effort and almost without thought.[2]

The "nonchalance" of which Canossa speaks is called *sprezzatura*, a term Castiglione employs to encapsulate the attitude and expressions that must be embodied to emanate inner and outer gentility.[3] Throughout his text, Castiglione frames sprezzatura as manifesting personal qualities such that one rises above the demeanor of common folk. Central to sprezzatura is ensuring that one conceals flaws while effortlessly conveying a dignified appearance and etiquette throughout one's daily activities, from dressing, dancing, and walking to exercise. Sprezzatura is underpinned by grace—a heightened sense of refinement that flows through an individual and guides their thoughts and actions. For Castiglione, possessing sprezzatura leads to the embodiment of an ideal of perfection that others would envy and seek to emulate. Throughout his text, sprezzatura is posited as an intentional and strategic, artful self-expression that emits effortlessness: a greatly desired quality despite the glaring implications of balancing truth and falsity.[4]

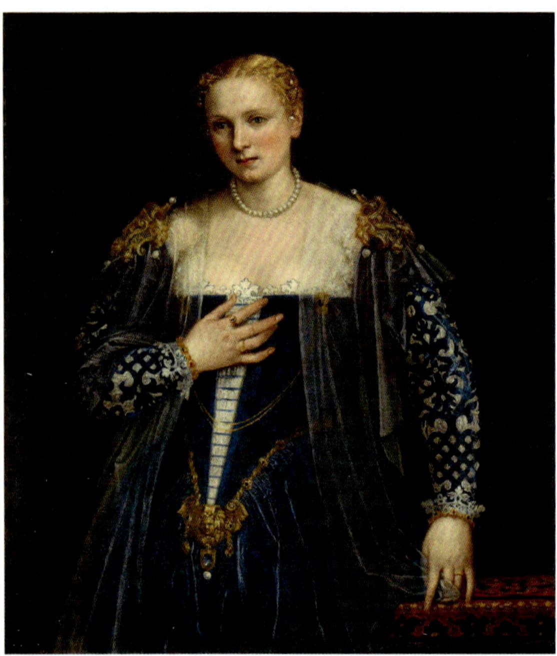

fig. 2   *Portrait of a Venetian Woman—La Belle Nani*, 1560. Paolo Veronese (Italian, 1528–1588). Oil on canvas; 119 x 103 cm. Musée du Louvre, Paris, RF 2111. Photo: © RMN-Grand Palais / Michel Urtado / Art Resource, NY

Although he allows that it can be acquired through discipline, Castiglione believed that such elegance and temperament were best evoked inherently.[5] He implies that true sprezzatura derives from the aristocracy, from which it makes its way to the lower echelons. This belief seems to anticipate the trickle-down theory of fashion advanced by sociologists such as Georg Simmel (1858–1918) and Thorstein Veblen (1857–1929) that claims that fashion begins with the elite and the adjacent creative cohort, then percolates down to the lower classes and their creative cohort.[6] In mainstream media, a hilarious elaboration of the trickle-down theory is seen in the famous "Cerulean Blue" scene in *The Devil Wears Prada* (2006), in which Meryl Streep's character, Miranda Priestly, wittily instructs Anne Hathaway's Andy Sachs on the trajectory of fashion: It originates in the office of the fashion editor, then makes its way to the runway, ultimately landing in the "clearance bin"—at which point such fashion is out of style.[7]

In Castiglione's formulation, there is an underlying element of manipulation in sprezzatura, whereby those who possess this quality become so attractive that they can use it to wield influence over other people.[8] This aspect is addressed in the second conversation in *The Book of the Courtier*, in which Cardinal Messer Bernardo recounts an anecdote that suggests that women abundant in sprezzatura can deceive their husbands, prompting them to commit unspeakable acts.[9] In line with the text's arguably sexist undertones, Castiglione distinguishes between feminine and masculine sprezzatura. He ascribes to women the primary responsibility of modulating their visual beauty, ensuring not to cross the line into depravity and what was perceived as unbecoming at the time.[10] For women, he writes, self-fashioning, combined with proper attire and accessories and mastery of the skills of hiding imperfections and emanating sensuality, was the true sign of sprezzatura (**fig. 2**).[11] Yet, refinement for women also involved wearing clothing styled in a way that subtly revealed parts of the body, leaving enough concealed to arouse men's imaginations (libidos).[12] Male sprezzatura, by contrast, is connected to athleticism and the demonstration of military prowess, although intellectualism plays a role as well. Castiglione writes that strategically wearing minimal clothing during moments of intense activity is an aspect of masculine sprezzatura (**fig. 3**).[13]

Along with the trickle-down theory, Castiglione's discussion seems to anticipate another later fashion concept: dandyism. The term "dandy" first appeared nearly three hundred years ago, receiving its most famous elaboration in the writings of Charles Baudelaire (1821–1867). In 1928, a writer in *The Sewanee Review* summarized Baudelaire's theory of dandyism thus: "he [a dandy] must determine his every action and thought in life by the nature of their reaction on his aesthetic and intellectual being."[14] Castiglione was keen on framing the social graces men should exhibit but noted that males should also be keyed in to the latest fashions. It is important, he continued, that young men reject the styles of older generations—who, for example, scoffed at young men donning newer styles such as skirted jerkins and fur-lined coats.[15]

Perhaps unsurprisingly, Castiglione was not only an acute observer of style but was also obsessed with his own appearance. Around 1504, when he was in the midst of relocating from the Mantua court to the Urbino court, he wrote to the Duke of Urbino asking that the latter send a master tailor named Antonio to create a new robe, presumably some sort of outerwear, before he was to embark on a diplomatic mission to Rome.[16] The letter implies that the tailor was in the duke's employ, possibly even a court tailor. Dismayed at the duke's failure to respond to his letter, Castiglione penned a follow-up missive of distress, warning that if the tailor did not arrive in a timely manner, he would "have to wear [his] old cloak with fur, which is worn out."[17] As he rhetorically asked: "Do you think this is a decorous dress to be worn in the company of so many gentlemen?"[18]

An early modern fashionista, Castiglione was not alone in his obsession with fashion and his appearance. During the early modern period, specifically between 1400 and 1630, fashion was in a nearly constant state of flux. From tight outer sleeves to barrel sleeves, draped mantles to tailored jackets, kirtle styles to separate corsets and far-thingales, and flats to high-heeled shoes, fashion exploded in Italy as well as throughout Europe as a whole. Early modern Italy encompassed an assortment of independent states, each with its own associated style signaling regional identity. For instance, during the High Renaissance, Florentines were relatively sober in their attire, whereas the Milanese and Venetians embraced more colorful and flamboyant styles. In another example: While the regional taste of many states had abandoned the stomacher by the turn of the sixteenth century in favor of a smooth bodice, by the mid- to late sixteenth century, Venetian women embraced long stomachers under open bodices that stretched from their bust to the top edge of their skirts.

Importantly, fashion in early modern Italy and Europe coincided with the emergence of the concept of self-determination beyond the confines of political entities that were unequivocally rooted in the Catholic Church. The changing trends of the period enabled people of different classes to participate to varying degrees in the creative expressions of fashion, making it more difficult to identify one's class associations by their attire. And with a nascent merchant class, access to luxury disrupted what was considered the natural order.

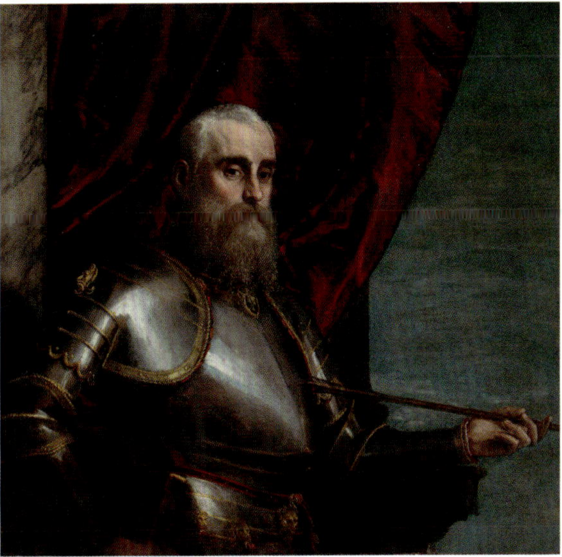

fig. 3 *Portrait of Agostino Barbarigo*, 1571. Paolo Veronese. Oil on canvas; 102.2 x 104.2 cm. The Cleveland Museum of Art, Gift of Mrs. L. E. Holden, Mr. and Mrs. Guerdon S. Holden, and the L. E. Holden Fund, 1928.16

As mentioned above, Castiglione is very clear on sprezzatura being the purview of the nobility, to which members of the lower classes can aspire but never truly achieve. The term *sprezzatura* as applied in today's context, however, is not class-specific. Whereas in Castiglione's time the word was used in relation to both men and women, since the twentieth century, *sprezzatura* has typically been employed in connection with masculine-facing and menswear codes.[19] In "Il faut être absolument maniéristes," his 1994 *Vogue Italia* article on the style of the modern-day man, philosopher Ugo Volli discusses the evolution of sprezzatura in relation to changing masculine codes of the modern age.[20] As the basis of contemporary attitudes, he invokes the artifice effects of Mannerism—the artistic movement that succeeded the Renaissance and lasted from the 1520s to about 1600—effects intensified nowadays by popular media platforms such as television. He even cites the correlation between sprezzatura and dandyism, implying that the essence of sprezzatura, a "slogan della modernità (slogan of modernity)," had laid the groundwork for dandyism.[21] Building on this argument, Volli writes: "And then there is the way people dress. With elegance, again after a long time. With a certain detachment (the Mannerist Baldassare Castiglione would say: with a certain disdain). But also, with the taste for bricolage, for mixing, for cross-breeding. Without entrusting their image to any demiurge, but deciding in a personal way."[22] In his article, Volli recognizes that even though fashion is personal and subjective, there still remains a collective understanding regarding the evocation of effortless elegance. In contrast to Castiglione, however, the elegance an individual exuded in the late twentieth century derived from deliberately combining a variety of influences instead of adhering to the type of trickle-down directive that underpinned fashion for many centuries. Volli adds that in the fashion industry, creative directors and industry leaders double down on fashion codes that amplify the legacy of their respective houses rather than allowing vernacular styles to guide their creative contributions.

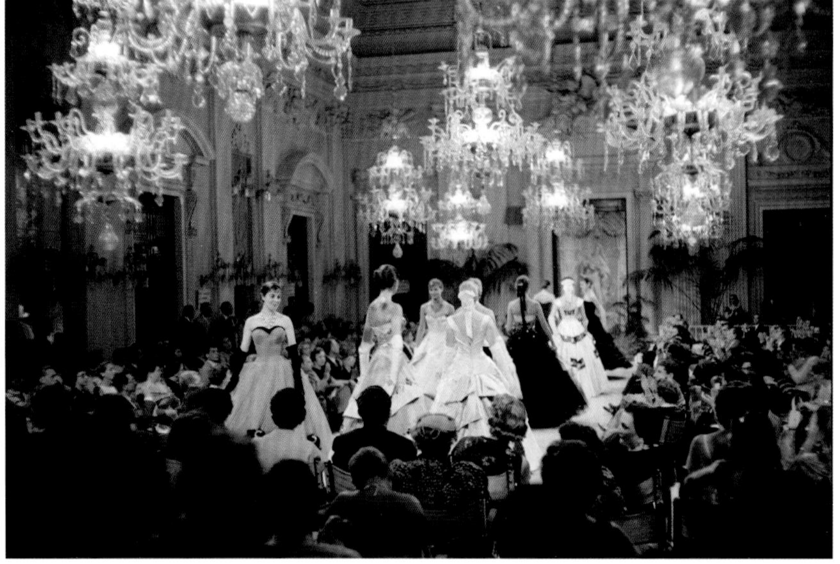

fig. 4   Fashion show at the Sala Bianca, Palazzo Pitti, Florence, c. 1952. Photo: Album / Alamy

Various designers, particularly Italian designers including Giorgio Armani (1934–2025) and Gianni Versace (1946–1997), have drawn inspiration from the needs of the changing world. Although polar opposites, Armani and Versace designed fashions that enabled men to be as flamboyant or as reserved as they wished, while still exhibiting the nonchalance that sprezzatura demanded. From the late 1970s into the 1980s, Armani defined an era of sprezzatura with his muted tones, relaxed tailoring, and wool suiting. In the movie *American Gigolo* (1980), Richard Gere's Julian, the

4

stylish and seductive main character, was outfitted by Armani, reigniting the power of sprezzatura through his laid-back demeanor. Versace also approached men's tailoring with relaxed proportions. But whereas Armani's sprezzatura was marked by subtle refinement, Versace's version, incorporating a plethora of Renaissance- and Baroque-inspired patterns, animal prints, and metal-hardware accents, radiated that same confident effortlessness, but with far greater exuberance.

Over time, sprezzatura evolved from being a narrowly identifiable quality to representing a broader spectrum of poise, a trajectory that also aligns with the gradual democratization of fashion in our global society.

Annotating Sprezzatura in Italian Fashion
In the aftermath of World War II, the Italian fashion industry attempted to reestablish itself as a preeminent arbiter of global taste.[23] Ever since, many burgeoning fashion houses have looked to the Renaissance and the early modern period as a creative framework for solidifying an Italian fashion identity, particularly as a way to offset Paris's status as the world's fashion capital. As seen throughout *Renaissance to Runway: The Enduring Italian Houses*, contemporary fashions consistently merge the Italian past and present. Fashion from the twentieth and twenty-first centuries acts as a portal to the Italian Renaissance and the early modern era, while the historical referents spark the contemporary imagination.

In the wake of World War II, especially in response to the Marshall Plan, the US federal program to revitalize the European economy, America sought to bolster the Italian textile and garment industry. Through the Marshall Plan, Italian manufacturers were supplied with hundreds of millions of dollars in cotton and machinery to subsidize the newly democratic nation's economic rebirth.[24] Soon after the war ended, American retail buyers began returning to Italy to make purchases; after the introduction of the annual Sala Bianca fashion shows, these buyers started coming in droves. Beginning in 1952, dressmakers and textile manufacturers, led by the Marquis Giovanni Battista Giorgini (1898–1971), came together to show collections in the Sala Bianca in Florence's famed Palazzo Pitti,[25] thereby launching the annual Sala Bianca fashion shows (**fig. 4**).[26] At the Sala Bianca's January 1953 iteration, Carmel Snow (1887–1961)—legendary editor in chief of *Harper's Bazaar*, who had coined the term "New Look" in reference to Christian Dior's (1905–1957) designs of several years prior—was astonished at the quality of the Italian textiles; their supreme blending of fibers rendered her unable to distinguish any of the individual fiber types.[27] With the start of the Sala Bianca shows, presentations of *alta moda*—"high fashion," Italy's answer to Parisian haute couture—were based there until 1982.[28] Throughout the 1960s and the early 1970s, designers like Valentino (b. 1932) and Roberto Capucci (b. 1930) gradually began debuting their collections in Rome.[29]

By 1958, the fashion trade organization Camera Syndicale della Moda Italiana was founded to oversee the Italian fashion industry.[30] Modeled on Paris's Chambre Syndicale de la Haute Couture, the organization—which four years later changed its name to the Camera Nazionale della Moda Italiana—sought to diminish Paris's centrality within the Italian fashion industry and creative norms.[31] The Camera Nazionale's first order of business in 1958 was instituting Milan Fashion Week. By the 1960s, the collections staged in Milan were beaming with ready-to-wear presentations, becoming a major category in Italian fashion; ready-to-wear was especially popular with American audiences, who consumed more ready-made fashions than any other country.[32] Today, most Italian houses show their women's collection in Milan, while since 1972, Florence has been the site of Pitti Uomo, which annually highlights spring and summer menswear. Sometimes, however, men's and women's collections are presented together in

Milan and Florence. For houses with alta moda lines, those fashions are presented in Rome and occasionally in Paris.[33]

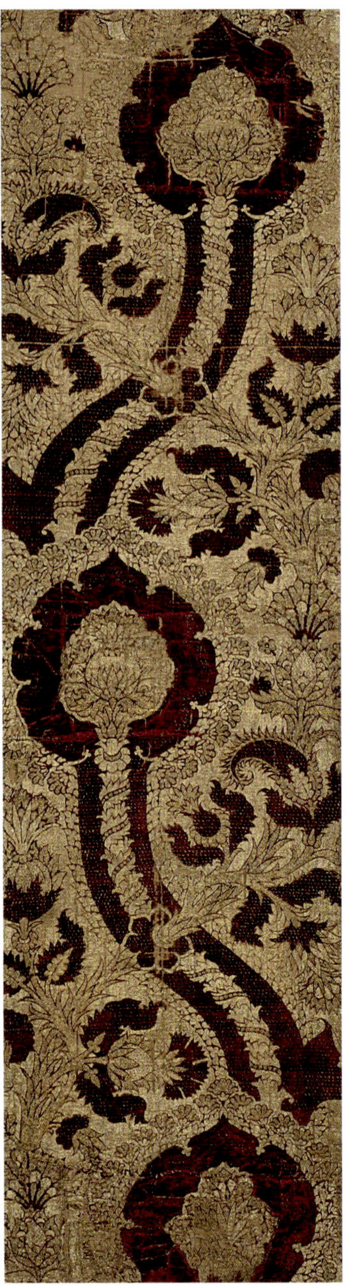

fig. 5 Velvet with pomegranate pattern, 1450–1500. Florence, Italy. Silk, gold thread, and velvet: three heights of cut pile, gold thread loops; 300.9 x 56.5 cm. The Cleveland Museum of Art, Purchase from the J. H. Wade Fund, 1973.20

The term *alta moda* derives from the Latin root *modus*, and *la moda* first appeared in everyday parlance as an umbrella term for fashion in the 1640s.[34] Like *sprezzatura* a century prior, *alta moda* implied appearance, demeanor, and an understanding of changing trends according to societal codes. *Alta moda* is one example of the various ways in which the language and scenic contextualization of the twentieth-century rebirth of Italian fashion are rooted in the early modern period. An even more striking example: This rebirth, as mentioned above, occurred at the Palazzo Pitti, the primary residence of the mighty Medici family, who ruled Florence with an iron fist in the early modern period and with whom the then-latest luxury trends originated. The most fashionable silhouettes were transmitted through figures such as the Palazzo Pitti's first Medici inhabitants, namely, Eleonora di Toledo (1522–1562), Duchess of Florence and wife of Duke Cosimo I de' Medici (1519–1574).

Prior to unification in 1861, Italy was a collection of city-states governed by noble families that both competed and allied with one another out of political expedience. During the early modern period and again from the twentieth century to the present, Italian families, or houses, have exerted considerable influence over design, in the process shaping fashion and culture more broadly, domestically and globally. As discussed earlier, Castiglione was in close proximity to fashion leaders in Northern Italy from all the major families, including the Sforza, Gonzaga, and Este. Through diplomatic missions, he likely also had dealings with members of the infamous Borgia clan and possibly the Medici as well.

Through their vigorous patronage of luxury and artisan industries, the houses that ruled over the Italian peninsula played a generative role in creative expressions of the period. For instance, at the height of Cosimo de' Medici's (1389–1464) power, in 1458, one of the businesses he funded through his family's bank was a wool bottega, or workshop. This workshop would prompt the large-scale manufacture of fine wool textiles—which would go on to become one of Florence's leading exports for much of the early modern period, alongside sumptuous gold-metal-threaded brocaded silk velvets (**fig. 5**).[35] Eager for Milan to keep pace with the silk and luxury textile industries of the neighboring states of Venice, Florence, and Genoa, Filippo Maria Visconti (1392–1447), Duke of Milan and grandfather of the future Duke of Milan, Ludovico Sforza, invited Florentine silk maestro Piero di Barolo and Genoese silk maestro Giovanni Borlasca to spearhead Milanese silk-weaving operations around 1442.[36] Soon after, the Milanese elite followed suit and began investing in silk workshops, helping realize the Milanese court's ambitions.[37] Textiles are transformed into fashion, which—again invoking Castiglione—speaks to the nobility's role in shaping fashion during the early modern era.

Incorporating aspects of her home country's style, the Spanish-born duchess Eleonora di Toledo famously ushered into Florence, and regularly donned, the *zimarra* (*ropa* in Spanish), a Turkish caftan–inspired long jacket that could also serve as an outerwear garment to wear in public instead of being casual, at-home attire.[38] The zimarra was also worn as an outer gown, embellished with the embroidered and appliqued frills of a typical gown, and some even had trains.[39] Upon Eleonora's death in 1562, she reportedly had seventy-nine zimarre in her wardrobe.[40] As for the queens of Renaissance fashion, Isabella and Beatrice d'Este, jewelry was their vice; in this, they took after their mother, Eleonora of Naples (1450–1493), Duchess of Ferrara. The Este sisters collaborated with goldsmiths and jewelry artisans on specific designs, placing the sisters in the role of creatives in the same way we would designers today.[41]

In contrast to the nobility-driven fashion trajectory of the early modern era, the twentieth century saw the emergence of family-run fashion houses, many of which started out as humble design firms, local ateliers, and bottegas but over time grew into coveted luxury brands. Mario Prada (1857–1958) opened his luxury luggage store in Milan's main shopping district, the Galleria Vittorio Emanuele II, in 1913.[42] His granddaughter Miuccia Prada (b. 1949), who assumed control of her family's business in 1978, went from introducing her coveted Vela nylon handbags, merging utility and luxury, in 1984, to her "Ugly Chic" womenswear collections of the mid-1990s, which mixed unconventional patterns in murky colors like lime green and brown and challenged traditional concepts of beauty. In the process, she turned Prada into a global juggernaut.[43]

Having founded his business in 1927, Salvatore Ferragamo (1898–1960), supported by his wife, Wanda (1921–2018), expanded his company after enduring the hardships of World War II and went on to become the world's preeminent shoe designer and retailer. With the added bonus of his scientific foot-anatomy studies at the University of Southern California prior to the war, he was committed to improving shoe designs that could comfortably fit a range of sizes while supporting the foot's arch.[44] After Ferragamo's sudden passing in 1960, his wife and children continued his legacy, eventually expanding into ready-to-wear fashion—today an integral component of Ferragamo's output—while maintaining Salvatore's concern with creating eloquent yet bodily conscious footwear. ETRO and Missoni are two of the many other Italian fashion houses that began as modest, family-founded ventures and that would ultimately become entities whose contributions epitomized Italian design.

Sprezzatura from Renaissance to Runway

Since the 1980s, there has been a consistent uptick in the number of contemporary Italian fashion designers looking to the early modern period for inspiration, drawing on evocations of sprezzatura in fine art to evoke the fantasy of the Italian past while creating designs that reflect modern tastes. Alessandro Michele (b. 1972), Valentino's creative director, is celebrated for his masterful deconstruction of early modern dress styles and artistic mediums. Michele was formerly the creative director at Gucci from 2015 to 2022. For the Cruise 2023 collection, he isolated and exaggerated various early modern fashion accoutrements and paired them with contemporary silhouettes, as evidenced in this diaphanous evening dress, coupled with a neck ruff (**fig. 6**). By the mid-sixteenth century, ruffled, high-neck collars were overtaken by separate pleated

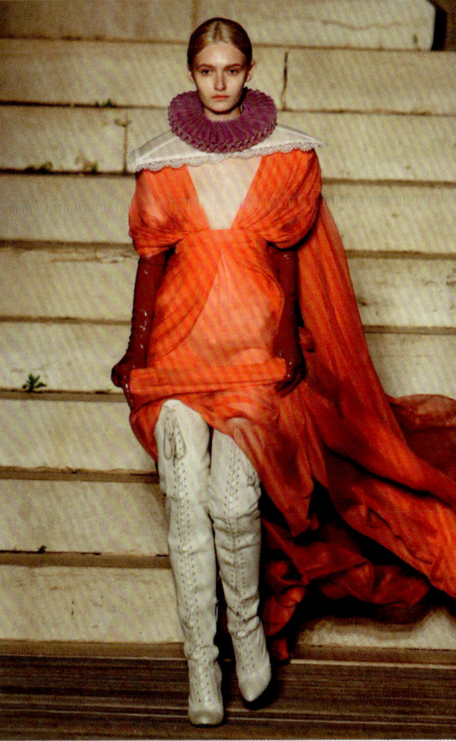

fig. 6 Evening gown, Gucci Cosmogonie, Cruise 2023. Alessandro Michele (Italian, b. 1972) for Gucci (Italian, est. 1921). Silk chiffon, silk georgette, lace, and crystal embroidery. © Gucci Archive

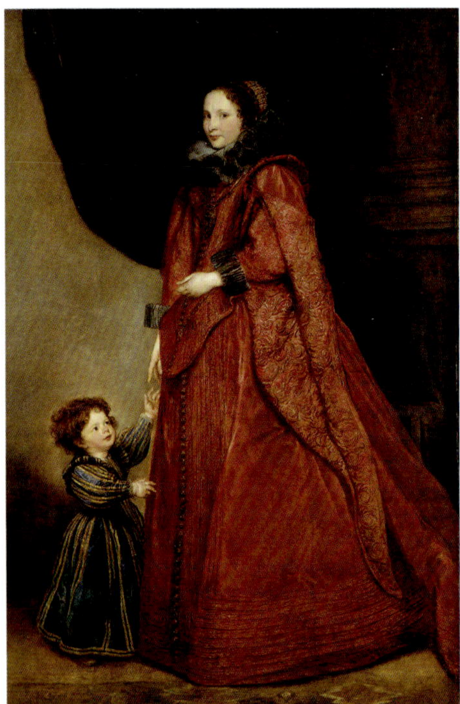

fig. 7   *A Genoese Lady with Her Child*,
c. 1623–25. Anthony van Dyck (Flemish,
1599–1641). Oil on canvas; 217.8 x 146 cm.
The Cleveland Museum of Art, Gift of the
Hanna Fund, 1954.392

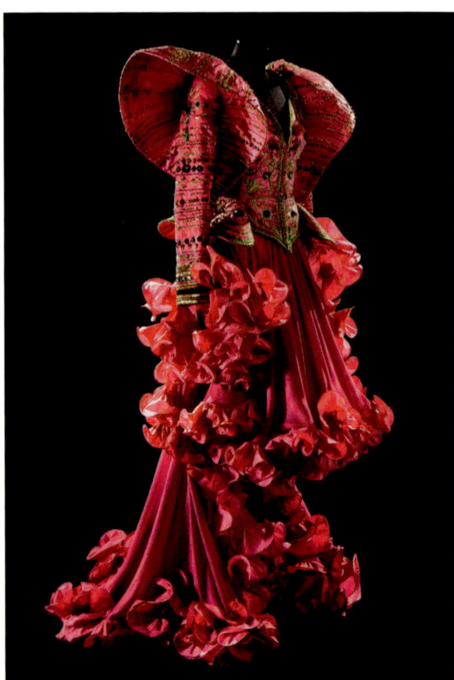

fig. 8   Gown, 1989. Roberto Capucci
(Italian, b. 1930). Silk satin and silk
georgette. © The Roberto Capucci
Foundation

and rounded linen neck attachments known as ruffs. The titular subject of Anthony van Dyck's (1599–1641) *A Genoese Lady with Her Child* dons a lavish layered ruff that makes it seem as if her head is resting on a cloud (**fig. 7**). With the sheer dress flowing behind her, the Gucci model evokes a walking nymph. Suggesting access to her body, the Gucci ensemble is informed by a sense of sexual liberality, whereas sensuality in the Castiglione vein encouraged the opposite approach for female sprezzatura. Even before Castiglione's time, fashion, as a concept extending beyond simple constructed clothing, featured the inclusion of elements to manipulate the body: internal elements such as padding and undergarment styles, as well as external accoutrements including complex embroideries and braided stitching. In some cases, these elements complied with codes related to sensuality such as those addressed by Castiglione.[45]

Van Dyck's Genoese noblewoman is bedecked in a velvet gown, exquisitely styled with a remarkable gem-set necklace, that features many internal elements. Her conical silhouette, emblematic of the height of 1620s fashion, hints at the presence of a corset. Suggested by her lace-capped cuffs, she wears a waistcoat under a matching mantle that has a train and a billowing skirt. At the time of this painting as well as in prior decades, Genoa was allied with Spain and adopted many of their fashions, including the hooped underskirt called the *verdugado/faldiglia*, or farthingale.[46] The latter undergarment eventually fell out of popularity in Genoa; hence, the folds illustrated along the noblewoman's skirt. A gown designed by maestro Roberto Capucci in 1989, with its silk-georgette pleated skirt and structured metal-thread-embroidered satin bodice with an angular front like that worn by the Genoese noblewoman, combines early modern styles with tropes of the contemporary period such as the desire for large, accentuated shoulders (**fig. 8**).

Apropos of contemporary designers who invoke early styles that link sprezzatura of past and present, Gianfranco Ferré (1944–2007) and Antonio Marras (b. 1961) also come to mind. Ferré's legacy is closely associated with his efforts to use Renaissance dress history as a creative vehicle, as seen in his Fall 2001 ensemble with its imposing puffed upper sleeve. Ferré was known for his manipulation and experimentation with the tailored white cotton shirt, and by pairing it with leather trousers, he breathed new life into this traditional garment (see **pl. 43**). The September 2001 issue of *Vogue Italia* heralded the ensemble as a brilliant interpretation of the latest in black-and-white tie trends.[47] The white shirt appears to have descended from the puffed sleeves that Castiglione would have seen and worn himself.

During the first few decades of the sixteenth century, having sleeves that gave a chemise (*camicia*) the effect of bursting outward was the height of sprezzatura at the time (**fig. 9**). The sleeves of women's outer bodices and men's doublets became more barrel-shaped during the first decade and gradually slimmed down as the century progressed, because sleeves were often separate attachments tied to the portion of the garment covering the torso, and chemises easily bulged. The emphasis on the *baragoni*, the upper sleeve of a garment, also became more fashionable by the 1530s; thus, Ferré's shirt could be making multiple allusions to the period's taste inclinations whether through the chemise or the sleeves of the outer garment.

Like many Italian designers, Antonio Marras has multidisciplinary artistic ambitions, with fashion as their root. The opening ensemble for his Fall 2024 line reflects his passion for early modern and modern art. Designed in wool using the fil coupé jacquard method, the ensemble adapts historical sprezzatura and translates it into a contemporary idiom, in the process raising sprezzatura to a whole new level (see **pl. 34**). The collection is inspired by a late medieval/early Renaissance figure, Eleonora d'Arborea (1347–1404), Princess of Sardinia. She was known for her promulgation of the Carta da Logu legislation, established to protect women's rights.[48] With its wide skirt, the ensemble also speaks to the expanding widths of skirts, stemming from the late fifteenth-century introduction of the farthingale,

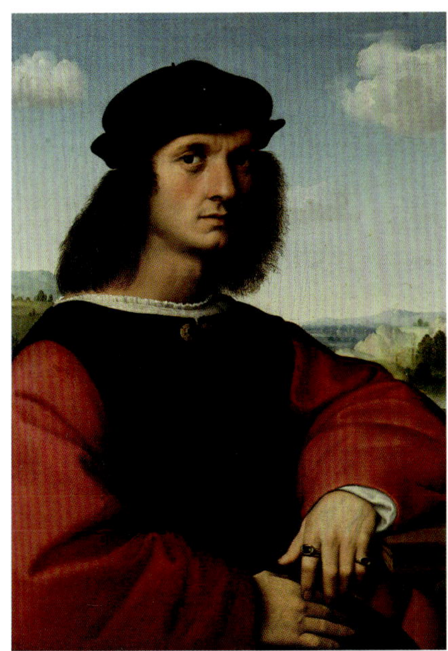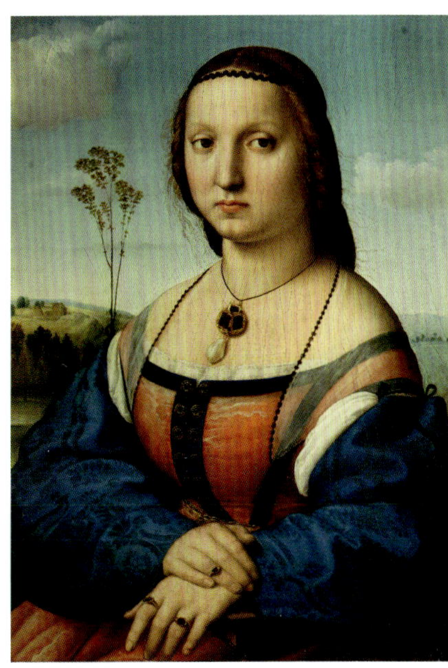

fig. 9 *Portraits of Agnolo and Maddalena Doni*, c. 1504–7. Raphel (Italian, 1483–1520). Oil on basswood panel; each 63.5 x 45 cm. Le Gallerie degli Uffizi, 1912 nn. 61, 59. Photos: © Gabinetto Fotografico delle Gallerie degli Uffizi

which made its way into style across the Italian peninsula throughout the sixteenth century. In Sofonisba Anguissola's (c. 1535–1625) *Portrait of a Noblewoman* (1570; The Klesch Collection), the subject's rounded farthingale is prominently captured by the rigid outlines of the overdress, whose conical silhouette anticipates the silhouette in Marras's design, created by the high-waisted skirt meant to billow as the wearer gallivants.

Building on sweeping designs, this menswear ensemble by Glenn Martens (b. 1983) from the Diesel Fall 2022 collection captures the contemporary mode of male sprezzatura evolving in our midst (**fig. 10**). Today, menswear codes have been informed by those of the early 2000s, embracing oversize garments and tailoring.[49] In its denim-on-denim presence, this ensemble includes, for example, a massive shredded denim coat that gives a distressed appearance; the design exudes a bravado not unlike that of the *chamarre*, the padded, fur-lined, thigh-length coat that was the height of European menswear during the 1520s and 1530s. A chamarre envelops the subject of Lorenzo Lotto's (1480–1556) *Portrait of a Man, Possibly Girolamo Rosati* (**fig. 11**).[50]

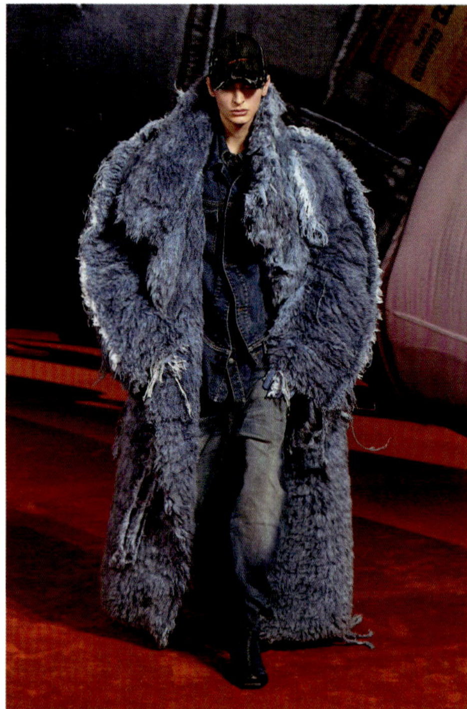

fig. 10 Ensemble, Fall 2022. Glenn Martens (Belgian, b. 1983) for Diesel (Italian, est. 1978). Cotton denim. Photo: Filippo Fior, *Vogue Runway*, © Condé Nast

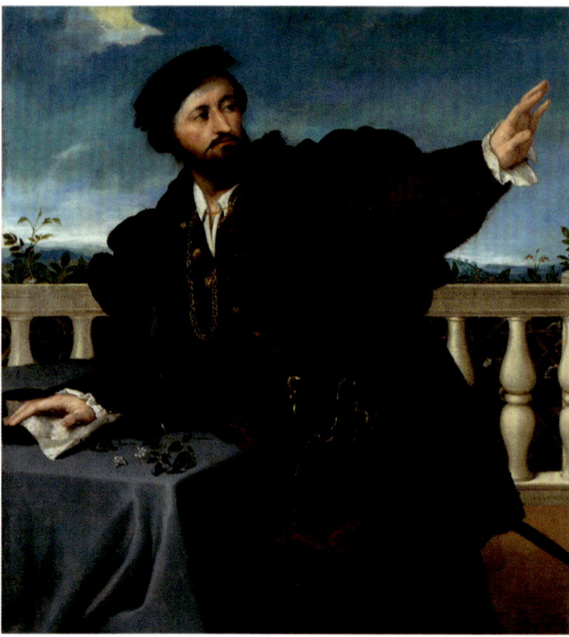

fig. 11 *Portrait of a Man, Possibly Girolamo Rosati*, 1533–34. Lorenzo Lotto (Italian, 1480–1556). Oil on canvas; 108.2 x 100.5 cm. The Cleveland Museum of Art, Gift of the Hanna Fund, 1950.250

Along with the concept of sprezzatura, Renaissance and early modern art have played a key role as a conduit of dress history in contemporary Italian fashion. From architecture and textile arts to decorative and fine arts, the creative arsenal from which Italian designers and houses have drawn is seemingly endless. The house of Buccellati, for instance, was built on the design styles of Renaissance goldsmiths and the culture at large.[51] Handcrafted in 2007 by Gianmaria Buccellati (1929–2015), son of Mario (1891–1965), the founder of the house, the Violante Pendant's rippling diamond inset is a nod to the *bugnato*, the facade of Renaissance palaces (**fig. 12**).

Works by Sandro Botticelli (1444/45–1510) are a significant reference point in twentieth- and twenty-first-century Italian fashion. His famous painting *Primavera* (c. 1480; see **pl. 6**) in particular has long been a fixture within the Italian fashion community. The various iterations of Gucci's floral motif, often interpreted in their scarves and sometimes in other apparel, were inspired by plants in much the same way Botticelli articulated flowers in *Primavera*. In addition, the embroidered silk flowers on a Spring 1971 Missoni dress and a 1989 Capucci gown also derive from Botticelli's floral display but via the favored silhouettes and decorative accoutrements popular during their respective decades (see **pls. 7** and **9**).

Botticelli is famously said to have based the female subject of *Primavera* and other paintings on the celebrated Florentine beauty Simonetta Vespucci (1453–1476; **fig. 13**; see **pl. 12**).[52] Several of Botticelli's images of anonymous women later identified as Vespucci feature a string of pearls that flow through a set of blonde locks.[53] In the Renaissance and early modern era, pearls were associated with feminine virtues, as seen in jewelry design and embroidery. In this string of pearls from around 1975, with their diamond-inset gold-coin links, Bvlgari, known for its storied mastery of gemstones, harkens back to pearls' early modern connection with feminine qualities (**fig. 14**).

Also modeled on Vespucci was perhaps Botticelli's *Birth of Venus* (c. 1485; see **fig. 30**). In contrast to Botticelli's more modest renderings of the sitter, Venus is unapologetically sensual.

10

After Botticelli painted it, there was an extreme Florentine movement condemning secular and sexual imagery led by Fra Girolamo Savonarola (1452–1498), who engineered the "Bonfire of the Vanities"—a literal bonfire in which people burned objects that, in Savonarola's view, represented the evils of the world.[54]

Embracing the unabashed feminine sexuality often seen in early modern art, most pronouncedly in the *Birth of Venus*, Versace sought to use fashion design to empower women to recover their sexual agency. In the Versace Atelier's Fall 1995 collection, entitled "Space Age," diamonds were used as witty indicators of the stars in the universe, but the gravitational pull was directed toward the dress and the woman's body. On the surface, Versace's design seems to suggest that a woman's power is almost cosmic, but the silhouette's form-fitting nature, which emphasizes the female body (albeit differently from the nudity of the Botticelli), is meant to encourage women to embrace their sensuality if they so desire.[55] In a 1990 *Women's Wear Daily* article on his design vision and the role of women within that vision, Versace is quoted as saying, "The message is to let your womanhood show and be proud of it."[56]

Early modern religious art is another major touchstone in contemporary Italian fashion, most famously exemplified in the blockbuster exhibition *Heavenly Bodies: Fashion and the Catholic Imagination*, held at the Metropolitan Museum of Art's Costume Institute in 2018. For his 2019 collaboration with Moncler, Pierpaolo Piccioli (b. 1967) designed the entire collection by manipulating the contemporary nylon lacquered puffer coat in many forms, from dresses to capes, recalling Renaissance-silhouette exemplars. Throughout his career, especially during his time as Valentino's creative director, Piccioli has looked to the Renaissance and early modern period. One of his ensembles, with a blue hooded overcoat and a red underdress, calls to mind depictions of the Virgin Mary, who, in the Catholic tradition, has consistently been rendered in a blue outer garment and a red underdress—blue symbolizing purity and her status as Holy Mother, and red signifying motherhood and the Passion (**fig. 15**).[57]

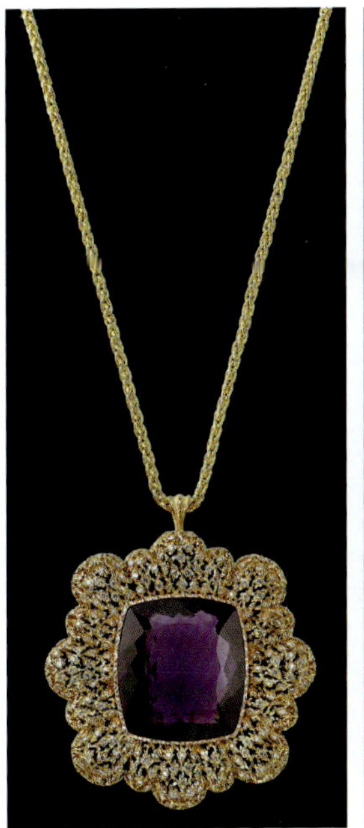

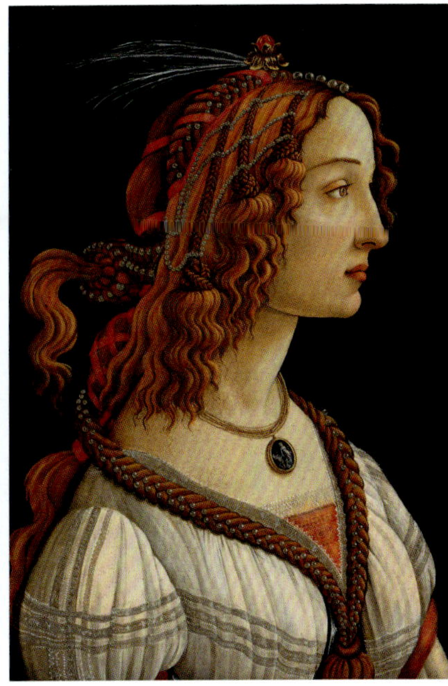

fig. 12   Violante Pendant, 2007. Gianmaria Buccellati (Italian, 1929–2015) for Buccellati (Italian, est. 1919). Diamonds, amethyst, yellow gold, white gold, and pink gold. Photo: © Aplomb Photo Studio

fig. 13   *Idealized Portrait of a Lady (Portrait of Simonetta Vespucci as Nymph)*, c. 1480–85. Sandro Botticelli (Italian, 1444/45–1510). Mixed technique on poplar; 81.3 x 54 cm. Staedel Museum, 936

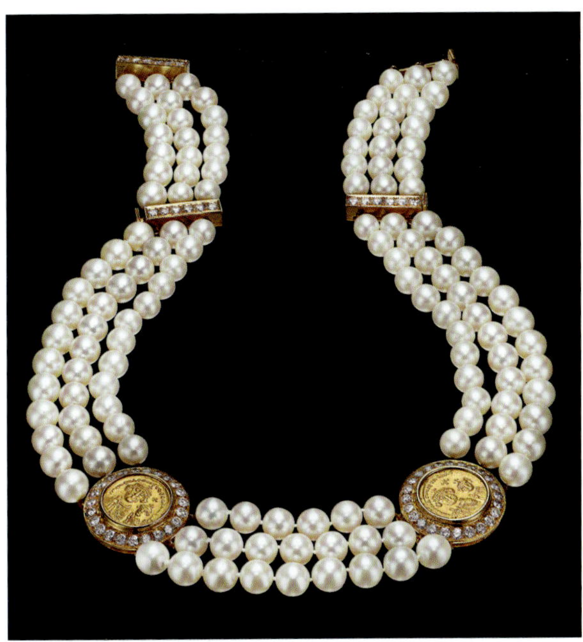

fig. 14   *Monete* necklace, c. 1975. Bvlgari (Italian, est. 1884). Gold with pearls, Byzantine gold coins, and diamonds. Bvlgari Heritage Collection. Photo © Bvlgari

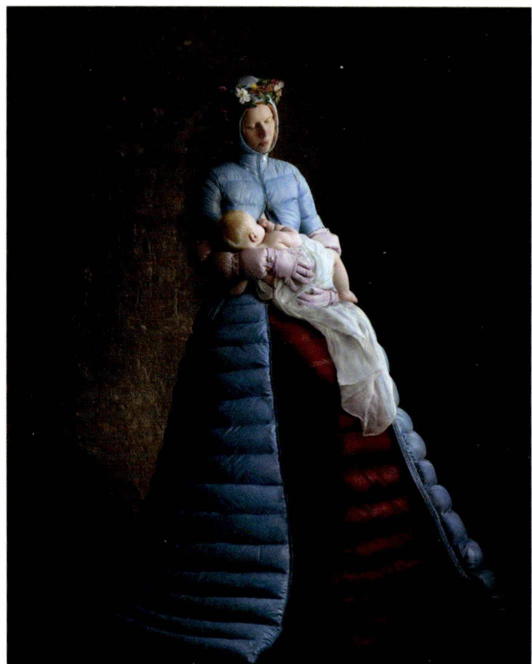

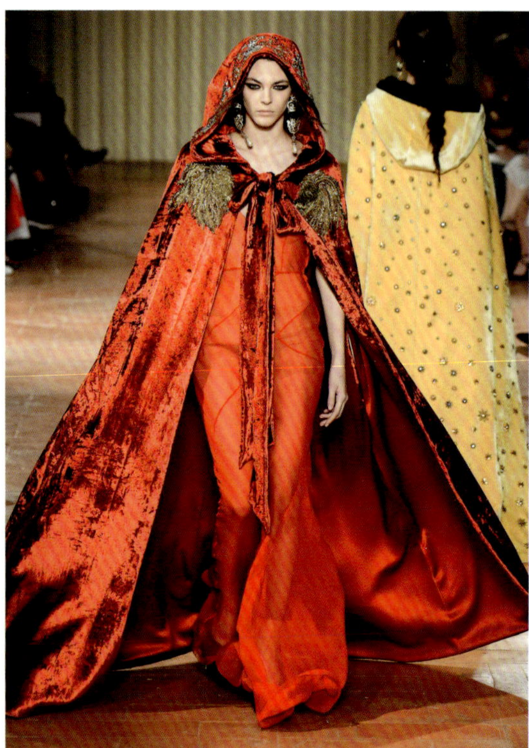

Utilizing a similar design approach, in this cape and dress from the Alberta Ferretti Fall 2017 collection (**fig. 16**); this sleek, black button front dress with its high, ruffled neckline from Giorgio Armani's Spring–Summer 2021 Privé line (**fig. 17**); and this expansive gown with a ruffled tulle crinoline from the Giambattista Valli Fall 2023 Couture collection, in its black-and-white colorway (**fig. 18**), the designers suggest Catholic vestments but in very alluring subversions (**fig. 19**). The Ferretti ensemble is aligned with cardinal vestments in particular, adapting the outer cassock to a cape form, whereas the Armani design alludes to the mantles worn by slightly lower-ranking, yet still powerful Catholic officials such as bishops. With its black-and-white color palette, the Valli gown evokes the sacred uniform worn by many Catholic officials over the centuries to convey piety.

Exploring the interplay between the early modern era and the present as a vehicle to delineate the rich legacy of Italian fashion, *Renaissance to Runway* is an adventure through the Italian cultural imagination. The first chapter, "Silky Smooth: Fabricating the Renaissance," interrogates the importance of silk velvets and the legal and operational factors that influenced their production as well as the crucial role of tailors, the unsung fashion heroes of the early modern period. Chapter 2, "The Original 'It Girls,'" focuses on several of the leading female fashion figures who shaped High Renaissance fashion and utilized fashion as a geopolitical tool. Chapter 3, written by Stefania Ricci, director of the Ferragamo Museum, explores the significance of Renaissance dress histories as a conduit for Salvatore Ferragamo's shoe-design genius. In chapter 5, Massimiliano Capella, director of the House Museum of the Paolo and Carolina Zani Foundation for Art and Culture, discusses Ottavio and Rosita Missoni, founders of Missoni, and their creative integration of Renaissance art to facilitate their early collection and set the course for one of Italy's, and the world's, most heralded fashion houses.

"Fashion Is a Family Business" travels back and forth between the historical and the contemporary, elaborating on the intertwining of fashion creation and family values across timelines. A conversation with major social media influencer Luke Meagher (@HauteLeMode) illuminates the generational cycles of Italian fashion and their impact on mainstream culture from the 1990s to the present, and a discussion with Dr. Matteo Augello, lecturer and Italian fashion curation aficionado, highlights the foundations of Italian fashion curatorial practice and related methodologies. In her contribution, noted archivist and curator Alessandra Arezzi Boza builds on the conversation with Dr. Augello, addressing factors integral to the preservation of Italian fashion, including collections management. Concluding the written portion of the journey is a discussion of Bonaveri, Italy's preeminent mannequin manufacturer, and the ways in which the firm's legacy continues to underpin the development of fashion exhibitions worldwide. Following this discussion is a series of photographs of several of the exhibition's highlights by Luca Stoppini, the creative director of *Vogue Italia* from 1991 to 2018 and the art director of the present publication, which beautifully capture the visual narrative at this project's core.

We hope you enjoy. Welcome to the Renaissance; your runway awaits!

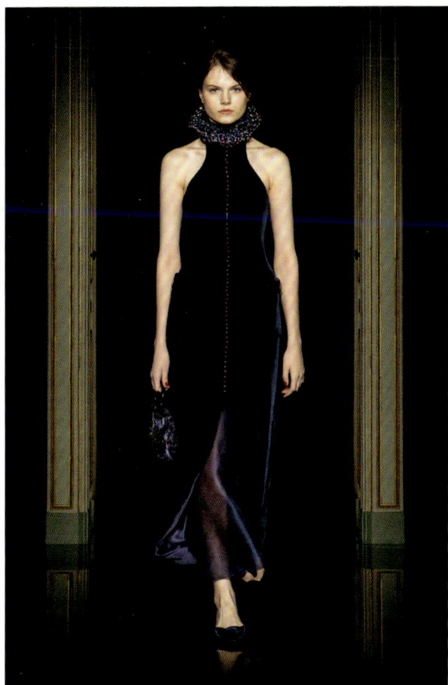

fig. 17 Evening dress, Spring–Summer 2021, Giorgio Armani Privé. Giorgio Armani (Italian, 1934–2025) for Armani (Italian, est. 1975). Silk velvet, silk organza, and crystals. Photo: David McKnight, Courtesy of Armani / Silos

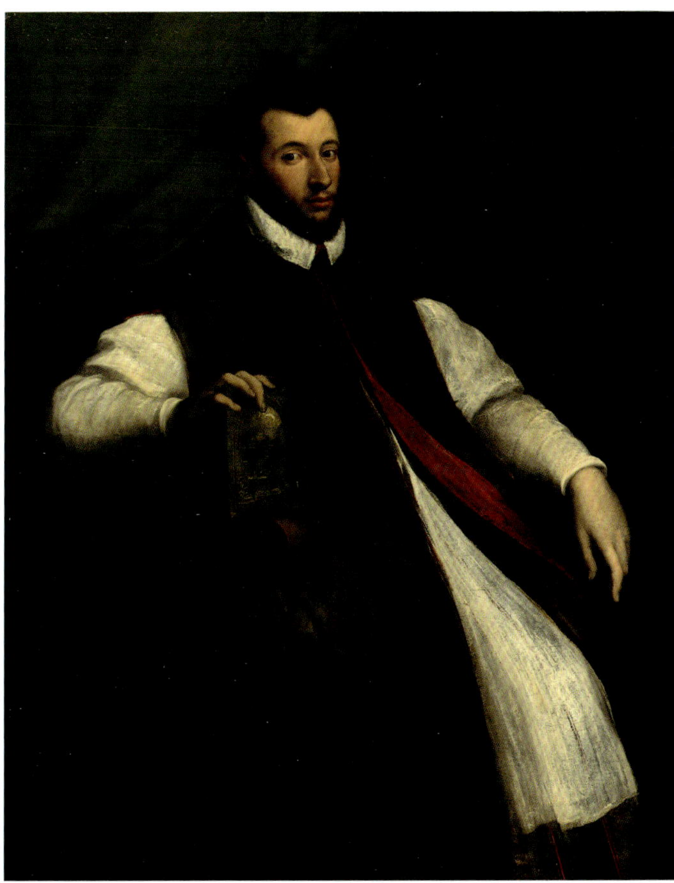

fig. 19 *Portrait of a Prelate*, mid-1500s. Girolamo da Carpi (Italian, c. 1501–1556). Oil on canvas; 140.4 x 108 cm. The Cleveland Museum of Art, Mr. and Mrs. William H. Marlatt Fund, 1947.210

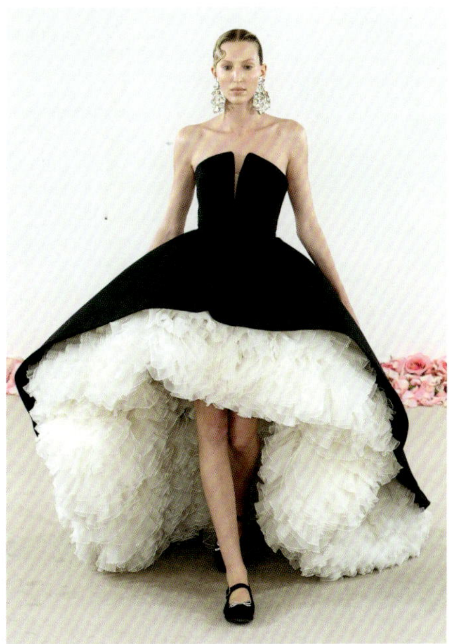

fig. 18 Gown, Fall 2023 Couture. Giambattista Valli (Italian, b. 1966) for Giambattista Valli (Italian, est. 2005). Silk faille and silk organza. Photo: © GoRunway

1 Eugenia Paulicelli, *Writing Fashion in Early Modern Italy: From "Sprezzatura" to Satire* (Farnham, Surrey, UK: Ashgate, 2014), 53.
2 Baldassare Castiglione, *The Book of the Courtier* (1528), book 1, 26, gutenberg.org/files/67799/67799-h/67799-h.htm#sec1.24.
3 Paulicelli, *Writing Fashion in Early Modern Italy*, 54. The popular phrase "Je ne sais quoi" is the French equivalent to sprezzatura.
4 Castiglione, *Book of the Courtier*, book 2, 40.
5 Castiglione, *Book of the Courtier*, book 1, 65.
6 Paulicelli, *Writing Fashion in Early Modern Italy*, 52.
7 *The Devil Wears Prada*, directed by David Frankel (20th Century Fox, 2006), streaming on Disney +.
8 Shola von Reynolds, "Mastering Sprezzatura: The Fashionable Art of Nonchalance," *AnOther*, May 19, 2016, anothermag.com/fashion-beauty/8699/sprezzatura-or-the-fashionable-art-of-nonchalance.
9 Castiglione, *Book of the Courtier*, book 2, 93.
10 Castiglione, *Book of the Courtier*, book 3, 8.
11 Paulicelli, *Writing Fashion in Early Modern Italy*, 66.
12 Castiglione, *Book of the Courtier*, book 1, 40.
13 Castiglione, *Book of the Courtier*, book 2, 8.
14 S. A. Rhodes. "Baudelaire's Philosophy of Dandyism," *Sewanee Review* 36, no. 4 (1928): 387–404, jstor.org/stable/27534321.
15 Castiglione, *Book of the Courtier*, book 2, 3.
16 Paulicelli, *Writing Fashion in Early Modern Italy*, 66–67.
17 Paulicelli, *Writing Fashion in Early Modern Italy*, 66–67.
18 Paulicelli, *Writing Fashion in Early Modern Italy*, 66–67.
19 Von Reynolds, "Mastering Sprezzatura."
20 Ugo Volli, "Il faut être absolument maniéristes," *Vogue Italia*, May 1994, 136–37, 183, proquest.com/magazines/il-faut-être-absolument-maniéristes/docview/1824204554/se-2.
21 Volli, "Il faut être absolument maniéristes."
22 Volli, "Il faut être absolument maniéristes."
23 Lucia Savi, *A New History of "Made in Italy": Fashion and Textiles in Post-War Italy* (London: Bloomsbury, 2023), 19.
24 Savi, *Made in Italy*, 27.
25 Savi, *Made in Italy*, 47.
26 Savi, *Made in Italy*, 47.
27 Savi, *Made in Italy*, 48.
28 Catherine Sabino, "The Legendary Pitti Palace in Florence Offers a New Take on Fashion," *Forbes*, January 12, 2024, forbes.com/sites/catherinesabino/2024/01/12/the-legendary-pitti-palace-in-florence-offers-a-new-take-on-fashion/.
29 "Rome's New Day," *Interview Magazine*, August 1, 2011, https://www.interviewmagazine.com/fashion/alta-moda-rome-summer-2011.
30 Savi, *Made in Italy*, 75.
31 Savi, *Made in Italy*, 75.
32 Rosalind Jana, "A Brief History of Milan Fashion Week," *Vogue*, September 18, 2019, vogue.co.uk/fashion/article/history-of-milan-fashion-week.
33 Before Florence became the center of fashion, for a period Rome was the center of alta moda.
34 Paulicelli, *Writing Fashion in Early Modern Italy*, 5.
35 Raymond de Roover, "The Medici Bank Organization and Management," *Journal of Economic History* 6, no. 1 (1946): 24–52, jstor.org/stable/2112995.
36 Chiara Buss, ed., *Silk Gold Crimson: Secrets and Technology at the Visconti and Sforza Courts* (Milan: Silvana Editoriale, 2009), 18.
37 Buss, *Silk Gold Crimson*, 18.
38 Roberta Orsi Landini, *Moda a Firenze, 1540–1580: Lo stile di Eleonora di Toledo e la sua influenza / Eleonora di Toledo's Style* (Florence: Pagliai Polistampa, 2005), 109–11.
39 Landini, *Moda a Firenze*, 109–11.
40 Landini, *Moda a Firenze*, 109–11.
41 Jacqueline Herald, *Renaissance Dress in Italy 1450–1500* (London: Bell & Hyman; Atlantic Highlands, NJ: Humanities Press, 1981), 172.
42 "History," Prada, last accessed February 1, 2025, pradagroup.com/en/group/history.html.
43 Lynn Yaeger, "A History of Prada and Nylon—How the Textile Earned Its Fashionable Place," *Vogue*, September 24, 2021, vogue.com/article/prada-nylon-handbag-history; and Sophie Bew, "When Mid-90s Prada Made Ugly Chic," *AnOther*, April 17, 2017, anothermag.com/fashion-beauty/9740/when-mid-90s-prada-made-ugly-chic.

44 Stefania Ricci, "Salvatore Ferragamo: Equilibrium and What It Means to Walk," Google Arts & Culture, last accessed February 1, 2025, artsandculture.google.com/story/salvatore-ferragamo-equilibrium-and-what-it-means-to-walk-museosalvatoreferragamo/oQXh4vrXcaLEIA?hl=en.

45 Anne Hollander, *Seeing Through Clothes* (New York: Viking, 1978), 90–91.

46 "1625–27 – Anthony van Dyck, Genoese Noblewoman," *Fashion History Timeline*, May 29, 2019, fashionhistory.fitnyc.edu/1625-27-van-dyck-genoese/.

47 Anna Piaggi, "Black Tie . . . White Shirt," *Vogue Italia*, September 2001, 542–45, proquest.com/magazines/black-tie-white-shirt/docview/1832516504/se-2.

48 Luis Zargani, "Antonio Marras Fall 2024 Ready-to-Wear: A Master in Storytelling," *Women's Wear Daily*, February 21, 2024, wwd.com/runway/fall-2024/milan/antonio-marras/review/.

49 Jonathan Borge, "11 Men's Fashion Trends to Watch for Fall 2025," *InStyle*, March 20, 2025, instyle.com/mens-fashion-trends-fall-winter-2025-11700048.

50 François Boucher, *A History of Costume in the West* (London: Thames & Hudson, 1967), 228.

51 Alba Cappellieri, *Buccellati: A Century of Timeless Beauty* (New York: Assouline, 2021), 18.

52 Zuzanna Stańska, "Simonetta Vespucci: The Renaissance Top Model," *DailyArt Magazine*, March 6, 2025, dailyartmagazine.com/simonetta-vespucci-the-renaissance-top-model/.

53 Emanuele Lugli, "The Hidden Meanings in Botticelli's Hair," Fine Arts Museums of San Francisco, January 11, 2024, famsf.org/stories/hidden-meanings-botticelli-hair.

54 Isla Phillips-Ewen, "3 Things You Might Not Know About Botticelli's Venus," *DailyArt Magazine*, May 2, 2023, dailyartmagazine.com/3-things-you-might-not-know-about-the-birth-of-venus/.

55 "Versace–Haute Couture–Runway Collection–Women," firstVIEW, last accessed January 1, 2025, firstview.com/collection_image_closeup.php?of=21&collection=656&image=260476.

56 Glynis Costin, "Gianni Versace: A Reflection on Pride, Honesty, and Women," *Women's Wear Daily*, March 1990, wwd.com/feature/article-1076461-1819641/.

57 Julia Fiore, "Why Jesus and Mary Always Wear Red and Blue in Art History," *Artsy*, December 19, 2018, artsy.net/article/artsy-editorial-jesus-mary-wear-red-blue-art-history.

CHAPTER 1

SILKY SMOOTH: FABRICATING THE RENAISSANCE

Ian Griffiths (British, b. 1961), the creative director of Max Mara, showcased the house's 2025 Resort collection in the Palazzo Ducale, the Venetian Republic's historical seat of power and the home of its former ruler, the doge, during the medieval and early modern eras. The ensemble shown here includes a coat of a silk, velvet, and wool blend, featuring a dense, Renaissance-inspired floral pattern created by a void of velvet piles using a burn-out technique to achieve its interface (**fig. 20**). Between the fashion show's setting and the influences incorporated into the ensemble's silhouette, Venice's legacy as an epicenter of textile and commerce during the early modern period hung in the ether. Around 1910, Mariano Fortuny (1871–1949), one of fashion's greatest trailblazers, designed the Delphos mantle. Created more than a century prior to the Max Mara ensemble, the Delphos design boasts a printed gold-pomegranate pattern on a red-velvet ground that recalls the legendary Florentine gold-brocaded velvets that swept the Italian peninsula throughout the 1400s (**fig. 21**).

During the late Middle Ages, Italian municipalities rose to prominence for the quality of their silk weaving. Prior to the fifteenth century, Lucca was the primary silk manufacturer; thereafter, silk cultivation spread across the Italian peninsula, laying the groundwork for what would become—and continues to be—one of Italy's leading exports.[1] Because of Lucca's political and economic instability arising from competition and wars with their neighboring Italian states, by the fifteenth century, it was eclipsed by Venice and Florence, which became the two major players in textile trade and production. Although Milan also had its own silk-weaving industry, its production was modeled after Florence's, affirming Florentine and Tuscan dominance over silk manufacture and design.[2] Another important player in the silk industry was Genoa, whose textiles, especially velvets and lace, were universally admired across Europe. Because of Genoa's access to European markets due to its advantageous location, similarly to Venice, they had a very prosperous economy.[3]

Balancing Vibrancy and Sobriety

To make silk, silkworm cocoons were boiled in water and then spun finely into thread. The threads were dyed and woven into complex fabrics that

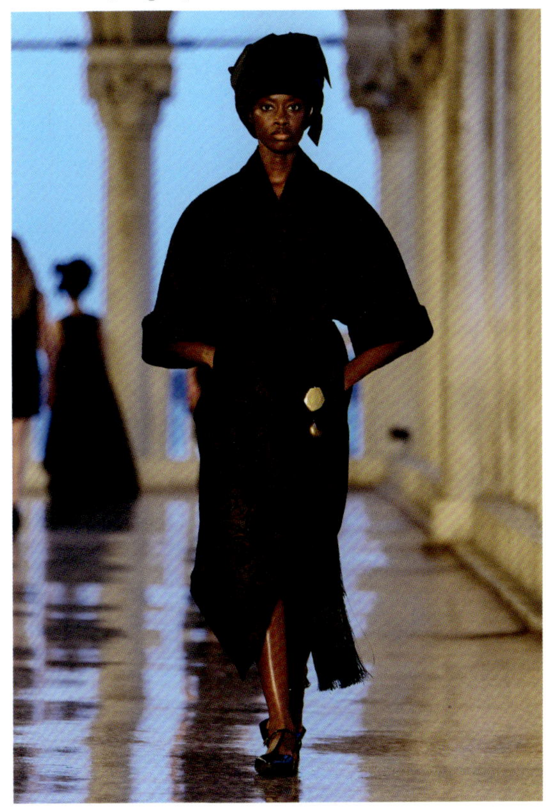

fig. 20   Ensemble, Resort 2025. Ian Griffiths (British, b. 1961) for Max Mara (Italian, est. 1951). Silk velvet, sablé wool, and cotton. Photo: Guy Marineau, *Vogue*, © Condé Nast

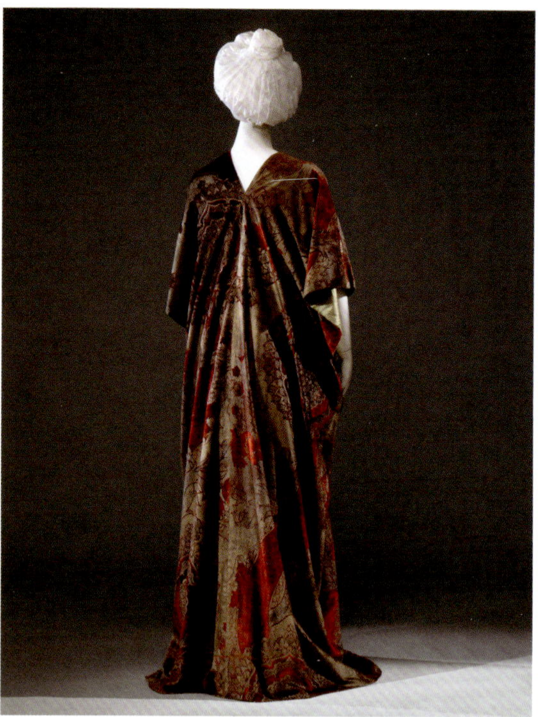

Fig. 21 Delphos Mantle, c. 1910. Mariano Fortuny (Spanish, 1871–1949). Silk velvet and silk *ermesino* with printed metallic pigment. Courtesy of the Museum of Costume and Fashion, Palazzo Pitti, TA 5843. Photo: © Gabinetto Fotografico delle Gallerie degli Uffizi

expanded the lexicon of textile arts during the early modern period. Throughout this era, Venetian crimson velvets were highly sought after across Europe. By the second half of the 1400s, crimson figured largely in Florentine fabrics as well. The base ingredient for the dye was the kermes, an insect native to the Mediterranean.[4] By the mid-1500s, however, cochineal, an insect native to Mexico and South America, was used alongside kermes to create crimson-colored dyes across the Italian peninsula.[5] Cochineal was imported from Spain because of the latter's dominance over what is today considered Latin America—one of many examples of fashion's close ties to geopolitics.

The Max Mara ensemble points to another color favored in Renaissance and early modern silks— black. Deep-black silks were especially valued. But the color black posed technical challenges. The materials needed to create black were difficult to apply to fine threads; as such, black fabrics were often redyed to create an illustrious appearance. The Genoese were lauded for their black silks, presumably because of their high degree of colorfastness—the ability to retain the originally dyed color.[6] The color quality of Venetian black silk was inferior to that in other regions, so despite local sumptuary laws limiting the use of black to widows in mourning, black silks were smuggled into the Venetian Republic.[7]

Another popular hue in Italian silks was violet. Renaissance and early modern Italy encompassed a broad palette, however, and velvets were dyed to reflect a myriad of colors including shades of blue, green, and yellow.

In the Milanese Republic during the late 1400s, colorful silks were not only adored; they were also adorned—with countless jewels for those who followed in the fashionable footsteps of Milan's leading lady, Duchess Beatrice d'Este (1475–1497). During the reign of her husband, Ludovico Sforza (1452–1508), Milanese sumptuary laws, such as the 1498 statute that allowed only grieving widows to wear a dark hue, gave way to the wide color palette of silks seen in the vibrant Milanese styles of the time.[8]

The Guild System

In addition to velvet, other revered fabrics in early modern Italy were silk satin and taffeta, which would create a sheen-like effect, brilliantly captured in painted portraits such as Agnolo Bronzino's (1503–1572) *Portrait of Lucrezia Panciatichi* (1541–45; see **pl. 45**). The creation of these fabrics was an arduous journey. The path to becoming a silk weaver was codified and prolonged. To become a master weaver and profit from velvet of one's own making, especially the *alto e basso*, pile-on-pile velvets, a weaver had to undergo between four and eight years of training.[9] Silk weavers also had to comply with the regulations of the powerful guild system. Every Italian municipality had its own guild that regulated various aspects of the silk industry, including the apprenticeship, the hierarchy of silks, and the types of silk products that could be imported and exported in order to safeguard the local economy.[10] At the core of the silk-guild

18

system was defining the caliber of silk, especially because marketing lower-grade silks affected the local economy. Each municipal guild established visual aids to indicate a fabric's content and value.[11] The Florentine silk guild, Arte della Seta, maintained silk-weaving and broader industry standards that shifted in relation to the republic's economic structure.[12]

Each city and republic also had its own codes to identify levels of quality. In Florence, multiple gold threads along the selvage, or the fabric's edge, signaled the highest-quality fabric, whereas in Venice, crimson velvets meeting the highest standard possessed green-and-gold-striped selvage.[13] In Lucca, white thread attested to the best fabric composition, while yellow thread denoted lower-quality fabric.[14]

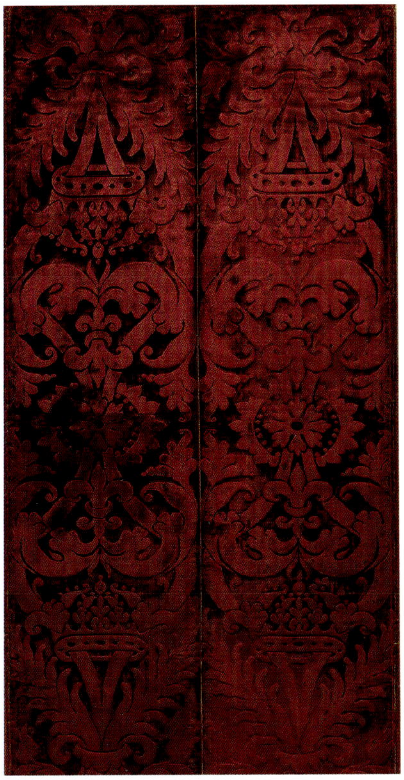

The drawloom was the primary piece of equipment needed to weave velvet. To produce silk velvets—the most prized fabrics—a supplementary warp, or additional vertical thread, was added to a ground weave (typically a satin, tabby, or twill) using a set of rods to create loops of the supplementary warp that were then cut to create the velvet's plush, fuzzy surface.[15] To fabricate the even more luxurious variety of velvet, alto e basso, instead of using single rods that lay horizontally underneath the supplementary warp to create the loops that would eventually be cut, two rods were inserted in order to create a double-raised pile.[16]

The consistency of the plush-cut area of velvets was heavily regulated by the guild system. In Venice during the 1460s, some merchants began supplying velvet weavers with improperly low-grade rods to make pile-on-pile velvets.[17] Using such rods to construct double-pile velvet resulted in having the pile with the lawfully correct height toward the ends of the fabric juxtaposed with an uneven, shorter pile at the center of the fabric. Anyone caught weaving using these types of rods had their looms confiscated and was expelled from the guild for a period of five years.

The Cleveland Museum of Art collection features a velvet stole from the late 1500s that had been part of the regalia of a procurator, a Venetian official second in importance only to the doge (**fig. 22**). The stole was dyed in the delectable Venetian crimson red and then woven in the alto e basso style. Its impeccable condition allows us to observe the higher and lower piles of cut velvet spread evenly across its interface. The higher pile forms the basis of the republican insignia surrounded by a foliage motif. The strips of green and gold thread along the stole's selvages indicate that this velvet was of the finest quality.

fig. 22   Procurator's velvet stole, c. 1575–1600. Venice, Italy. Silk velvet; 142.2 x 71.1 cm. The Cleveland Museum of Art, Bequest of John L. Severance, 1942.829

Beyond the Velvet Piles

By the 1500s, a fabric called *ermisino* was all the rage.[18] Ermisino is similar to the tabby woven silk known as taffeta; instead of using the same color for the warp and the weft, an ermisino fabric places complementary colors alongside one another, creating an iridescence in the finished fabric.[19] Ermisino is also lightweight, which made it perfect for the warm Italian summers, and with its iridescence, ermisino garments would have glistened in the sun.

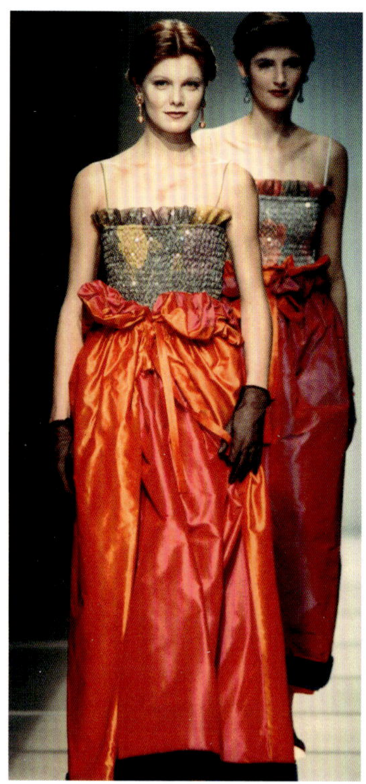

fig. 23 Dress, Fall–Winter 1988.
Giorgio Armani (1934–2025)
for Armani (Italian, est. 1975).
Silk. Courtesy of Armani / Silos.
Photo: Sergio Caminata

Expense records for aristocratic Italian families, an important tool in researching early modern material culture, attest that ermisino was a commonly purchased fabric among the Florentine elite. Duchess Eleonora di Toledo (1522–1562), wife of Cosimo I de' Medici (1519–1574), the Duke of Florence, had many ermisino fashions made for her and the family. Records suggest that she and the other female members of her family wore lighter shades of ermisino, while her husband's wardrobe featured darker hues of the fabric.[20]

While they formerly had an unsung legacy, ermisino and iridescent taffeta fabrics have come to the fore in recent fashion design. Throughout his career, Maestro Roberto Capucci (b. 1930) has utilized both types of silk fabric for his house because their malleability allows him to achieve dynamic silhouettes through pleating, draping, tucking, and ruffling. For his Fall–Winter 1988 collection, Giorgio Armani (1934–2025) played with iridescent taffetas in a series of strapless dresses with fifteenth- and early sixteenth-century-inspired high waistlines (**fig. 23**).

Cloth of Gold

Cloth of gold, another Florentine favorite, is the general term for silks woven with gold or silver metal threads within the foundational ground of a fabric or as the supplementary thread to create the luscious brocades that flooded the early modern Italian market.[21] Velvets with metal-thread brocades were undoubtedly extremely sought after. The metallic thread employed in woven designs was created by wrapping metal around a silk core. To fabricate brocades that integrated metal threads, the ends of supplementary weft metal threads were fastened to supplementary warps, creating the design juxtaposed to the velvet piles.[22]

The CMA collection includes a Florentine silk velvet dripping in a gold metallic thread that forms the period's famed pomegranate pattern at the middle (**fig. 24**). A broadly fashionable motif, the pomegranate generally appeared in several versions, sometimes in a thistle-like illustration, as seen here, at other times in the form of a pine cone.[23] Remnants of the pile's heights suggest that it is an alto e basso, but due to many of the worn-down regions of the textiles, the metallic thread loops transfixing the brocaded wefts peer through; on its fabrication, this textile's pile would have been high enough to conceal such remarkable details. Another important feature of the CMA's Florentine silk velvet is the slight, curved cut at the top, suggesting this was a fabric used in a garment of some sort. Prior research on the textile indicates that it could have served as the back of a chasuble, a Catholic vestment.

The Tailor

Another vital aspect of Italian Renaissance silks—not to mention fashion in general—was the tailor. Depicted in glorious portraiture of aristocrats, a tailor's artistry speaks to a specific moment in time. There is little evidence of published fashion plates circulating in Italy until the turn of the 1700s, but again, by examining the records left behind by aristocratic families, we learn that entire wardrobes were composed by specialized artisans. Often identified as *maestro*, a term that far outlived its original Renaissance context and was adopted by the most prominent mid-1900s courtiers such as Roberto Capucci and Emilio Schuberth (1904–1972), early modern tailors were not as acclaimed as artisans in other major industries; indeed, they were often situated at the bottom rung of the hierarchy of material culture.[24]

Although not regarded as highly as weavers, tailors, particularly in the 1400s, still had to operate a studio and shop and adhere to official industry standards.[25] Each textile sector typically registered and regulated tailors within their respective guild. For instance, in Florence, silk tailors were aligned with the silk guild, Arte della Seta, while wool or linen tailors were registered with the Arte de Lana. Even though much of their work was custom, tailors did produce ready-made accessories such as hats and gloves. In further similarity to their fabric-weaver counterparts, tailors had an apprenticeship system, price caps on the cost for designing each garment, and continual inspections by the guild to ensure that their practices were up to code.

Unlike in prior generations, by the 1500s silk tailors were able to embellish fabrics and customize their clients' garments, adding elements like slashing and braiding.[26] Throughout the sixteenth century, as the fashion lexicon began to expand, the role of the tailor also expanded, and his status rose such that the price per garment increased considerably. The laws evolved so that tailors were able to purchase fabrics, including silk, on behalf of their clients; formerly, they had acted as consultants who were only allowed to purchase silk before handing it off to be transformed into fashion.[27] Based on correspondence found in aristocratic families' account ledgers, tailors sometimes proposed designs to their clients.[28] There are even records of tailors speaking with their clients about employing family members and friends.

The relationship between tailor and client, especially aristocratic clients, could vary widely. In *The Material Renaissance* (2007), Michelle O'Malley and Evelyn Welch examine the early-1600s account records of the Magalotti family; these indicate that the tailor Maestro Domenico Bossoli spent 133 lira on silk, yet did not complete the requested custom order of garments for the family.[29] O'Malley and Welch identified the silk merchant from whom Bossoli had purchased the silk, Alessandrino Covoni. Covoni referred to Bossoli as a "one-time tailor" for the Magalotti, suggesting that the family and Bossoli had parted ways.[30]

Giovanni Battista Moroni's (1520/24–1579) painting *The Tailor* shows a subject dressed in the finest fashions of the period, including a slashed, cream-colored, presumably wool doublet (*giubonne*) and ballooned trunk hose (*calze*; **fig. 25**). More glamorous than the usual tailor, his elegant presence identifies Moroni's sitter as the probable maestro of his studio. The tailor's slashes on his doublet highlight his design capabilities, which would have instilled confidence on the part of potential clients in his ability to provide high-quality fashions.

Sumptuary Laws

Renaissance and early modern production and consumption were governed by sumptuary laws, but those who had the ability to defy those laws undoubtedly did so—providing space for fashion innovations to develop exponentially—and to such an extent that sumptuary laws could not keep pace with fashion developments arising from this defiance. A sumptuary law was

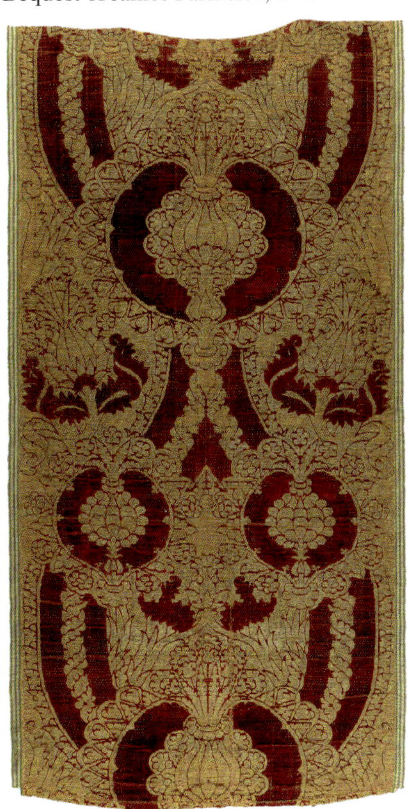

fig. 24 Silk velvet with gold in pomegranate pattern, 1450–1500. Florence (possibly), Italy. Silk velvet and gold thread; 118.7 x 60.6 cm. The Cleveland Museum of Art, Bequest of James Parmelee, 1940.596

passed in Florence in 1464 dictating that a dress had to be worn for a minimum of three years before it was eligible to be traded in and transformed into a new garment.[31] The same law permitted women to wear only one overgarment at a time that was dyed in kermes red. This reinforced the sober fashion sense of Renaissance Florence compared to its more exuberant regional neighbors. As mentioned, in vibrant Milan in 1498, for example, dark-colored attire could be worn only by the wife of a deceased husband or the brothers and sisters of the deceased.

In line with constant economic fluctuations, sumptuary laws tried to tamp down the growing consumption of fashion. In a far cry from the fashion consumption we see today, in the early modern period (and other historical eras), textiles were treasured. When a garment was too distressed to wear, it would be taken to tailors and seamstresses to be refashioned into something else. Put differently, upcycling was not a marketing tactic, as corporations nowadays use that term to engage contemporary audiences; it was a way of life throughout much of human history.

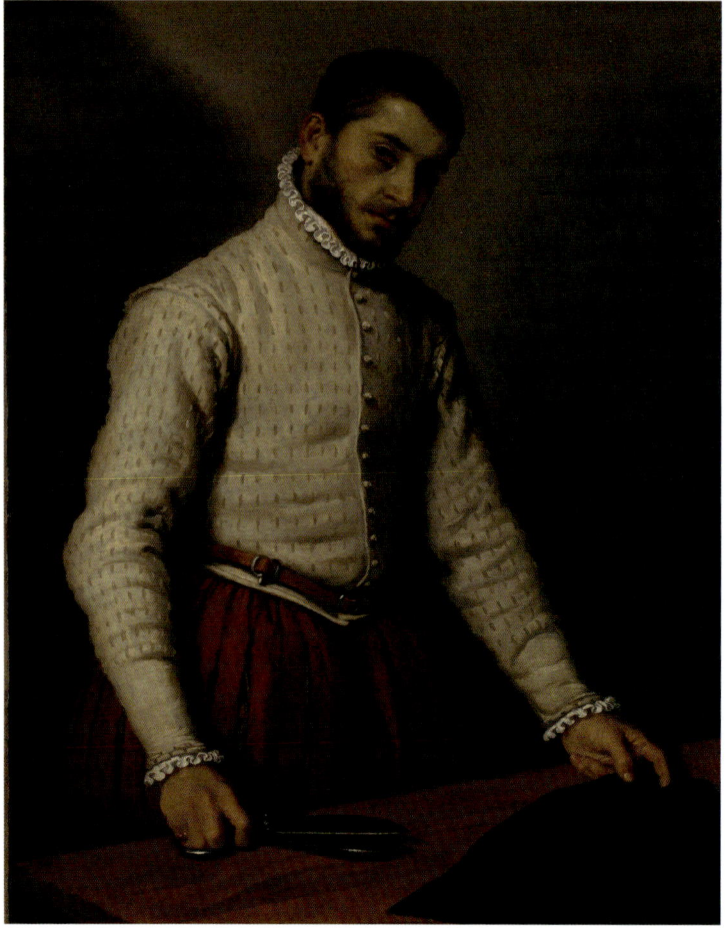

fig. 25 *The Tailor*, 1565–70. Giovanni Battista Moroni (Italian, 1520/24–1579). Oil on canvas; 99.5 x 77 cm. The National Gallery, London, Bought, 1862, NG697. Photo: © The National Gallery, London

1   Richard A. Goldthwaite, "The Economy of Renaissance Italy: The Preconditions for Luxury Consumption," *I Tatti Studies in the Italian Renaissance* 2 (1987): 15–39, doi.org/10.2307/4603651.

2   Melinda Watt, "Renaissance Velvet Textiles," *Timeline of Art History*, Metropolitan Museum of Art, last modified August 1, 2011, metmuseum.org/essays/renaissance-velvet-textiles.

3   Watt, "Renaissance Velvet Textiles."

4   Timothy McCall, "Materials for Renaissance Fashion," *Renaissance Quarterly* 70, no. 4 (2017): 1449–64, jstor.org/stable/26560612.

5   McCall, "Materials for Renaissance Fashion."

6   Watt, "Renaissance Velvet Textiles"; and Lisa Monnas, *Renaissance Velvets* (London: Victoria & Albert Museum, 2012), 39.

7   Monnas, *Renaissance Velvets*, 25.

8   Jacqueline Herald, *Renaissance Dress in Italy 1450–1500* (London: Bell & Hyman; Atlantic Highlands, NJ: Humanities Press, 1981), 39.

9   Monnas, *Renaissance Velvets*, 20.

10   Monnas, *Renaissance Velvets*, 8.

11   Luca Molà, *The Silk Industry of Renaissance Venice* (Baltimore: Johns Hopkins University Press, 2000), 132.

12   Carole Collier Frick, *Dressing Renaissance Florence: Families, Fortunes, and Fine Clothing* (Baltimore: Johns Hopkins University Press, 2005), 15.

13   Frick, *Dressing Renaissance Florence*, 15.

14   Monnas, *Renaissance Velvets*, 26.

15   Monnas, *Renaissance Velvets*, 16.

16   Monnas, *Renaissance Velvets*, 16.

17   Monnas, *Renaissance Velvets*, 23.

18   Frick, *Dressing Renaissance Florence*, 98.

19   Frick, *Dressing Renaissance Florence*, 98.

20   Roberta Orsi Landini, *Moda a Firenze 1540–1580: Lo stile di Eleonora di Toledo e la sua influenza / Eleanora di Toledo's Style* (Florence: Pagliai Polistampa, 2005), 78–79; and Landini, *Moda a Firenze, 1540–1580: Cosimo I de' Medici's Style / Lo stile di Cosimo I de' Medici* (Florence: Mauro Pagliai, 2011), 25.

21   Gertrude Townsend, "A Fifteenth Century Italian Velvet," *Bulletin of the Museum of Fine Arts* 29, no. 174 (1931): 63–65, jstor.org/stable/4170325.

22   Monnas, *Renaissance Velvets*, 18.

23   "Velvet with Pomegranate Design," Walters Art Museum, last accessed January 1, 2025, art.thewalters.org/object/83.742/.

24   Frick, *Dressing Renaissance Florence*, 64.

25   Michelle O'Malley and Evelyn Welch, *The Material Renaissance* (Manchester: Manchester University Press, 2007), 158.

26   O'Malley and Welch, *Material Renaissance*, 158.

27   O'Malley and Welch, *Material Renaissance*, 164.

28   O'Malley and Welch, *Material Renaissance*, 164.

29   O'Malley and Welch, *Material Renaissance*, 157.

30   O'Malley and Welch, *Material Renaissance*, 157.

31   Herald, *Renaissance Dress in Italy*, 151.

CHAPTER 2
THE ORIGINAL "IT GIRLS"

After Lucrezia Borgia (1480–1519) married her third husband, Alfonso d'Este (1476–1534), the soon-to-be Duke of Ferrara, she arrived at her husband's home for the first time in 1502 with no less than 1,700 Roman, Spanish, and Ferrarese courtiers.[1] Equal to the spectacle, she wore a velvet dress of gold bouclé, called *broccato riccio sopra riccio*, featuring a turquoise taffeta lining and robust sleeves in the French style.[2] Lucrezia's gown was so astonishing that another Renaissance "it girl," her sister-in-law Isabella d'Este (1474–1539), warily admired Lucrezia's procession, presumably thinking about the future and potential threats to her status as the most fashionable woman in the world.

Defining the "It Girl"

These stately women of the Renaissance were the fashion plates of their era. Their impact on style far outlasted their historical period, however, as they continue to provide inspiration for contemporary fashion into the twenty-first century. In Alessandro Michele's (b. 1972) Fall–Winter 2016 collection for Gucci, accompanying his mint-green silk evening dress was a ravishing pearl-embroidered partlet covering the neckline (**fig. 26**). Well known for creatively integrating a Renaissance repertoire within his design process, Michele has looked to figures such as Duchess Eleonora di Toledo (1522–1562), who famously donned glistening pearl-embroidered partlets and a gown in the Spanish style during the mid-1500s, as seen in her legendary portrait by Agnolo Bronzino (1503–1572; **fig. 27**). The following narrative will illuminate the fashion contributions of some early modern leading ladies whose style shaped the foundations of luxury that we still build on today.

The moniker "it girl" was originally bestowed on Clara Bow (1905–1965), star of the 1927 film *It Girl*. Bow's character was a young saleswoman named Betty Lou, whose enticing demeanor beguiled her boss, Cyrus.[3] When the film premiered, the press proclaimed Bow an "it girl" because, as F. Scott Fitzgerald (1894–1940) put it, she possessed "something to stir every pulse in the nation."[4] Outside of her character, the actress was known for her sexually liberal, controversial "flapper" fashions, outspokenness, and refusal to conform to Hollywood dogma. Bow's legacy eventually laid the groundwork for feminist movements later in the twentieth century and beyond, but since her passing, there have been a string of women with global recognition who have also stood above the rest, possessing qualities that culturally revolutionized and embodied their respective zeitgeists.

Centuries prior to the coining of the term in 1927, there were many special women who exerted such an impact, largely through the vehicle of fashion. During the early modern era, women such as Isabella and Beatrice d'Este (1475–1497), Lucrezia Borgia, Simonetta Vespucci (1453–1476), and Eleonora di Toledo set the tone for taste

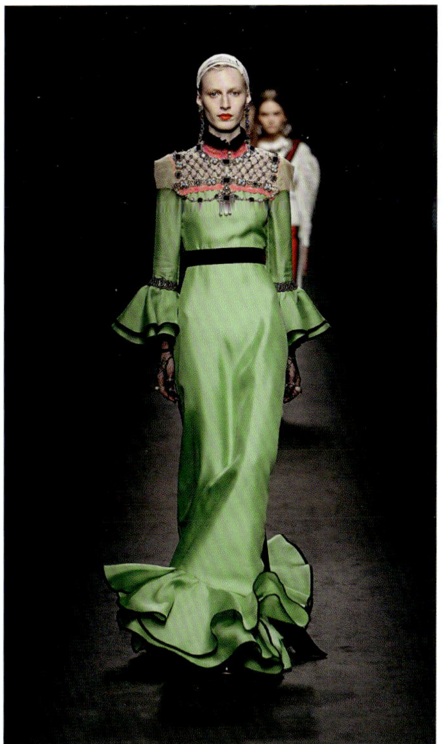

fig. 26   Evening dress, Fall–Winter 2016. Alessandro Michele (Italian, b. 1972) for Gucci (Italian, est. 1921). Silk gazar, shearling, lace, and jeweled embroidery. © Gucci Archive

while utilizing their style prowess to wield considerable political and cultural influence. Moreover, these original "it girls" set the standard for regality while shaping how scholars today understand and reconstruct the early modern period.

Many of these "it girls" had lives that were closely intertwined because they all came from powerful Italian aristocratic families in which, through marriages and alliances, they had overlapping associations. As mentioned, Isabella and Beatrice d'Este were sisters-in-law to Lucrezia Borgia. Additionally, the most powerful aristocratic families had access to vast wealth, maintaining a financial pipeline that allowed them to consume and experiment with fashion on a magnitude impossible for the rest of the population. Each "it girl" had her own preferred facets of style, especially in regard to her home municipality, but in every case, these women embodied the period's highest forms of creative expression.

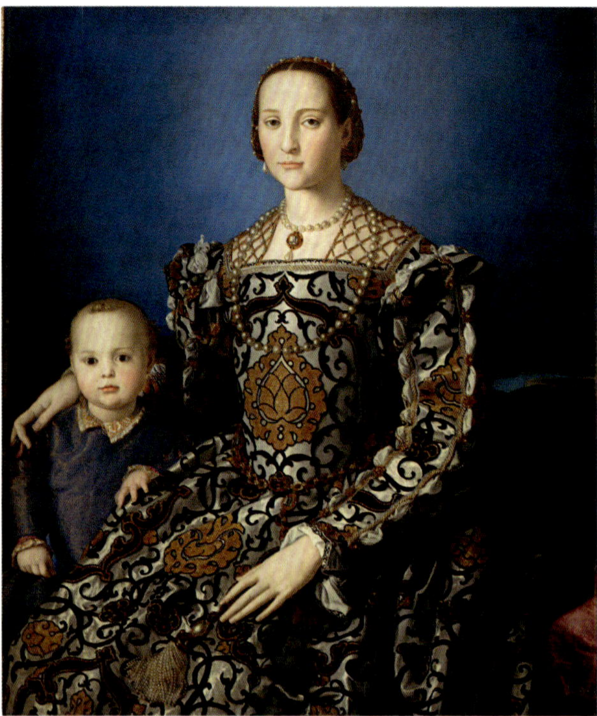

fig. 27 *Portrait of Eleonora di Toledo with Her Son Giovanni,* 1545. Agnolo Bronzino (Italian, 1503–1572). Oil on wood; 115 x 96 cm. Le Gallerie degli Uffizi, 1890 n. 748. Photo: © Gabinetto Fotografico delle Gallerie degli Uffizi

Isabella and Beatrice d'Este

For the Este sisters, the most desired accoutrement was jewelry. Similar to many aristocratic women of the Renaissance, their love of jewelry came from their mother, Eleanor of Naples (1450–1493), Duchess of Ferrara, who had a jewelry collection so enormous it was difficult for even her daughters to keep pace with her consumption.[5] In 1490, Isabella, nicknamed "First Lady of the World," married her betrothed, Francesco II Gonzaga (1466–1519), Marquis of Mantua, while the following year her sister Beatrice wedded Ludovico Sforza (1452–1508), Duke of Milan. Throughout the years, gem and jewelry gifts as well as recommendations went back and forth between the sisters and their relatives, bolstering this industry.[6]

Isabella and Francesco often worked with gem engravers within and outside of Mantua, whereby gems would be imported and then sent to preferred goldsmiths and gem cutters to execute their requested designs. Isabella was so particular about jewelry that she would return jewels containing any hint of a flaw and even sent artisans sketches of her desired jewels.[7] Titian's (c. 1488/90–1576) portrait of her captures the remarkable silhouette of her *balzo,* or headdress (a popular Northern Italian fashion); at the front of the balzo glistens a massive gem surrounded by a setting of pearls (**fig. 28**). The gem's darkly illustrated visage suggests it could have been a ruby. As for Beatrice, her Milanese court had a master gem engraver, Domenico dei Cammei.[8] Her love of jewelry was memorably captured in Giovanni Angelo Mirofoli's Sforza Altarpiece (**fig. 29**; see **pl. 16**). The artist depicted Beatrice wearing a Spanish-style cap called a *trinzale* embroidered with pearls and gems and a pearl necklace that overlaps a gold choker and pours down her narrow bodice: the very epitome of high style of the 1490s. Her hair is tucked into a

cone called a *coazzone*, tied with crossing ribbons.[9] Exemplifying how taste norms pass from one generation to the next,
Beatrice's daughter Bianca Sforza (1472–1510) inherited the
jewelry bug. A 1493 portrait of Bianca by Ambrogio de Predis
(c. 1455–after 1508) in the National Gallery of Art, Washington, DC, depicts her wearing jeweled attire including a pearl-
and gem-embroidered trinzale and coazzone.

Even though gemology was the Este family's obsession,
clothing was not far behind. Within two years of her marriage
to Ludovico Sforza, Beatrice reportedly had more than eighty
gowns commissioned for her.[10] Beatrice's fashions were so
awe-inspiring, they even enchanted Charles VIII (1470–1498),
King of France, who visited the Milanese Republic in 1494,
presumably for peace talks amid the start of the Italian Wars.[11]
French courtiers reported that on the first day of the king's
visit, she wore a gown featuring gold metallic thread with
green brocade lined in georgette and had her hair in a coazzone.[12] What King Charles did not know is that two years earlier, the Milanese ambassador to France, Antonio Calco, sent
back fashion reports on the French monarch and his wife, Anne
of Brittany (1477–1514).[13] Ever since, Beatrice incorporated
French taste in her wardrobe, and in the ensemble she wore
to host King Charles, he would have immediately discerned
her political savvy through her fashionable taste. (Isabella
also enjoyed integrating French styles in her wardrobe; in one
instance, she was angry at the tailor Alberto da Bologna for
executing a subpar interpretation of the long, draped French-
style sleeves on one of her dresses.[14]) On the second day of the Milanese court meeting with King Charles, Beatrice was attired in a gown embroidered with diamonds,
pearls, and rubies, with her chemise noticeably peering through her slashed sleeves.[15]
Clearly, Beatrice was presenting a glamorous show of strength to Charles in the face
of his military subjugation of various Italian states as he and his military forces continued their southward march to Naples.

It is important to note that from the late fifteenth century into the sixteenth, fashion
throughout the Italian peninsula was modeled on the tastes of Italy's French and Spanish neighbors. Oftentimes, the women closest to, or at the heart of, political intrigue,
like the Este sisters, were the first to experiment with foreign fashions, mixing them
with their preferred local styles.

Because fashion changes so quickly, artistic depictions of personalities from the
past help enable scholars to reconstruct the taste of a given era. The depiction of
Beatrice d'Este in the Sforza Altarpiece (see **fig. 29**), notably, the fitted bodice and
the sleeve silhouette, illustrates the vibrant silk colorways favored in Milan at the
turn of the sixteenth century. In addition, researchers have discovered that the dress
had a gold-metal-thread ground with silk strips that could have been brocaded or
were separate strips couched on top of the ground.[16] Furthermore, the smooth surface
and the angularity of the bodice seem to indicate either that her garment included
a stiffening material such as buckram, a layer of fabric that has been coagulated, or
that she was wearing a kirtle-like underbodice with a stiffening material so that her
overgown fell smoothly on top. The Spanish *vasquine*—the predecessor to the corset
and the farthingale—was not a popular undergarment in Italy, but both successors

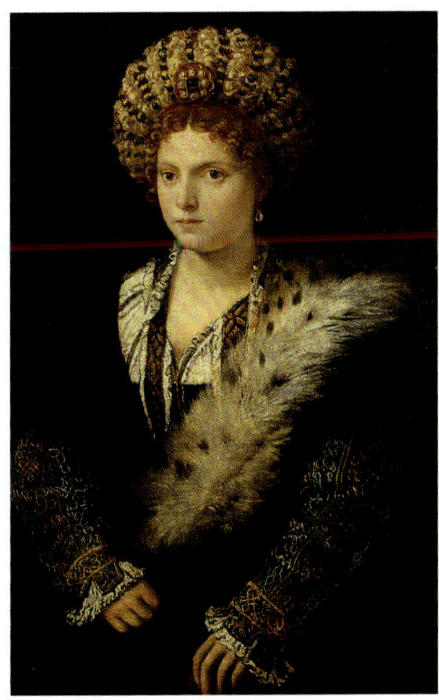

fig. 28 *Isabella d'Este*, 1534/36.
Titian (Tiziano Vecellio; Italian,
1488/90–1576). Oil on canvas;
102.4 x 64.7 cm. Kunsthistorisches
Museum, Gemäldegalerie, 83.
Photo: © KHM-Museumsverband

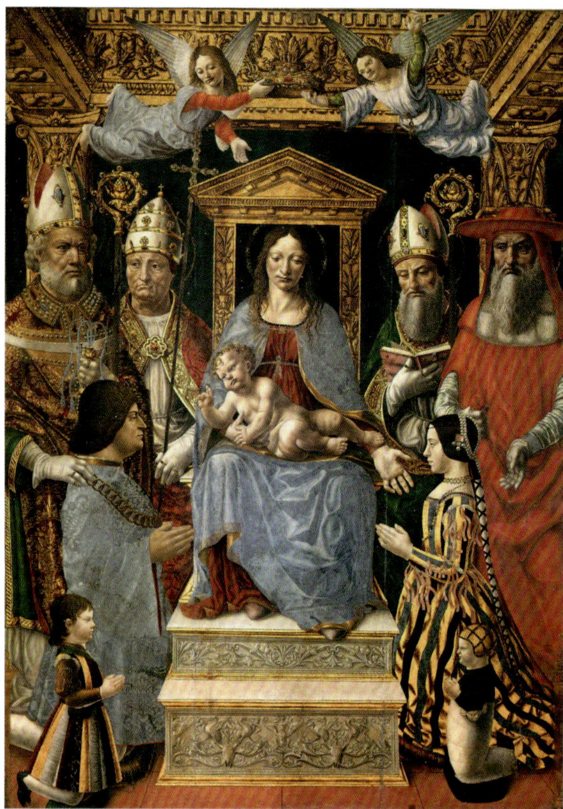

fig. 29 *Virgin and Child Enthroned with the Doctors of the Church and the Family of Ludovico il Moro* ("Sforza Altarpiece"), 1494–95. Giovanni Angelo Mirofoli (Master of the Sforza Altarpiece; Italian, 15th century). Tempera and oil on panel; 230 x 165 cm. Pinacoteca di Brera, 451. Photo: Scala / Art Resource, NY

of the vasquine eventually became mainstays throughout the peninsula.[17]

Beatrice's conical skirt suggests the possible presence of an early farthingale, or *verdugado/faldiglia*.[18] Another style of Spanish origin, the farthingale emerged in Spain in the late fifteenth century. Ironically, in 1498, a year after Beatrice's death, a Milanese sumptuary law was established prohibiting women from wearing the farthingale; the law was intended to prevent excessive luxury consumption.[19] Across the Italian peninsula, many states either banned or did not broadly adopt the farthingale until the mid- to late sixteenth century, around the time early corsets became more popular in Italy.

Around 1500, Gian Cristoforo Romano (c. 1465–1512) produced a sculptural portrait of Isabella d'Este, housed in the Kimbell Art Museum in Fort Worth, depicting her from her head to her upper bust. The sculpture captures the fitted nature of her bodice—presumably because Romano rendered the visual effect of the popular undergarments that produced such slimming effects—whereby a segment of her *camicia*, or chemise, peers out from underneath her bodice across her neckline. The sleeves of her outer gown, which are depicted as being tied to the bodice, are portrayed in a scrunched manner that Romano emphasized by making the chemise appear as if it were bursting outward from Isabella's body—an effect signaling access to sumptuousness. About thirty years after Romano's rendering, toward the end of her life, Titian painted the earlier-discussed portrait of Isabella (see **fig. 28**). In this image, a black velvet outer gown, padded upper sleeves, plunging neckline revealing a lace-lined chemise, brocaded sleeves, and fur stole come together, showcasing the latest 1530s fashions. Titian's portrait affirms that the Este sisters were forever stylish, even late in life.

Lucrezia Borgia

The Estes' sister-in-law, Lucrezia Borgia, was likewise no shrinking violet when it came to her appearance. When Lucrezia married Isabella and Beatrice's brother, Alfonso, Lucrezia owned 84 gowns, 20 cloaks, 22 headdresses, 13 belts, 33 pairs of slippers, 50 pairs of shoes, 1,900 pearls, and 300 gemstones.[20] Daughter of Rodrigo Borgia (1431–1503), later Pope Alexander VI, the most infamous papal figure in history, Lucrezia and her family had a lot to prove to situate themselves among the Italian and other European nobility. The Borgia family was notorious for its nefarious ways, including using the Catholic Church to enrich themselves, making their entrée to the center of European politics controversial. Lucrezia was her father's sole daughter; he used her in the game of politics, marrying her off to men from families who possessed the most advantageous economic, political, and military status.[21] She was barely a teenager when she was married off to her first husband, Giovanni Sforza (1466–1510), and several years later, when the Sforza family's political stature no longer suited Alexander VI, he fabricated a reason to annul Lucrezia and Giovanni's marriage.[22] A year after the annulment, she was married off to Alfonso of Aragon (1481–1500), a son of Alfonso II, King of Naples (1448–1495), but two years after the wedding, papal allegiances shifted toward France, enemy of the Neapolitans, and Alfonso was mysteriously murdered. Scholars suggest that Lucrezia had fallen in love with Alfonso, so his death affected her greatly.[23]

Alexander VI believed his daughter's third marriage, to Alfonso d'Este, the soon-to-be Duke of Ferrara, would provide the wealth and political stability needed to maintain his family's hold on power, especially given the Estes' close ties to the French court.[24] Lucrezia's sister-in-law Isabella d'Este as well as most of the Este family were wary of associating with the Borgias, making all of Lucrezia's initial interactions with the Este clan highly fraught. Despite Lucrezia being highly educated and even-keeled compared to her relatives, she was overshadowed by her family's notoriety. Thus, fashion became the key to her success in winning over her new family.

Lucrezia was technically married by proxy to Alfonso in December 1501. Alfonso's brothers, Ferrante and Cardinal Ippolito (1477–1540; 1479–1520), officiated the wedding ceremony at the Vatican on Alfonso's behalf while he remained in Ferrara.[25] When the Ferrarese party arrived, contemporary accounts recorded that Lucrezia wore a gown of white fabric, probably silk bleached white, with gold metal embroidery, sleeves brocaded in gold metal thread in the Spanish style, and a cloak of dark-brown velvet trimmed with sable.[26] The account also notes that she topped off her ensemble with a green gauze headdress. Lucrezia's prominent incorporation of Spanish fashion highlighted Spain's, France's, and other European powers' increasing influence over Italian style. In addition, Lucrezia's family was Spanish by heritage. The nod to Spanish fashion could thus have been a way of signifying her family's legacy; the use of clothing to convey such ties was not an uncommon fashion practice. Conversely, the nod to Spanish style may have been a subtle means of signaling the Borgias' ability to leverage their relationship with Spain amid the Este family's allegiance to France.

Alfonso and his sister, fashion queen Isabella, had informants report back to them on Lucrezia's dress and demeanor.[27] On one occasion, as Lucrezia was preparing to depart Rome for her new home of Ferrara, El Prete, one of Isabella's spies, who was captivated by Lucrezia's charm, wrote that when she was entertaining in her quarters, she wore a remarkable black velvet gown with gold borders (probably gold embroidery or embroidered trim), a trim of fur, and slashed sleeves, and was dripping in pearl and ruby necklaces.[28] El Prete even noted that her ladies-in-waiting were not as fashionable as Lucrezia, implying that her taste stood high above the rest. After Lucrezia moved to Ferrara, she ultimately won over the hearts and minds of her new family, and her father's passing in 1503 enabled her to separate herself from the looming scandal that enveloped the Borgia clan.

Simonetta Vespucci

South of the Sforza and Este–controlled regions of Milan, Mantua, and Ferrara lay the Florentine Republic, which became subsumed under the Duchy of Florence in 1532 and, later, the Duchy of Tuscany in 1569. This region had its own share of "it girls." Prior to the fashion reign of Isabella and Beatrice d'Este, a young woman of striking beauty named Simonetta Vespucci had a brief moment in the sun. Originally from the Genoese Republic, she married into the Vespucci family of Florence, making her a cousin-in-law of Amerigo Vespucci (1454–1512), for which the Americas were named in honor of his voyages at the turn of the sixteenth century.[29] Despite Simonetta's married status, the Medici brothers Lorenzo the Magnificent (1449–1492) and Giuliano de' Medici (1453–1478) vied for her attention.[30] Although she lived a very short life, dying around the age of twenty-two allegedly of tuberculosis, she was an electrifying and celebrated figure during her lifetime and after her death.

Florence was one of the leading centers, if not the leading center, of the Italian Renaissance; scholars often point to the iterations of Vespucci's beauty in Florentine art of this period. She served as muse to the preeminent artists of the time including Sandro Botticelli (1444/45–1510) and Piero di Cosimo (1462–1521). Scholars have proposed that the figure of Venus in Botticelli's *Birth of Venus* (**fig. 30**) captures Vespucci's essence; she died in 1476, however, years before it was completed, calling into question whether she was the sitter for that painting and others bearing resemblance to Vespucci or whether the likenesses were visual "muscle memories" of her.[31] Botticelli artworks for which scholars ascribe her as the muse often center on her supple skin and her long, flowing blonde hair, falling in luscious locks or twisted into braids with strings of pearls to amplify her radiance. Although not much is recorded about her clothing, Vespucci's presence exuded a high degree of sensuality, framing the young woman as a cultural icon and premier symbol of Florentine artistry and beauty.

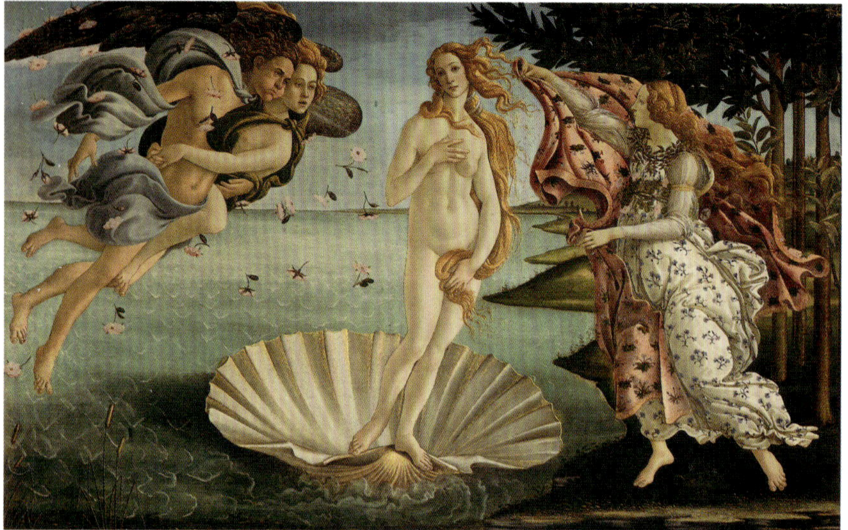

fig. 30 *Birth of Venus,* c. 1485. Sandro Botticelli (Italian, 1444/45–1510).Tempera on canvas; 203 x 314 cm. Le Gallerie degli Uffizi, 1890 n. 878. Photo: © Gabinetto Fotografico delle Gallerie degli Uffizi

Eleonora di Toledo

Following Vespucci's premature death, even though Florentine fashion styles were revered, and notable women whose stylistic impact on culture occasionally came to the fore, the newly recontextualized duchy's next "it girl" did not emerge until the following century with the rise of Eleonora di Toledo, Duchess of Florence, who ascended to the throne as the new queen of fashion in the 1530s. Eleonora was a Spanish-born princess whose father was the Viceroy of Naples.[32] Around the time of Eleonora's birth in 1522, Italy was embroiled in various military conflicts that were succeeded by the War of League of Cognac (1526–30), in which the Spanish swept through the Italian peninsula, reclaiming the region as a vassal of the Holy Roman Empire. The second year of the military campaign witnessed the Sack of Rome in 1527, in which the Medici pope Clement VII (1478–1534) was famously held under siege at the Castel Sant'Angelo. After the war ended, the Vatican was under the thumb of Charles V (1500–1558), King of Spain and Holy Roman Emperor. Peace talks ensued, and in 1530, Clement VII used Spanish forces to reconquer Florence and reinstall the Medici family in power, establishing Alessandro de' Medici (1510–1537) as the first Duke of Florence and ending Florence's status as a republic.[33] Alessandro was murdered in 1537, and having no heirs, the line of succession passed to the junior hereditary line of the Medici family, making Cosimo I de' Medici (1519–1574) the new Duke of Florence. Against the political backdrop of Medici expansion amid Spain's global dominance, Pope Clement VII orchestrated Cosimo I's betrothal to Eleonora di Toledo.[34] Eleonora's family wielded tremendous power, making the match advantageous both militarily and economically.

As with Lucrezia Borgia and many other Renaissance and early modern women, festivals, weddings, and other events were vehicles to galvanize respect. Because the Medici had conspired with the Spanish to retake Florence, Florentines were not supportive of Eleonora, so she had to work hard to gain their trust. Furthermore, instead of going straight to Florence, Eleonora took a ship to Livorno and conducted a procession through the Florentine-controlled city of Pisa to meet her betrothed for the first time.[35] Unabashedly Spanish in her taste, she wore a black silk satin gown with glistening gold-metal-thread embroidery.[36] Such embroidery, however, was also an aspect of local Neapolitan high style, speaking to her lived experience as a Spanish lady in an Italian region; thus, Eleonora's ensemble in the procession anticipated how she sought to use fashion as duchess—as a tool for communicating political affiliations. Accounts indicate that during various festivities, she wore violet-colored velvet gowns with remarkable gold embroidery, a necklace gifted to her by her new husband, a diamond ring, and a pearl snood, or hairnet, another notable Spanish court fashion at the time.[37] Eleonora's entrance into Florentine society was quite audacious, and her fusion of Italian and Spanish styles only intensified over the years, highlighting a message of political unity that was meant to align with her husband's.

Continuing her wholehearted public embrace of Spanish fashion, for Eleonora's next procession, into Florence itself, she reportedly wore a kermes-dyed red gown with "designs beaten of gold."[38] In 1539, Agnolo Bronzino, the Medici family court painter who ushered in the Mannerist art movement, depicted Eleonora in what is said to be her processional gown, in a portrait now housed in Prague's Národní Galerie. The gown's slight sheen in Bronzino's painting implies that it was probably a silk satin; and the artist also captured the swirling gold-thread embroidery across her bodice and sleeves. Her netted gold-metal-threaded partlet is embroidered with pearls, matching her snood and earrings. The combined effect of the ensemble: an unequivocal expression of Eleonora's Spanish fashion leanings.

As the Medici's relationship with the Spanish strengthened, the alliance was not looked upon kindly by the Florentines. They resented the Medici for aligning with Spain and using its armies to retake control. Eleonora's marriage to Cosimo was essentially a social hurdle that needed to be overcome for him to have a successful reign. In 1544, when Cosimo left the state in Eleonora's charge during his illness, she wrote to him: "I see myself in danger staying here without you in a hostile city with a Spanish name and under the present government."[39]

At the start of Cosimo's rule, Florence had endured years of economic uncertainty. In response, Cosimo sought to revive the textile sector. Backing her husband, Eleonora spearheaded this effort, commissioning all the major local workshops to produce extravagant decorative textiles as she renovated the various palaces in which her family lived over the years including the Palazzo Vecchio and the Palazzo Pitti.[40]

Via her Spanish roots, Eleonora introduced and donned numerous styles that swept the region. These include the *zimarra*, or overcoat, of which she was a proponent, as the outermost garment in public settings (**fig. 31**).[41] Virtually the same as the Spanish *ropa*, these jackets were considered informal, but Eleonora's style profile created a permission structure for men and women to wear such fashions in public. Eleonora even had a court tailor, Maestro Agostino, who, wardrobe records reveal, designed many of her known styles. Scholars have combed through these records to try to determine which fashions pictured in paintings of her were real or fictional. These include the gown depicted in Bronzino's earlier-discussed portrait of Eleonora and her son (see **fig. 27**). The painting was acclaimed as Eleonora's state portrait.[42] The complicated structure of the illustrated textile has prompted questions as to the gown's existence, but after the revelation of the duchess's burial gown, which is remarkably similar to the gown in the Bronzino painting, many scholars are inclined to affirm its existence. One layer of the burial gown includes a velvet underbodice that fastened at the front, a feature whose function was similar to that of the earliest generation of corsets that began to populate the European fashion lexicon by the time of her passing in 1562.[43]

The Bronzino painting presents the gown as having a silk satin–damask ground, bleached white, with a black silk–velvet brocade that subsumes the patterned regions of the damask.[44] Additionally, gold metal threads were used in the pomegranate brocades to reemphasize the outlines of the foliage patterns throughout the design. Her chemise spills outward, small gold closures line her sleeves, which have shortened in size compared to those of previous decades, and she dons a matching pearl-embroidered partlet and snood. The luxurious blackwork embroidery, a very Spanish-leaning style element, along her chemise may be seen at the edge of the bodice. Altogether, the emphasis on black–velvet brocades and the pomegranate thistle style reflects, balances, and amplifies, the emergent *ferronerie*, or ironwork style, popular in Florence at the time the painting was commissioned.[45] Conversely, because the black–velvet brocade presumably fills the damask pattern, researchers assert that the fabric is Florentine rather than a Spanish import; Spanish textiles produced brocaded textiles in the reverse.[46] The silhouette, with a padded bodice and a square neckline, elicits the Spanish style. In sum, Eleonora's dress combines Spanish fashion with Florentine textiles, conveying a unification she longed to achieve in the political realm. This painting, especially as a state-sanctioned image, promoted Florentine textiles alongside her husband's efforts to bolster the local economy. Eleonora was a very politically savvy spouse, and over the years, the Florentine people began to warm up to her remarkable, formidable spirit.

From Isabella d'Este to Eleonora di Toledo, "it girls" shaped the glamorous profile of the Renaissance and early modern period, leaving our contemporary world with clues to reconstruct the evolution of fashion and its role in the cultural landscape. Fashion was not merely a burgeoning industry during this historical period but a vital means of communication and political influence.

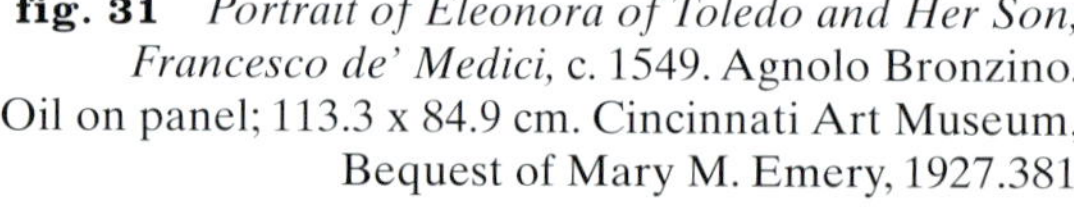

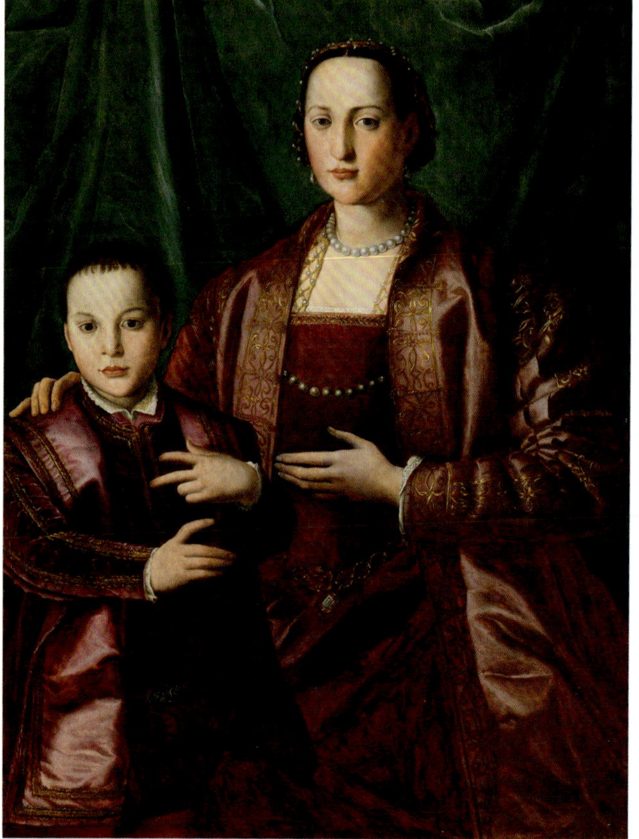

fig. 31 *Portrait of Eleonora of Toledo and Her Son, Francesco de' Medici,* c. 1549. Agnolo Bronzino. Oil on panel; 113.3 x 84.9 cm. Cincinnati Art Museum, Bequest of Mary M. Emery, 1927.381

1   Meredith K. Ray, *Twenty-Five Women Who Shaped the Italian Renaissance* (Abingdon, Oxon, UK: Routledge, 2024), 58.

2   Lisa Monnas, *Renaissance Velvets* (London: Victoria & Albert Museum, 2012), 20.

3   "The History of the It Girl," *Women's Wear Daily*, wwd.com/eye/people/gallery/the-history-of-the-it-girl-10437638/clara-bow-in-1927-bow-starredin-the-silent-film-it-after-which-she-was-nicknamed-the-it-girl-she-is-considered-hollywoods-first-sex-symbol/.

4   "History of the It Girl."

5   Jacqueline Herald, *Renaissance Dress in Italy 1450–1500* (London: Bell & Hyman; Atlantic Highlands, NJ: Humanities Press, 1981), 172.

6   Herald, *Renaissance Dress in Italy*, 171.

7   Herald, *Renaissance Dress in Italy*, 171.

8   Herald, *Renaissance Dress in Italy*, 169.

9   Lourdes Font, "1490–1499," *Fashion History Timeline*, June 28, 2021, fashionhistory.fitnyc.edu/1490-1499/.

10 Herald, *Renaissance Dress in Italy*, 38.

11 Herald, *Renaissance Dress in Italy*, 202.

12 Herald, *Renaissance Dress in Italy*, 202.

13 Herald, *Renaissance Dress in Italy*, 201.

14 Herald, *Renaissance Dress in Italy*, 202.

15 Herald, *Renaissance Dress in Italy*, 202.

16 Chiara Buss, ed., *Silk Gold Crimson: Secrets and Technology at the Visconti and Sforza Courts* (Milan: Silvana Editoriale, 2009), 25.

17 Valerie Steele, *The Corset: A Cultural History* (New Haven, CT: Yale University Press, 2001), 6.

18 Steele, *Corset*, 6.

19 Buss, *Silk Gold Crimson*, 25.

20 Carole Collier Frick, *Dressing Renaissance Florence: Families, Fortunes, and Fine Clothing* (Baltimore: Johns Hopkins University Press, 2005), 113.

21 Ray, *Twenty-Five Women*, 56.

22 Ray, *Twenty-Five Women*, 56.

23 William Waldorf Astor, "Lucretia Borgia," *North American Review* 142, no. 350 (1886): 68–73, jstor.org/stable/25118572.

24 Ray, *Twenty-Five Women*, 58.

25 Ferdinand Gregorovius, *Lucrezia Borgia: Daughter of Pope Alexander VI* (Las Vegas: Vita Histria, 2020), 174.

26 Gregorovius, *Lucrezia Borgia*, 177.

27 Gregorovius, *Lucrezia Borgia*, 178.

28 Gregorovius, *Lucrezia Borgia*, 179.

29 Zuzanna Stańska, "Simonetta Vespucci: The Renaissance Top Model," *DailyArt Magazine*, March 6, 2025, dailyartmagazine.com/simonetta-vespucci-the-renaissance-top-model/.

30 Tim Brinkhof, "Art Bites: Who Was Simonetta Vespucci, Botticelli's Enduring Muse?" *Artnet*, August 17, 2024, news.artnet.com/art-world/art-bites-simonetta-vespucci-botticelli-2523589.

31 Stańska, "Simonetta Vespucci."

32 Joe A. Thomas, "Fabric and Dress in Bronzino's Portrait of Eleanor of Toledo and Son Giovanni," *Zeitschrift für Kunstgeschichte* 57, no. 2 (1994): 262–67, doi.org/10.2307/1482735.

33 Stephen D. Bowd, "The Republics of Ideas: Venice, Florence and the Defence of Liberty, 1525–1530," *History* 85, no. 279 (2000): 404–27, jstor.org/stable/24424949.

34 Roberta Orsi Landini, *Moda a Firenze, 1540–1580: Cosimo I de' Medici's Style / Lo stile di Cosimo I de' Medici* (Florence: Mauro Pagliai, 2011), 24.

35 Janet Cox-Rearick, "Power-Dressing at the Courts of Cosimo de' Medici and François I: The 'Moda Alla Spagnola' of Spanish Consorts Eléonore d'Autriche and Eleonora di Toledo," *Artibus et Historiae* 30, no. 60 (2009): 39–69, jstor.org/stable/25702881.

36 Cox-Rearick, "Power-Dressing at the Courts."

37 Cox-Rearick, "Power-Dressing at the Courts."

38 Cox-Rearick, "Power-Dressing at the Courts."

39 Cox-Rearick, "Power-Dressing at the Courts."

40 Roberta Orsi Landini, *Moda a Firenze, 1540–1580: Lo stile di Eleonora di Toledo e la sua influenza* (Florence: Pagliai Polistampa, 2005), 24.

41 Cox-Rearick, "Power-Dressing at the Courts."

42 Thomas, "Fabric and Dress in Bronzino's Portrait."

43 Steele, *Corset*, 6.

44 Thomas, "Fabric and Dress in Bronzino's Portrait."

45 Thomas, "Fabric and Dress in Bronzino's Portrait."

46 Thomas, "Fabric and Dress in Bronzino's Portrait."

CHAPTER 3

FERRAGAMO'S NEW RENAISSANCE

by STEFANIA RICCI

With its clothing's opulent fabrics, vibrant colors, refined details, and almost architectural forms, the Renaissance represents an extraordinary period for exploring the centuries-long connection between art and fashion. This connection finds its most intense expression among Italian designers, from Dolce & Gabbana to Alessandro Michele, drawing from the vast repertoire of necklaces, luxurious fabrics, and embroidered garments depicted in Renaissance paintings. In their fashions, Italian designers celebrate the roots of their cultural tradition, utilizing their imagination, technical expertise, and extraordinary ability to communicate through art. In this way, they amplify the impulses of Rosa Genoni (1867–1954), a dressmaker, historian, and teacher of fashion who, with two dresses shown at the Milan International Exposition of 1906—one inspired by a drawing by Pisanello (c. 1395–1455) and the other by Sandro Botticelli's (1444/45–1510) *Primavera* (c. 1480; see **fig. 63** and **pl. 6**)— maintained that Renaissance art provided a crucial vehicle for imbuing Italian fashion with a national identity, differentiating it from then-predominant French fashion.

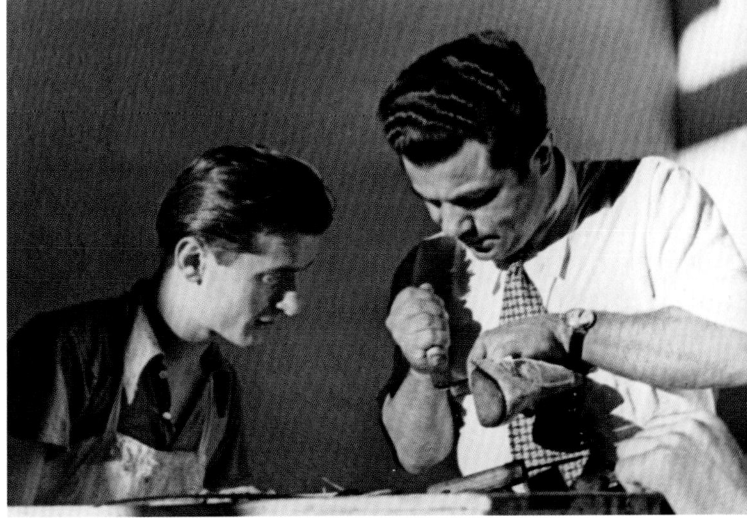

fig. 32 Salvatore Ferragamo teaching a young apprentice how to assemble a shoe. Courtesy of Museo Ferragamo. © Ferragamo

Florence, the heart of the Renaissance, has long been known for its concentration of textile manufacturing and history of tailoring. During the early modern period, its textile workshops and tailors were regulated by guilds, which constantly monitored the protocols around the execution of all fabric-based products and garment-creation services emanating from each respective municipality in the Italian peninsula.[1] In 1770, Leopold II, then the Grand Duke of Tuscany (and later the Holy Roman Emperor), abolished the guild system; thereafter, such workshops began departing from historical manufacturing techniques in favor of new technologies in their artisanal productions. Yet, these textiles created by using more current methods still elicited aesthetic qualities of the early modern era: a development that laid the groundwork for today's Italian fashion industry, becoming a globally beloved creative approach that continues to enhance Italian fashion's presence on the world stage.[2]

In 1927, when Salvatore Ferragamo (1898–1960; **fig. 32**) founded his eponymous firm, the Italian government, supported by the state-run media, recognized in the artisanal experience the essence of what could become a distinctive national fashion, separate from foreign models. By sponsoring the establishment of trade schools, the government promoted research in the textile field and on the decoration of garments and accessories; these efforts helped advance the revival of historical techniques and repertoires while also encouraging artisanal engagement with the realm of art and design.[3] This fertile terrain favored conditions whereby a new generation of fashion designers, who would gain traction in Florence in the early 1950s, could recognize in those processes, creative repertoires, quality of materials, and, above all, attention to detail the distinctive elements of an Italian style: a style that evoked historical references to Italian art and culture—most of all, the Renaissance—but with a contemporary approach. This was the very goal pursued by Giovanni Battista Giorgini (1898–1971), who, as head of an important buying agency in Florence beginning in the early 1920s, fostered the organization and promotion of fashion shows and accompanying Florentine events throughout the 1950s, utilizing the city's artistic past as an ideal backdrop to confer a clear identity and international aspirations upon Italian clothing and accessories.

Salvatore Ferragamo was among the protagonists in this fundamental chapter of Italian fashion, and, to this day, the brand he created remains a symbol of "Made in Italy." Ferragamo's story, his education, his aesthetic and business-related decisions, and the international success of his creations, particularly in the area of women's footwear, beautifully embody the "new Renaissance" that Americans identified as the postwar revival of Italian design, in which design innovation was combined with the culture of materials and artisanal expertise. On November 29, 1950, thirteen models of Ferragamo shoes, signed by the man himself (and now housed in the Metropolitan Museum of Art in New York), were exhibited alongside works in ceramics, glass, furniture, fabrics, and other Italian handicrafts in the exhibition *Italy at Work: Her Renaissance in Design Today*. The goal of *Italy at Work*, which was organized by the Brooklyn Museum in New York and subsequently traveled to twelve US cities, including Chicago and Providence, Rhode Island, was to demonstrate how the rebirth of Italian design in the post–World War II years was guided not only by architects and designers but also by artisans; the exhibition emphasized the fundamental role the latter played in restoring Italy's centrality within the global panorama of design and fashion.[4]

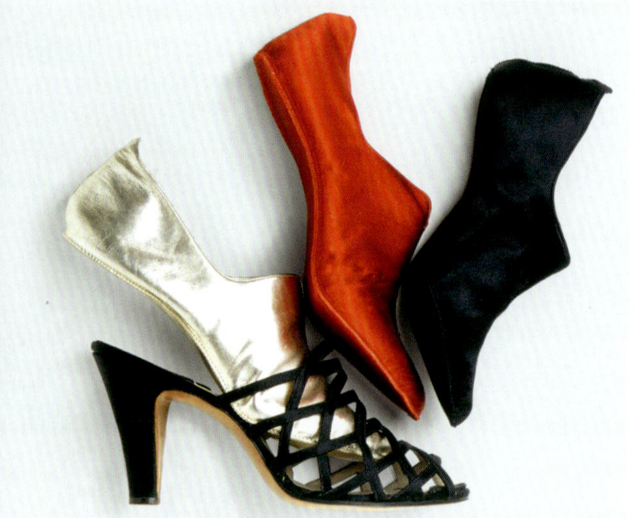

fig. 33 *Kimo* sandal, 1951. Salvatore Ferragamo (Italian, 1898–1960 for Ferragamo (Italian, est. 1927). Sandal in kidskin with silk satin and leather socklets. Courtesy of Museo Ferragamo. © Ferragamo

When Giorgini organized the first postwar Italian fashion show at his home on Via de' Serragli in Florence, launching a national trend, Ferragamo could not ignore his friend's invitation to participate. For the occasion, he created his now-famous *Kimo*: a high-heeled kidskin sandal worn with leather or satin socks. Inspired by the *tabi*, a form of Japanese footwear consisting of a sock and a sandal-like shoe, and by fifteenth-century Italian soled stockings, the *Kimo* exemplifies the shifting influences that would subsequently characterize Italian style, while invoking a historical past that had given the country its primacy (**fig. 33**).[5]

By the 1930s, Ferragamo had become a prestigious brand known abroad, especially in the United States, where its models were sold in leading department stores such as I. Magnin and Saks. Born in Bonito, a small town in Southern Italy, in 1898, Salvatore

Ferragamo learned the shoemaker's craft at a young age. After emigrating to California in 1915, he rapidly built his fortune, first in Santa Barbara and then in Hollywood, creating exclusive footwear for the emerging American film industry and its actresses. In the United States, he came to the realization that the success of his shoes—made entirely by hand—could be further expanded, thanks to his bond with Italian art and culture, embodied by the Renaissance and Florence. The Tuscan city's prominence was powerfully shaped by the patronage of the mercantile-turned-aristocratic Medici family. As the Medici's wealth and power were initially amassed through banking and political savvy, they represented, for Americans as well as for the young Ferragamo, a notion akin to the "American Dream," whereby talent, initiative, and moxie could enable anyone, even those without noble origins, to achieve success.[6]

In 1927, Ferragamo returned to Italy, settling in Florence. Near the Campo di Marte train station and operating under the name Ferragamo Incorporated, he opened up a factory that produced handmade shoes for the American market. Due to both commercial success and the favorable Italian political climate, which encouraged the development of craftsmanship, he decided to remain there permanently. The global financial crisis triggered by the US stock market crash of 1929 adversely affected the start-up, which was closely tied to the US market. Increasing financial difficulties, pressure from American partners, and the sale of the Hollywood store—an option Ferragamo had long attempted to avoid—pushed him to establish a company based wholly in Italy, of which he remained the sole owner. This did not suffice to save the firm, however, and in 1933, Ferragamo was forced to declare bankruptcy. Despite this serious blow, he did not allow himself to become discouraged. He resumed operations, expanding his clientele throughout the rest of Italy and Europe. Before long he regained his footing and, even with the outbreak of World War II, led the company to new heights, establishing Ferragamo as a touchstone for innovation and quality craftsmanship in the world of footwear fashion. In 1947, Ferragamo received important international recognition when he was given the first Neiman Marcus Award for the creativity of his footwear. This would be the first in a series of accolades that Italian fashion would celebrate.

Because of his vast knowledge of the American market and his ability to interpret its tastes and needs, in Florence Ferragamo had the foresight to associate his high-quality handmade shoes with the image of the Tuscan capital, establishing numerous collaborations with local artisans: from craftspeople working with semiprecious stones to those specializing in fine embroidery and precious jewelry. For many of his clients, especially foreigners, purchasing a Ferragamo shoe signified possessing a piece of Florence, with its glorious artistic and cultural past. Advertising for his creations centered on an evocative image of Ferragamo, seated before a cobbler's studio in elegant attire, in a pose analogous to that of a Renaissance artist in the workshop of Lorenzo

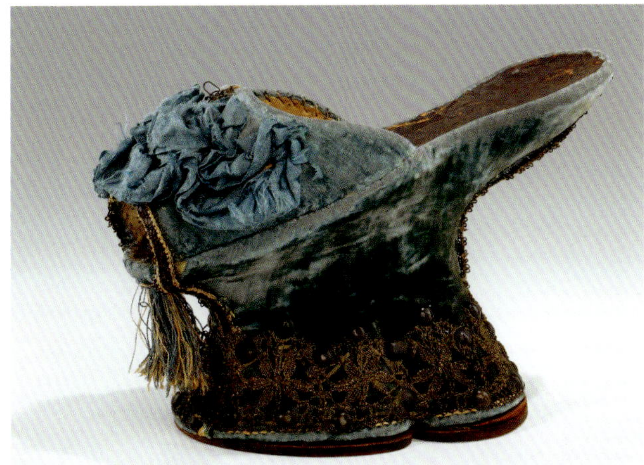

fig. 34　Chopines, 1590–1610. Italian. Silk and metal thread. Brooklyn Museum Costume Collection at The Metropolitan Museum of Art, Gift of the Brooklyn Museum, 2009; Gift of Mrs. Clarence R. Hyde, 1928, 2009.300.1408

Ghiberti (1378–1455) or Andrea Verrocchio (1435–1488). This shrewd branding spoke to his technical ability, his passion for his work, and a design insight that merged architecture, anatomy, and mechanics.

In the artisanal world from which he hailed, Ferragamo ushered in a wave of renewal, blending Italian artisanal traditions with American production savvy acquired during his years in Hollywood. He introduced a manufacturing system inspired by the assembly line, transforming it into a human process in which every artisan specialized in a specific phase of production. He also innovated the fitting system, adopting the American standard that offered a wide range of sizes, differentiated not only by the length but also the width of the foot. Ferragamo transformed the shoe into a creative laboratory of research into forms and colors. He utilized precious and innovative materials such as cellophane in addition to reinterpreting traditional ones like leather and cork, employing them in novel ways: upper portions of shoes decorated with straw threads from hats or Tavarnelle lace, or otherwise embracing surprising chromatic combinations and original decorative motifs. One of his most revolutionary inventions was the *cambrione*, an insole covered in metal foil; light and resistant, the cambrione replaced the traditional leather insole, providing greater support for the arch of the foot. In another major innovation, in 1937 he invented the renowned cork wedge heel, a creative response to the economic sanctions imposed on Italy amid the war against Ethiopia, which limited imports of German steel needed for constructing shanks.[7] In addition to being a practical solution, the wedge heel also revealed the extent to which Ferragamo studied history books and museum collections. With the high sole, he evoked the fifteenth-century female shoes known as *chapins*, or chopines (**fig. 34**), which, with their 50 centimeters of height, gave their wearers the appearance of being well-born and slender (**fig. 35**).

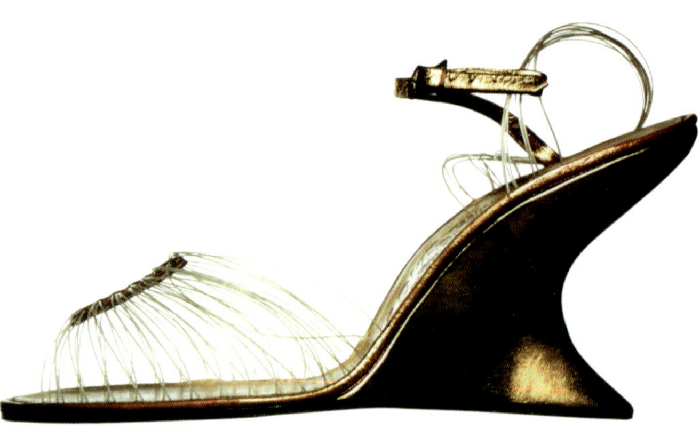

fig. 35   *Invisibile*, 1947. Salvatore Ferragamo (Italian, 1898–1960) for Ferragamo (Italian, est. 1927). Sandal with nylon and kidskin with wedge heel in covered wood. Courtesy of Museo Ferragamo, © Ferragamo

The reopening of international borders and the resumption of trade following World War II provided conducive circumstances for Ferragamo to further develop his creative vision, especially with regard to heels and soles. Among his most extraordinary creations, the 18-carat gold sandal stands out as a manifesto of the Ferragamo philosophy.[8] Equipped with a complex metal sole that maintained the comfort typical of leather shoes, this model boasted exuberant decoration, created with incisions and chisels. Commissioned by an American client for $1,000, the sandal was created in collaboration with the goldsmiths of the Casa dell'Orafo, near Florence's Ponte Vecchio. With the four-petal flower and the squared corolla of the upper shoe, the sandal was inspired by sacred goldworks in fifteenth-century Florence, while the serpent-dragon that twists around the heel derived from the handles and ornamental motifs of vases in the Medici Treasury, housed at the Palazzo Pitti.[9] Thus, the sandal encapsulates the inextricable bond between Italian fashion and the decorative patrimony of its rich cultural past, rooted in the interaction between artisanal skill and design culture dating back to the Renaissance. In 2021, Maximilian Davis (b. 1995), an

Englishman, began working as the firm's new creative director at Ferragamo's headquarters in Florence. As expected, he immersed himself in the fashion house's rich history; he zeroed in on the story of the gold sandal, the brand's icon, reintroducing it into present-day collections but with a more contemporary heel (see **pl. 10**).

Since Salvatore's death in 1960, the Ferragamo company has been led by his wife, Wanda (1921–2018), and his six children, who, fulfilling the founder's dream, transformed the firm into a world-renowned fashion house that attires men and women. The transition to the family's leadership has enabled the Ferragamo legacy to be maintained and supported over time. This legacy is further promoted thanks to the establishment, in 1985, of the house archive, which preserves records of the brand's long history, and, in 1995, the opening of a museum, the Museo Ferragamo, devoted to celebrating the Ferragamo vision.

The connection to Florence's artisanal and artistic traditions in which Ferragamo immersed the business has not only been continuous; it has also been reinforced over the decades by advertising campaigns and fashion collections emphasizing the house's ties to local handicrafts and the city's artistic and architectural masterworks. Paintings in the Uffizi Gallery such as Francesco Granacci's (1469–1543) *Joseph Conducted to Prison* (1515) or Giorgio Vasari's (1511–1574) *Portrait of Alessandro I de' Medici* (1534) entered Davis's creative mood board for the Fall–Winter 2023 collection (**fig. 36**) and became backdrops for the advertising campaign, while photos by Juergen Teller (b. 1964) situated the 2024 collection amid the sculptures of the Loggia dei Lanzi in the Piazza della Signoria.

Salvatore Ferragamo left an important legacy rooted not only in models that express his creative, forward-looking approach to shapes and colors. Above all else, he taught us that the past is always contemporary, and that only by looking to the past can we design the future.

fig. 36 Ensemble, Fall–Winter 2023. Maximilian Davis (British, b. 1995) for Ferragamo (Italian, est. 1927). © Ferragamo. The backdrop is Giorgio Vasari's *Portrait of Alessandro I de' Medici*, Galleria delle Statute e delle Pitture degli Uffizi, Gallerie degli Uffizi, Florence, 1890 n. 1563. By concession of Ministero della Cultura–Le Gallerie degli Uffizi

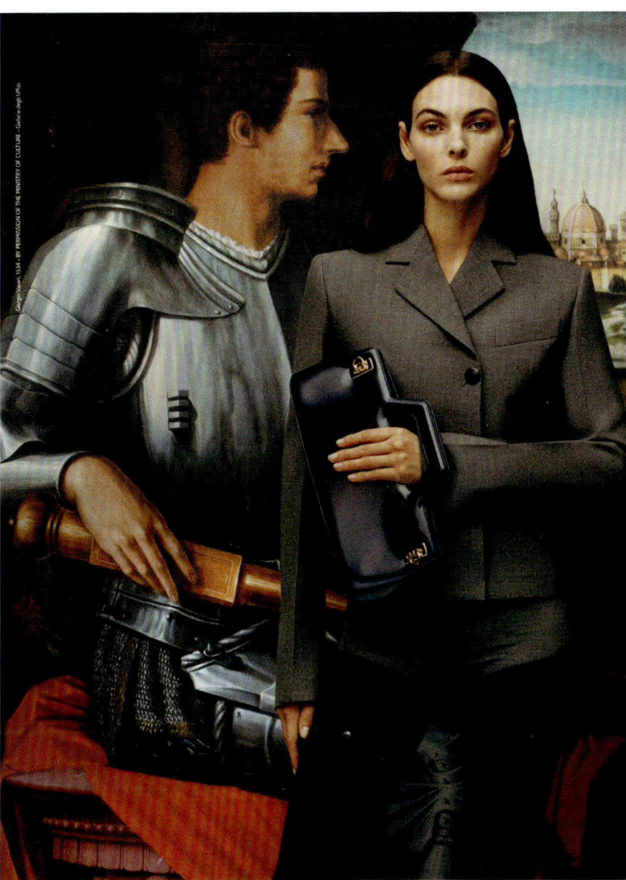

1 Stefania Ricci, "L'artigianata della moda," in *La grande storia dell'artigianata*, vol. 6, *Il Novecento*, ed. Gloria Fossi (Milan: Giunti, 2003), 229–95; and Ricci, "Florence Fascinates the World," in *Fashion in Florence: Through the Lens of Archivio Foto Locchi, 1934–1970*, by Erika Ghilardi and Matteo Parigi Bini (Prato: Gruppo Editoriale, 2017), 47–66.

2 Aurora Fiorentini Capitani and Stefania Ricci, "The Winning Cards of Italian Fashion," in *The Sala Bianca: The Birth of Italian Fashion*, by Guido Vergani, ed. Giannino Malossi, trans. Antony Shugaar (Milan: Electa, 1992), pl. 118; Paolo Colombo, "Il mestiere dell'arte e il Made in Italy, tra un passato lontano e un futuro assai prossimo," *Quaderni di ricerca sull'artigianato* 60 (2012): 54; and Maria Luis Frisa, Anna Mattirolo, and Stefano Tonchi, eds., *Bellissima: Italy and High Fashion, 1945–1968*, exh. cat. (Milan: Electa, 2014).

3 Stefania Ricci and Carlo Sisi, eds., *1927: The Return to Italy; Salvatore Ferragamo and Twentieth-Century Visual Culture*, exh. cat. (Milan: Skira, 2017).

4 Chiara Faggella, "The New Renaissance in Italian Fashion: Ferragamo and the Post-War Era," in *Salvatore Ferragamo, 1898–1960*, ed. Stefania Ricci, exh. cat. (Milan: Electa, 2024), 482–89.

5 Stefania Ricci, "Salvatore Ferragamo, 1898–1960," in Ricci, *Salvatore Ferragamo, 1898–1960*, 416–81.

6 Stefania Ricci, ed., *Italy in Hollywood*, exh. cat. (Milan: Skira, 2018).

7 Stefania Ricci, ed., *Ideas, Models, Inventions: The Patents and Company Trademarks of Salvatore Ferragamo from 1929 to 1964*, exh. cat. (Livorno: Sillabe, 2004).

8 Sandra Salibian, "Ferragamo Stages Exhibition Celebrating the Brand's Founder," *Women's Wear Daily*, October 27, 2023, wwd.com/fashion-news/fashion-features/ferragamo-stages-not-to-miss-exhibition-on-brands-founder-life-shoes-florence-1235890869/.

9 Elisabetta Nardinocchi, "From the Golden *Primavera* Footwear to Salvatore Ferragamo's Golden Sandals," in Ricci, *Salvatore Ferragamo, 1898–1960*, 490–99.

CHAPTER 4

FASHION IS A FAMILY BUSINESS

In Italy, fashion is a family business. Whether speaking about the early modern period or the contemporary fashion world, family ties have always powered the creative engine of Italian style. From the production of luxury textiles to the evolution of garment silhouettes, fashion in the Renaissance was central to the image and influence of the Italian aristocratic clans that governed their respective municipalities. In various Italian fashion houses currently in operation, many of which arose during the post–World War II period, families have typically united behind a lead relative and, like their early modern predecessors, have played a significant role in forging our current taste regime.

Further uniting these two eras of Italian history, numerous Italian fashion houses have looked to the Renaissance for inspiration, linking the rebirth of Italian influence in fashion to the historical renewal of culture to define their "Italianness," as Dr. Matteo Augello has explained. In his acclaimed book, *Curating Italian Fashion: Heritage, Industry, Institutions* (2022), Augello writes: "Organizations, whether public or private, may build upon existing narratives or develop new ones, in order to stress the connection which the organization has with local or national communities, cultures and events."[1] Houses such as Buccellati, ETRO, and Missoni have linked their creative aesthetics, literally or conceptually, to the Renaissance and the early modern period, incorporating historical elements into contemporary fashion while maintaining their operations through the involvement of the families whose surname appears in the firm's moniker.

Even earlier than most modern-day Italian houses, the house of Bvlgari was founded by the Greek-born Italian silversmith Sotirios Voulgaris (1857–1932) in Rome in 1884. Opening stores throughout the Eternal City, he embedded, ancient classical, medieval, Byzantine, and early modern artistic references into his creations, references that have become a bedrock of the house's design code. For example, around 1984, the house produced a striking necklace with a silk chord band and a sardonyx cameo, set in diamonds and a ruby, evoking the Medusa (**fig. 37**). As a Greek mythological creature, the Medusa speaks to the Bvlgari founder's Greek origins. At the same time, the

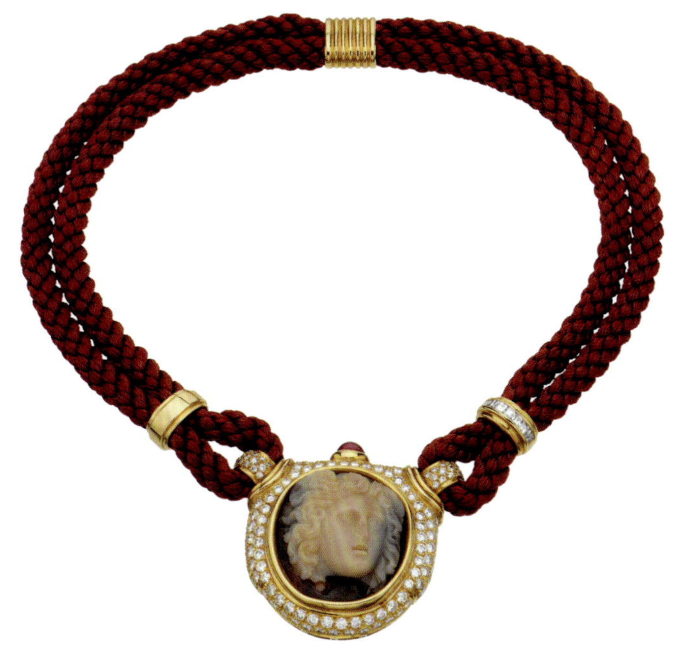

fig. 37   Necklace, c. 1984. Bvlgari. Gold with silk cord, sardonyx cameo, ruby, and diamonds. Bvlgari Heritage Collection. Photo © Bvlgari

Medusa is more broadly a Greco-Roman reference, given its widespread appearance in ancient Roman visual culture. In addition, the cameo was a popular Greek and Roman accessory that received renewed attention in the early modern era. The layering of influences in the Bvlgari necklace comprises a mere fraction of the historical artistic expressions that underpin Italian contemporary creativity. After Voulgaris's death, his son Giorgio (1890–1966) continued the family legacy, and he was later succeeded by his sons Gianni (b. 1935), Paolo (b. 1937), and Nicola Bvlgari (b. 1941). Paolo remained involved in the business until 2011, by which time the Bvlgari aesthetic had become thoroughly entrenched in global fashion due to the family's sustained involvement in the firm and the continual homage to their storied ingenuity by those who have contributed, and continue to contribute, to the house's longevity.

As Stefania Ricci discussed in the previous chapter, Salvatore Ferragamo's (1898–1960) house and design prowess embody the intersection of history, family, and modern creativity. Building his fashion house in the center of Florence, the crown jewel of the Renaissance, Ferragamo looked to an array of early modern cultural forms to inspire modern innovations, such as chopines (high platform shoes) serving as the inspiration for his famed wedges (see **figs. 34, 35** and **pl. 20**). Salvatore's wife, Wanda (1921–2018), played a crucial role in building the business. Upon his passing in 1960, Wanda assumed control over the firm and continued to draw on the same wellspring of sources, fusing them with each new generation's fashion inclinations.[2] Although the house's creative director, Maximilian Davis (British, b. 1995), is not part of the family lineage, the Ferragamo clan is still very much involved in the firm's day-to-day operations. Moreover, Davis continues to develop the Ferragamo brand through codes developed amid the family's origins, amplifying the significance of familial collaboration and legacy in creative expression.

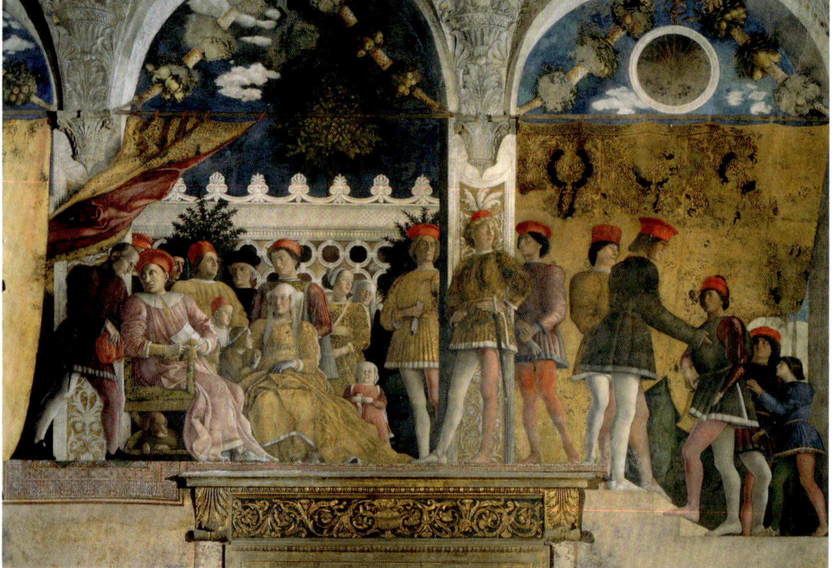

fig. 38   *The Court of the Gonzaga*, 1474. Andrea Mantegna (Italian, c. 1431–1506). Walnut oil on plaster; 805 x 807 cm. Camera degli Sposi, Palazzo Ducale, Mantua. Photo: Scala / Art Resource, NY

With its incredible display of fashion, Andrea Mantegna's (c. 1431–1506) fresco *The Court of the Gonzaga* showcases fashion's role as a signifier of power in the Renaissance, while also promoting its production and consumption (**fig. 38**; see **pl. 18**). The fresco is located on the north wall of the Camera degli Sposi in the Palazzo Ducale in Mantua. "Camera degli Sposi" translates to "bridal chamber," but in reality the camera was a space for conducting Gonzaga court business during the reign of Marquis of Mantua Ludovico III (1412–1478), making the Palazzo Ducale home base for the Gonzaga clan. As a side note, Ludovico was the grandfather of Marquis Francesco II

(1466–1519) and grandfather-in-law of queen of fashion Isabella d'Este (1474–1539), the earliest patrons of Baldassare Castiglione (1478–1529)—attesting that personal style was integral to the Gonzaga family long before Castiglione came along and codified *sprezzatura*. Moreover, during the 1460s and 1470s, Ludovico III ruled alongside his wife, Barbara of Brandenburg (1422–1481), establishing a flourishing court that sponsored artistic production on an increasingly vast scale.

The Camera degli Sposi fresco depicts Ludovico III, his family, and the Mantuan court in an audience-reception room, exquisitely attired in the height of Italian fashion of the mid- to late fifteenth century. Seated on the far left, Ludovico wears a decadent wool or velvet red *veste*, a garment typical of mature-aged statesmen at the time. Seated to his right, Barbara wears a voluminous golden-colored gown, presumably velvet, brocading across her bodice and sleeves, its train sweeping the floor. From her sleeves, her chemise slightly peers out, while her veil pours down from her head and over her bodice. The Gonzaga children are all attired in a manner similar to their parents, and the palace servants and courtiers around the marquis and his family are also dressed in garments of comparable richness. Several servants at the right of the fresco wear what appear to be brocaded, velvet-pleated, long-sleeve jackets called *cioppa*. The mismatched red and white hoses that run up the men's legs betray their servant status; in addition, the male servants wear the same circular hat as Ludovico, indicating that those individuals are his personal butlers and security detail.[3] Behind Barbara is a woman, also luxuriously attired, in a brocaded high-waist gown, who is possibly the marquise's lady-in-waiting. More than a family portrait, Mantegna's fresco was meant to portray the Gonzaga as a dignified, fashionable family who, as purveyors of taste, occupied the same socioeconomic echelon as the Sforza and Este clans. The fresco also illustrated the Gonzaga's access to vast wealth, enabling them to purchase and participate in the creation of fashion. And it highlighted the importance of the principal family member and their subjects by adorning them in an equally sumptuous manner—showcasing the principal's power in life and in art. As we recall, Lucrezia Borgia (1480–1519) made her entrance into Ferrara with 1,700 fabulously dressed courtiers.

In the twentieth century, fashion houses emerged decade after decade, fueled by innovative designers and their families, reasserting Italy's place as a fashion hub. An especially notable connection between past and present is seen in the house of Pucci. During the Renaissance, the aristocratic Florentine Pucci family were close allies of the Medici. Building their wealth through their political connections, the Pucci family remained a powerful force throughout the early modern period only to see their status decline in the nineteenth century amid the dawn of Italian unification. A descendant of the clan, Emilio Pucci (1914–1992) began designing ski uniforms in 1947—uniforms informed by his career as an Olympic skier.[4] The publication that same year of photographs of Pucci wearing his own designs in *Harper's Bazaar* launched his new career as

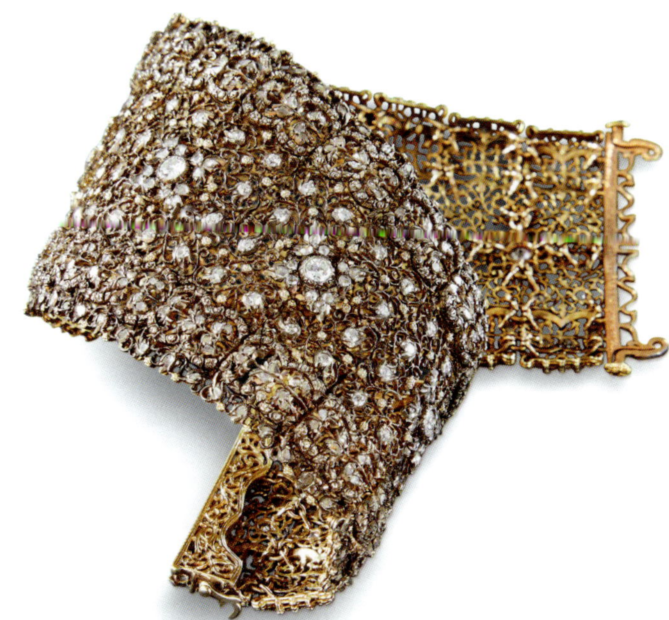

fig. 39   Ramage Bracelet, 1920s. Mario Buccellati (Italian, 1891–1965) for Buccellati (Italian, est. 1919). Diamonds, silver, and gold. Photo: © Aplomb Photo Studio

a designer and marked the beginning of one of Italy's most enduring houses.[5] Pucci was heralded as the "Prince of Prints," creating graphic geometric designs that fused motifs from Balian batiks with patterns from North African and Sicilian mosaics; this combination of influences recalls early modern Italian textiles, which also adapted arabesque forms from regions such as North Africa. It is important to note that prior to Emilio's rise, the Pucci family had earlier dealings in textile production.[6] In the late eighteenth century, the Pucci were among the handful of Italian families whose ancestors dated back to the early modern era and who still possessed in-house looms from previous generations. In 1786, these families came together to form Antico Setificio, which is still in existence today, one of the only manufacturers using handlooms to produce textiles using authentic Renaissance and early modern patterns.

On establishing the new design house, Emilio Pucci acquired the majority of Antico Setificio, establishing a pipeline for his design aspirations. As such, it was through his family's legacy that Pucci came to found the eponymous fashion house. His daughter, Laudomia (b. 1961), followed in his footsteps in the 1980s, taking over the business in 1992. Today, the firm's creative director is Camille Miceli (b. 1972), who is upholding Emilio Pucci's legacy while adding her own imprint to the house by combining different prints from the 1960s and 1970s and redrawing them by hand.[7] For the Pucci Spring 2024 collection, she reproduced Emilio Pucci's 1965 Vivara print, rendering it in the form of silhouettes that draw on popular Italian fashions of the late 1400s (see **pl. 17**).

The house of Buccellati even more concretely exemplifies the notion of the family as a core conduit for creating fashion. The four-generation, family-run organization has fabricated a wide range of jewelry and decorative arts that combine various art historical elements, translating them into the highest form of design. Opening his first store in 1919 and greatly inspired by Renaissance goldsmiths—the leading jewelers of

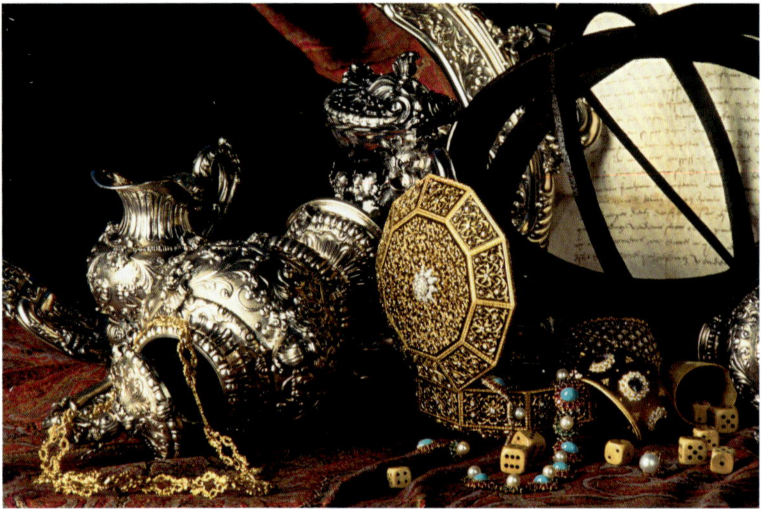

fig. 40   Medici Casket with other Buccellati jewels by photographer Frank Horvat, 1980s. Gianmaria Buccellati (Italian, 1929–2015) for Buccellati (Italian, est. 1919). Diamonds, gold, and steel. © Frank Horvat Studio / Buccellati

their day—Mario Buccellati (1891–1965) built his practice around capturing the visual essence of early modern decorative arts in the form of jewelry.[8] For instance, the house's classic Ramage Bracelet features a tree-foliage (ramage) design that mimics openwork textiles and lace (**fig. 39**). Four of Mario Buccellati's five sons joined him to expand the business, with his son Gianmaria (1929–2015) succeeding him.[9] Similar to Pucci prints and psychedelic patterns of the 1960s, Gianmaria looked to mosaics from a wide range of cultures as his major contribution to the Buccellati lexicon.[10] In addition to jewelry, the Buccellati house is also known for its vibrant decorative arts. In 1970, Gianmaria famously designed the decagonal silhouetted Medici Casket, which references the angularity of Florentine Renaissance architecture, specifically Santa Maria del Fiore (the Duomo), and goldwork inspired by the sketches of Filippo Brunelleschi (1377–1446), the architect of Santa Maria's dome (**fig. 40**).[11] Gianmaria son's Andrea (b. 1958) became an apprentice to his father in 1978, assuming additional creative responsibilities in the decades since; his design outlook took a slight detour from Renaissance undercurrents to embrace a more Rococo-referential design. Since 2013, Andrea's daughter, Lucrezia (b. 1989), has been collaborating with her father and his creative team on new designs. Like her father, Lucrezia applies many of the design methods of her grandfather and great-grandfather, albeit in a more streamlined and subtle manner, balancing whimsical connections to the past with an awareness of the minimalist present.

The house of Missoni was founded by the loving couple Ottavio Missoni (1921–2013) and Rosita Jelmini (1931–2025), whose vision lives on in the house's eclectic patterns, utilized in designs that have stood the test of time. As discussed in greater depth in the next chapter, the Missoni aesthetic, with its famed zigzag motifs, exudes a contemporary-art adjacency, blurring the boundary between fine art and fashion. When the founders' daughter, Angela (b. 1958), assumed creative control with the help of her brother Luca (b. 1956), the two took a keen interest in revitalizing patterns and experimenting with new design principles in the same spirit as their parents.

ETRO is another significant player in contemporary Italian fashion whose practice was built on interpreting early modern patterns and modern prints. Gerolamo "Gimmo" Etro (b. 1939) established his eponymous house in 1968 with the intention of providing textiles to other ready-to-wear companies.[12] Inspired by his wife, Roberta's, textile and dress collection of paisley shawls and dressing gowns, Gimmo Etro built his vision around the various textile expressions that span the globe and historical eras, especially focusing on nineteenth-century Indian exports.[13] The family launched the ready-to-wear arm of their business in 1990, and the Etro siblings, Jacopo (b. 1962), Kean (b. 1964), Ippolito (b. 1967), and Veronica (b. 1974), took charge of daily operations throughout the following decade, creating luxuriously made designs that serve as art historical journeys through time and space.[14] The four siblings been integral to keeping their parents' legacy alive. Today, Marco De Vincenzo (b. 1978), the house's first creative director outside of the Etro family, champions the strong referential component that Gimmo Etro and his children trailblazed. Like Camille Miceli of Pucci, De Vincenzo seeks to balance the dynamic print heritage of ETRO with the minimalist attitudes of the present, expanding Gimmo's legacy in ways that resonate with contemporary audiences.[15] For the Fall 2024 collection, a set of ensembles featured laminated gold motifs reminiscent of the pomegranates pictured in many silk textiles from the Renaissance (**fig. 41**). During the early modern period, gold metal threads would have been brocaded to elicit the most luxurious interface, imbuing the textile with a sheen-like quality. As such metal threads would be too cumbersome for contemporary audiences to wear, De Vincenzo's use of lamination was a technologically savvy means of achieving the same visual effect as historical textiles. De Vincenzo

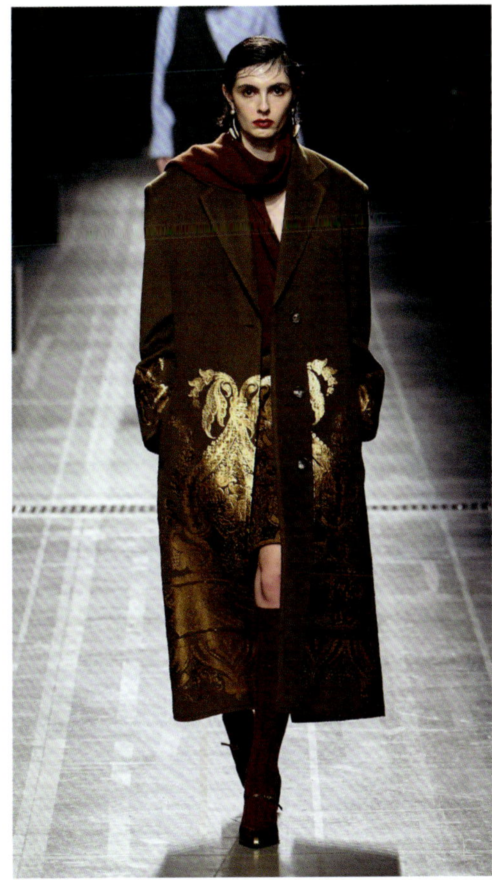

fig. 41 Ensemble, Fall 2024. Marco De Vincenzo (Italian, b. 1978) for ETRO (Italian, est. 1968). Wool, cashmere, and laminated floral print. Photo: Daniele Oberrauch, *Vogue*, © Condé Nast

thereby upholds the Etro family's legacy, his own design prowess, and both his and the ETRO house's affinity for reinterpreting early modern aesthetics as a core value of Italian identity and fashion.

Of course, no discussion of fashion as a family business would be complete without mentioning Versace. The house was started in 1978 by Gianni Versace (1946–1997) in partnership with his sister Donatella (b. 1955) and his brother, Santo (b. 1944). Gianni oversaw the creative direction of the house with Donatella's help, while Santo headed up the house's administration. After Gianni's passing in 1997, Donatella continued to expand Versace into the global powerhouse it is today. Inspired by his mother, Francesca (d. 2008), who was a seamstress, Gianni Versace was enamored of the practice of draping, melding references to dress histories from the classical period to the Renaissance.[16] When he launched his Atelier Versace haute couture line, he amplified his practice through various medieval and early modern art historical references. This is evidenced in his Spring 1991 Atelier Versace collection, which included printed images of medieval- and Renaissance-inspired depictions of the Madonna and crystal-embroidered crucifix accoutrements; it is also seen in his chainmail mesh dresses embroidered with metal-thread crosses in his Fall 1997 Atelier collection (**fig. 42**).[17] Most famously, Gianni designed the Versace logo to resemble the mythological figure of the Medusa, in much the same spirit in which Renaissance and early modern artists such as Caravaggio (1571–1610) and other houses, including Bvlgari, looked to classical mythology for artistic experimentation.[18]

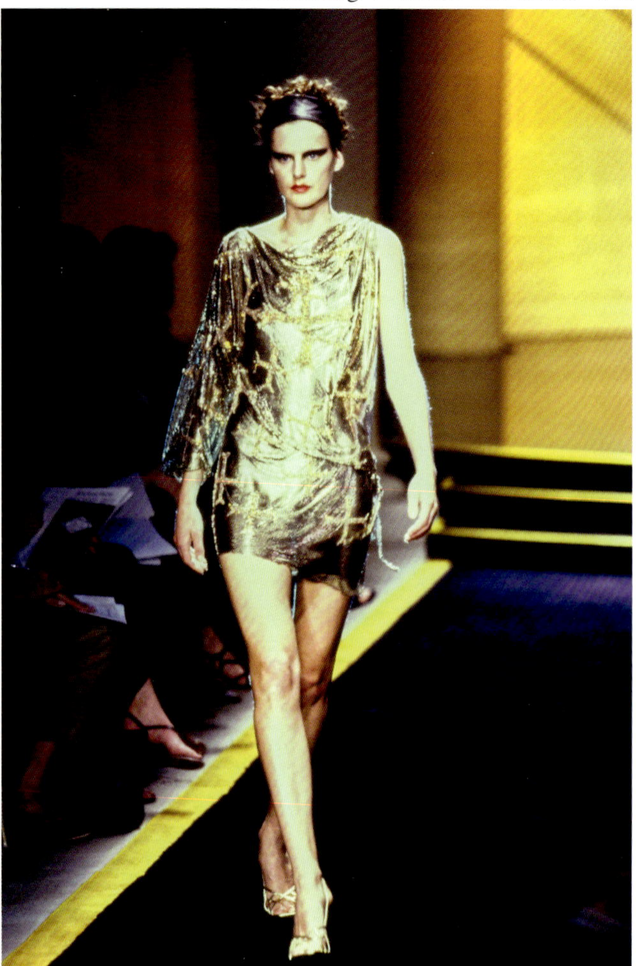

fig. 42 Evening dress, Fall 1997 Atelier. Gianni Versace (Italian, 1946–1997) for Versace (Italian, est. 1978). Metal mesh. Photo: Guy Marineau, *Vogue*, © Condé Nast

In a notable continuity of designing with Renaissance-referential intentions, for the Atelier Versace Spring 2018 collection, Donatella conceived sweeping silk chiffon and velvet A-line gowns with crystal and metal-thread embroideries in motifs that mimic the fanciful embroideries of fifteenth- and sixteenth-century luxury fashions. The lavender gown from this collection even has a netted décolletage that mirrors the netted partlets used to cover a woman's neckline and upper bust (see **pl. 36**). Gianni's vision surrounding his Baroque-inspired foliage motif is another major code that descended from his creative arsenal to Donatella's, as seen in the Versace Spring 2018 collection (**fig. 43**). Along with the Baroque floral-printed ensembles seen in the Fall 1991 and Spring 1992 collections, the Spring 2018 collection brought together many of the house's codes, from Renaissance Madonna imagery and mid-twentieth-century Pop Art Warholian homages as implemented in the Spring 1991 collection to draped high-slit, chainmail-like dresses as seen in the Fall 1994 collection. Moreover, Gianni's impact and love of the Renaissance and the early modern era has been wholeheartedly embraced through Donatella's tenure as creative director, positioning the house of Versace at the center of Italian fashion.

fig. 43 Ensemble, Spring 2018. Donatella Versace (Italian, b. 1955) for Versace (Italian, est. 1978). Cotton denim, printed silk twill, silk satin, gold metal thread, lace, leather, and metal. Photo: Shutterstock

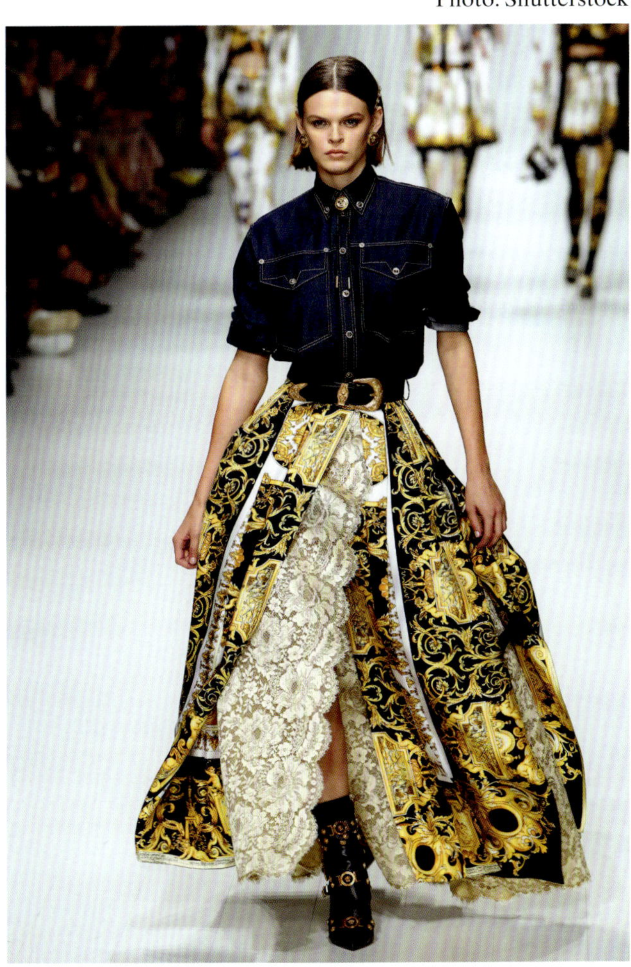

1   Matteo Augello, *Curating Italian Fashion: Heritage, Industry, Institutions* (London: Bloomsbury, 2022), 18.

2   Miles Pope, "How Wanda Ferragamo's Strength and Determination Built a Fashion Empire," *Vanity Fair,* December 21, 2021, vanityfair.com/style/2021/12/how-wanda-ferragamos-strength-and-determination-built-a -fashion-empire.

3   Lane Eagles, "'Beauty Adorns Virtue': Italian Renaissance Fashion," *Fashion History Timeline,* January 16, 2018, last updated March 5, 2019, fashionhistory.fitnyc.edu/beauty-adorns-virtue-italian-renaissance-fashion/.

4   "Timeline," Emilio Pucci Heritage Hub, last accessed January 1, 2025, emiliopucciheritage.com/timelinepucci/.

5   *The Fashion Book* (London: Phaidon, 2013), 422.

6   Lorena Meouchi, "How Emilio Pucci Became the Prince of Prints," *L'Officiel,* April 15, 2021, lofficielusa.com /fashion/emilio-pucci-prints-history-book.

7   Giampietro Baudo, "Camille Miceli Talks Taking Over Pucci and Self-Confidence," *L'Officiel,* February 24, 2023, lofficielusa.com/fashion/camille-miceli-pucci-creative-director-fashion-designer.

8   Alba Cappellieri, *Buccellati: A Century of Timeless Beauty* (New York: Assouline, 2021), 18.

9   Cappellieri, *Buccellati,* 22.

10   Cappellieri, *Buccellati,* 23.

11   Cappellieri, *Buccellati,* 24.

12   Alexandra Marshall, "How an Italian Family Turned Paisley Prints and Haute-Hippe Garb into a 50-Year-Old Fashion Legacy," *W Magazine,* February 23, 2018, wmagazine.com/story/etro-family-50-year-anniversary-italy.

13   Marshall, "How an Italian Family Turned Paisley Prints."

14   Marshall, "How an Italian Family Turned Paisley Prints."

15   Sarah Maisey, "Paisley Patterns and Power Bags: Marco de Vincenzo's New Vision for Etro," *National,* April 18, 2024, thenationalnews.com/lifestyle/luxury/2024/04/19/etro-creative-director-marco-vincenzo/.

16   Tim Blanks, *Versace: The Complete Collections,* Catwalk (New Haven, CT: Yale University Press, 2021), 11–14.

17   Blanks, *Versace,* 11–14.

18   Blanks, *Versace,* 13.

CHAPTER 5

THE MISSONI HOUSE: FAMILY AND ITALIAN FASHION

by MASSIMILIANO CAPELLA

And then the Missonis "arrive . . . and overwhelm everything . . . when models are like these, they have the power to move you like all works of art.[1]

When journalist Maria Pezzi described Missoni fashion as a true art form to be worn, the fashion house, founded in Gallarate in 1953 by Ottavio Missoni (1921–2013) and Rosita Missoni (1931–2025), had already been in existence for over twenty-five years (**fig. 44**). A glorious history, an authentic expression of "Made in Italy" at its finest, where craftsmanship, technical research, creativity, and, above all, a novel linguistic code meet, transforming fashion into the most widespread form of contemporary art: Missoni embodies all of this. Since the 1950s, the Missoni aesthetic has been distinguished by experimentation with graphics, colors, and lines that, over the course of decades, have become a genuine linguistic patrimony, encapsulated in 1994 by the coining of the neologism *Missonologia* on the occasion of the establishment of the Premio Pitti Immagine (Pitti Image Prize).[2] The reason for this recognition is unquestionable; the Missonis articulated a fashion vocabulary that includes the words "research," "knitwear," "stripes," "color," "fantasy," "invention," "tradition," "culture," and "fashion," elevating the garment to a new art form, as Maria Pezzi had already intuited in 1979 when she proclaimed: "They are museum pieces, yet wear them all the same."

Thanks to Ottavio and Rosita Missoni,[3] in the late 1950s, just a few years after founding the fashion house, stripes—their signature motif—were already appearing in every possible manner, in a wide array of colors and modes: horizontals, verticals, diagonals, zigzags (**fig. 45**). And in April 1970, they were incorporated into what Americans christened the "Put-Together" style. The 1958 fashion collection Milano Sympathy, shown at La Rinascente in Milan, was already emblematic of this dynamic look, with the recognizable Missoni monogram centered on a garment conceived as a knitted-wool shirt with brightly colored vertical stripes, a style immortalized that year by the illustrator Brunetta (1904–1989) in an advertisement in *Corriere della sera* (March 4, 1958). Exuding an unprecedented sense of sartorial freedom, the Missoni knitted shirt can be considered the right creation at the right moment: a perfect response to a new need by the younger generation for an independent, informal, and colorful fashion, anticipating the great revolution of Swinging London of the 1960s.

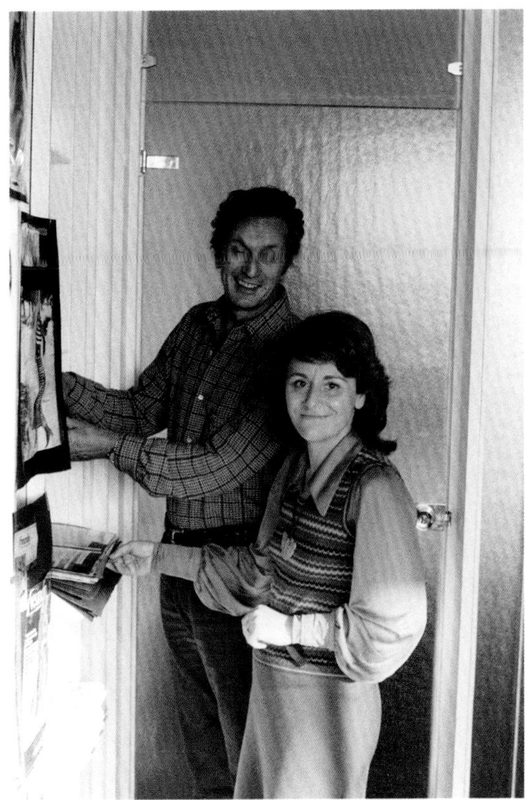

fig. 44   Ottavio and Rosita Missoni, Missoni studios, Milan, October 10, 1972. Photo: Bill Raser / WWD / Penske Media via Getty Images

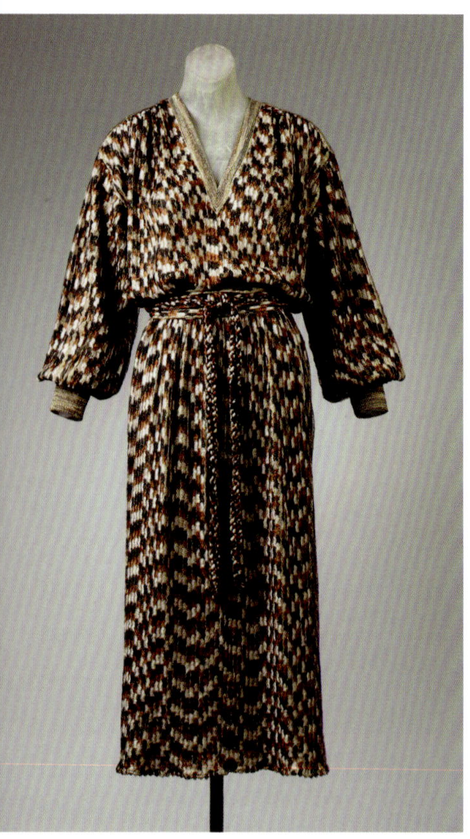

It was not the color, however, but the modernity of the garments in knitted white wool that would cause Missoni to appear on the covers of top fashion magazines, from *Arianna* (August 1969) to *Elle France* (February 1968). White alternating with bolder hues, an outburst of stripes, and the first zigzags were glimpsed in the Spring–Summer 1966 collection, presented at the Teatro Gerolamo in Milan with Emmanuelle Khanh; the full-blown styles exploded in the 1968 Spring–Summer collection, enshrined on the cover of *Grazia* (June 23, 1968).

Prior to this recognition, the Missonis had brought about a true aesthetic and cultural revolution when they were the protagonists in a now-famous scandal. In April 1967, they were invited to present on the runways of the Palazzo Pitti in Florence, the center of the contemporary "Italian Look." But a few moments before her entrance, Rosita realized that, beneath the extremely light black-lamé blouses, the models were not wearing the appropriate color of undergarments. Her solution: Rosita sent them out on the runway sans bras, creating a sensation. Under the spotlights, the clothes appeared transparent, unabashedly exposing the young women's nudity. This nude look was as unexpected as it was unprecedented, predating many runway collections of succeeding design generations. This Missoni collection was branded "Crazy Horse," after the famed Parisian cabaret, prompting the house to be excluded from the schedule of Palazzo Pitti runway shows for the remainder of the year. This dramatic turn of events prompted the Missonis to display the Spring–Summer 1968 collection directly in Milan, in the historic Solari swimming pool, with a "unique aquatic runway show" (*Panorama*, December 28, 1967; **fig. 46**).

By this point, everyone wanted to know more about the Missonis, their output, and their unique presentations, authentic performances closer to artistic happenings than to the traditional world of fashion. In an effort to expand the reach of the new fashion house, the-then editor in chief of *American Vogue*, Diana Vreeland (1903–1989), took it upon herself to organize various industry meetings for the pair in New York in 1969. In April 1972, Bernadine Morris, writing in *The New York Times*, acknowledged their uniqueness: "They make the best knits in the world. Some say the best clothes in the world." This was only a preview of the international triumph that was soon to come, in Dallas in 1973, when they were awarded the highly prestigious Neiman Marcus Fashion Award, and in February 1975, when their creations were included in the article "The Best Clothes in the World," listing the top ten European designers (*American Vogue*, February 1975).

By the time *The New York Times* resumed celebrating the Missonis as creators of a true art form, in 1979, Ottavio and Rosita's brand had already made its entrée into the world of cinema, then that of theater.[4] In 1972, Liza Minelli (b. 1946) wore Missoni in the film *Cabaret*, while in 1983 Sean Connery (1930–2020) appeared on the cover of *Rolling Stone* magazine wearing an unmistakable Missoni knit. Their relationship with cinema would be continuous and long-lasting, including, in recent years, collaborations of great splendor such as the Spring–Summer 2012 collection, involving Spanish director Pedro Almodóvar (b. 1949), who would also feature iconic Missoni bath sponges with zigzag motifs in posters for his film *Julieta* (2016). In theater productions, Missoni wools became authentic, evocative works of art, for example, featuring obvious Scottish references in

54

their costumes for the 1983 production of Gaetano Donizetti's *Lucia di Lammermoor* at the Teatro alla Scala in Milan.[5]

For the 1990 FIFA World Cup inaugural ceremony, several fashion houses were asked to create collections that reflected the essence of each continent; Gianfranco Ferré was assigned Europe, Valentino was assigned America, Mila Schön was given Asia, and Missoni, Africa. In this collection, mixing global cultural aesthetics, Missoni fused the art of Piet Mondrian (1872–1944) and Paul Klee (1879–1940) with aspects of the visual cultures of the native Akan, Dogon, and Senufo communities in West Africa, of Bantù-speaking regions in Central Africa, and of Maasai and East African regions.[6]

It is thus no coincidence that the most perceptive writing on Missoni has frequently emphasized the close relationship between the house's coloristic and compositional harmonies and those of great artists, especially after the presentation in Florence in April 1970 of the collection—the one hailed by Americans as the "Put-Together" line—where we find kaleidoscopic juxtapositions of lines, zigzags, and bold chromatic backgrounds (**fig. 47**). The pattern is unique and so recognizable that throughout Missoni's history, including in more recent years, under the creative direction of Ottavio and Rosita's daughter, Angela Missoni (b. 1958), Filippo Grazioli (b. 1981), and, since 2024, Alberto Caliri (b. 1970), the fashion house has contributed to a genuine revolution in style and communication that has always mixed past, present, and future.

After all, as Ottavio frequently and ironically observed, the Missoni style is one that "they have been copying for three thousand years!" and that earned him the moniker "Master of Color." In fact, as early as the 1970s, Missoni creations had proceeded from international runways to the halls of museums with important exhibitions celebrating creations from past and present.[7] These include *Missoni and the Magician Machine*, the acclaimed exhibition on Ottavio's work at the Naviglio Gallery in Venice in 1975 and, in 2015, a permanent installation of a unique series of the firm's patchwork tapestries made out of fabric cuttings that was dedicated in the Museo MAGA in Gallarate,[8] a town in the province of Varese, precisely where the Missoni story began.

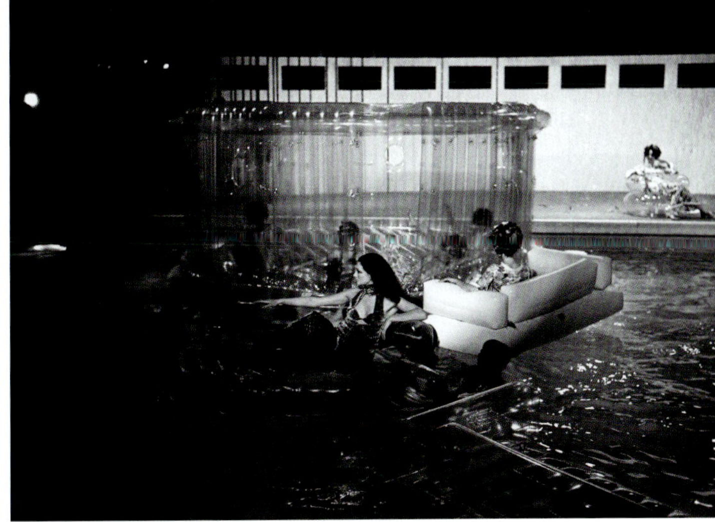

fig. 46 Missoni Spring–Summer 1968 presentation, Piscina Solari, Milan, 1967. Photo: Alfa Castaldi, © Missoni

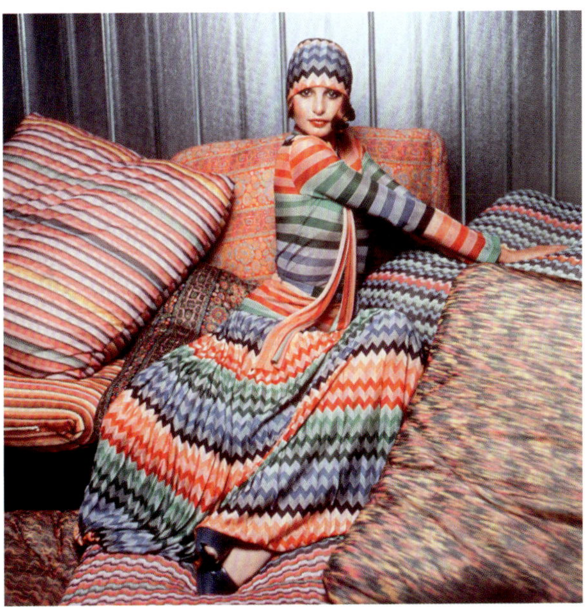

fig. 47 A model posing in a "Put-Together" Missoni outfit on pillows covered in Missoni fabric, 1975. Photo: Hulton Archive/Getty Images

1 Maria Pezzi, "Sono pezzi da museo, ma indossateli pure," *Il Giorno*, March 26, 1979.

2 Isa Tutino Vercelloni, ed., *Missonologia: Il mondo dei Missoni* (Milan: Electa, 1994).

3 On the artistry and history of Missoni, see Guido Vergani, "Missoni," in *Dizionario della moda* (Milan: 1999; Baldini Castoldi Dalai Editore, 2009), 796–800; Ottavio Missoni, *Una vita sul filo di lana* (Milan: Rizzoli, 2011); and Massimiliano Capella, *Missoni: The Great Italian Fashion* (New York: Rizzoli, 2019).

4 "The Missonis, who have elevated knitted clothes to a form of art, scored the first big success of the fall ready to wear shows here. The Italian fashion openings will be followed by market weeks in London, Paris and, toward the end of April, in New York. The shape of next winter's clothes will be established long before summer sets in." Bernadine Morris, "Missonis' Clothes a Hit as Milan Showings Open," *New York Times*, March 26, 1979, 16.

5 *Lucia di Lammermoor* (1835) is an opera by the Italian composer Gaetano Donizetti inspired by the 1819 historical novel *The Bride of Lammermoor* by Sir Walter Scott, one of the most celebrated British writers and poets. The novel is set in Scotland during the reign of Queen Anne (1702–14).

6 Anna Piaggi and Gianni Brera, *Africa di Missoni per Italia 90* (Milan: Electa, 1990).

7 *La Galleria del naviglio presenta i nuovi arazzi di Missoni: Marzo–Aprile 1981*, exh. cat. (Milan: La Galleria del Naviglio, 1981); Raffaella Sgubin and Mariuccia Casadio, *Caleidoscopio Missoni* (Gorizia: Musei Provinciali di Gorizia, 2006); Massimiliano Capella, *Il Teatro alla moda: Theater in Fashion; Costumes for the Stage by Italy's Haute Couture Designers; Armani, Capucci, Coveri, Fendi, Ferretti, Gigli, Marras, Missoni, Ungaro, Valentino, Versace* (Beverly Hills, CA: Wallis Annenberg Center for the Performing Arts, 2011); and Ottavio Missoni, et al., *Ottavio Missoni: Il genio del colore* (Ljubljana: Unione Italiana, 2012).

8 Luciano Caramel, et al., *Missoni: L'art; Il colore* (Milan: Rizzoli, 2015).

THE STATE OF ITALIAN FASHION

DARNELL-JAMAL LISBY in conversation with LUKE MEAGHER (@HauteLeMode)

Luke Meagher, founder of the social media company HauteLeMode, is one of the most sought-after fashion critics in the industry. Across several platforms, and growing rapidly, HauteLeMode boasts well over 1.4 million followers and counting, who crave authentic takes on various aspects of the industry, from corporate news to red-carpet reviews (**fig. 48**). In our conversation, Luke and I discussed the present and future of Italian fashion within the contemporary zeitgeist and the impact of its reach in the mainstream. Some of the most famous red-carpet and pop-culture moments have undoubtedly revolved around Italian fashion, but this realm of the industry also speaks to cultural evolution, from heralding gender nonconformity to sexual liberation, making this a particularly exciting time in the world of fashion.

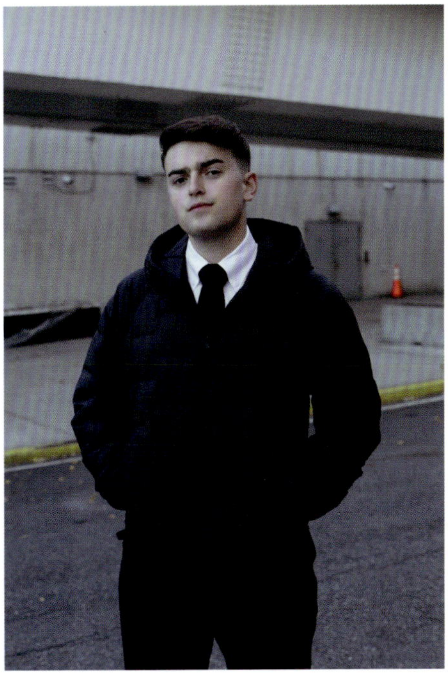

DARNELL-JAMAL LISBY: Jumping right into the heart of our discussion: With your background as a premier fashion critic in the industry, your work is a translation of the fashion industry's dense environment into an accessible format many people engage with, so I would love to get your thoughts on various moments that defined the state of Italian fashion in very recent decades!

fig. 48   Luke Meagher (@HauteLeMode). Photo: Luke Meagher

LUKE MEAGHER: Absolutely! Let's do it.

D-JL: Let's take a step back to the '90s. Especially with this current mainstream gravitation toward, and affinity for, this decade, what do you see as the role of Italian fashion at that point? At that time, of course, Prada ascended, and there was the Gianni Versace takeover, and they had such polar-opposite aesthetics: minimal and maximal, respectively.

LM: In a general sense, we actually have to go back to the 1970s, which was a time that creatively and operationally laid the foundations of the '90s and the turn-of-the-twenty-first-century period for Italian fashion, particularly with a heavy emphasis on manufacturing and creating collections that had a mass-aesthetic quality and appeal. As everyone knows, Italy has the best production, making this era a balance between shock value and streamlined, sublime design. As you mentioned, there was Prada and

Versace, and legends like Giorgio Armani spearheading this movement but without the fussiness we traditionally see in French fashion.

I also want to add, there is a marketing genius among Italian fashion houses that we all witnessed that highlights that balance I mentioned and gave rise to necessary cultural conversations. There's the FENDI Baguette, for instance, in which FENDI capitalized on the popularity of the handbag due to its appearances on *Sex and the City* [1998–2004]. Patricia Fields, the costume designer of the show, probably said something along the lines of, "Oh, I love that FENDI bag. We need to have that FENDI bag." Then, with its consistent appearance, and contextualized within the "go, go, go" urban lifestyle, FENDI used the moment to propel the Baguette, and it became a household name. Another example is the Prada Spring 1996 "Pretty/Ugly," often nicknamed "Ugly/Chic" collection that sidestepped the usual glamor tropes in favor of constructing fashion that used colors and geometric patterns that aren't often seen as the sexiest, but that collection represented Miuccia [Prada]'s way to confront patriarchal gender, class, and beauty classifications [**fig. 49**]. On the other end, there were creatives like Gianni Versace with his Fall 1992 "Miss S&M" collection or Tom Ford with his collections at Gucci, who used their aesthetics to signal that women should be as sensually liberal as they desire, possibly with the intentions of criticizing the patriarchy from a different angle.

D-JL: There was also, certainly, the emphasis on commerciality, which obviously has historical post–World War II origins in Italy. How do you assess that impact within the growing desire for newness through dynamic creative expressions?

LM: I believe the answer lies within Italian history. You bring up the case of commerciality, which is connected to quality around manufacturing that we can connect to Italy's past as a bedrock of design process. Luxury textiles and leathers are inherent in Italian history, dating back to the Renaissance. But also during that time, as we can see through art such as within portraits, the different ways those by-products were turned into avant-garde silhouettes of the time, signaling the shock and awe balanced with quality production.

D-JL: Additionally, thinking about production, there are funny parallels between the infrastructure of a fashion house today and artistic/artisanal production during the Renaissance.

LM: In a weird way, when I think of different fashion houses, they mirror the idea of the studios of Renaissance artists and artisans. There's the principal designer, similar to the level of the artistic master, and then their atelier, which would be equivalent to the artist studio. These correlations probably fuel the "Is fashion art?" debates, but we won't get into that today.

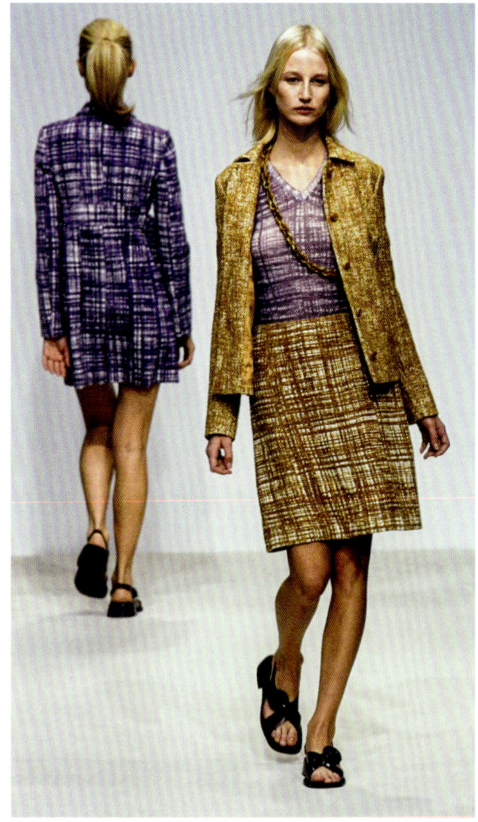

fig. 49   Ensemble, Spring 1996. Miuccia Prada (Italian, b. 1949) for Prada (Italian, est. 1913). Photo: Guy Marineau, *Vogue*, © Condé Nast

D-JL: I agree; that's an entirely different conundrum. Anyhow, connecting the insular aspects of the industry with the broader world, how do you see pop culture coalescing around Italian fashion versus the other major capitals?

LM: I think Italian designers are especially great at curating pop culture. I don't remember who said this: that Italian fashion and culture adore pop culture and celebrity. Giorgio Armani is the reason that celebrity dressing became the force that it's become. One instance that comes to mind is Los Angeles Lakers coach Pat Riley, who became a style icon because of the Armani suits he wore back in the '80s, and even around the same time, Armani was surging because of his relaxed tailoring, amplified in the "costumes" worn by Richard Gere's character in *American Gigolo* [1980]. Circling back to the Italian fashion houses being so good at marketing, creative directors like Armani understood how to predict and leverage pop-cultural moments. We can say the same thing about Gianni Versace when Elizabeth Hurley wore the famed safety-pin dress to the premiere of *Four Weddings and a Funeral* [1994], which cemented Elizabeth Hurley in the cultural landscape and projected Versace as this—again—vehicle for celebrating women's sensual liberality and put Versace at the heart of the '90s pop lexicon [**fig. 50**].

D-JL: Well, building on the Elizabeth Hurley and Versace red-carpet moment: From your purview, research, and recent work, are there particular environments, for lack of a better term, that you observe are momentous as far as putting and keeping Italian fashion at the center of the mainstream conversation, even in recent years?

LM: The first thing that comes to mind is the sheer amount of Italian fashion that you see on celebrities at the Met Gala, in which it's the Italian designs that most everyday people remember over the years. There's always a Dolce & Gabbana look on the red carpet; there's always a Gucci one; there's always a Prada; and there's always a Valentino. Versace certainly is a Met Gala celebrity and celebrity stylist favorite, i.e., Blake Lively, Olivia Rodrigo, or Zendaya [**fig. 51**]. Undoubtedly, there's an unabashed showmanship to Italian fashion design—a sort of campiness. Creative directors of Italian brands know fashion doesn't have to be so serious all the time.

D-JL: I agree; there's this proverbial wink and a nod embedded within Italian fashion that makes the style feel a lot less complicated but still sassy. I think my first introduction to the impact of Italian fashion was the Versace dress worn by Jennifer Lopez at the 2000 Grammy Awards.

LM: There's a reason Google Images was invented; you know what I mean?

D-JL: You're preaching to the choir. Speaking about J.Lo, and this twenty-first-century era of big-budget music videos

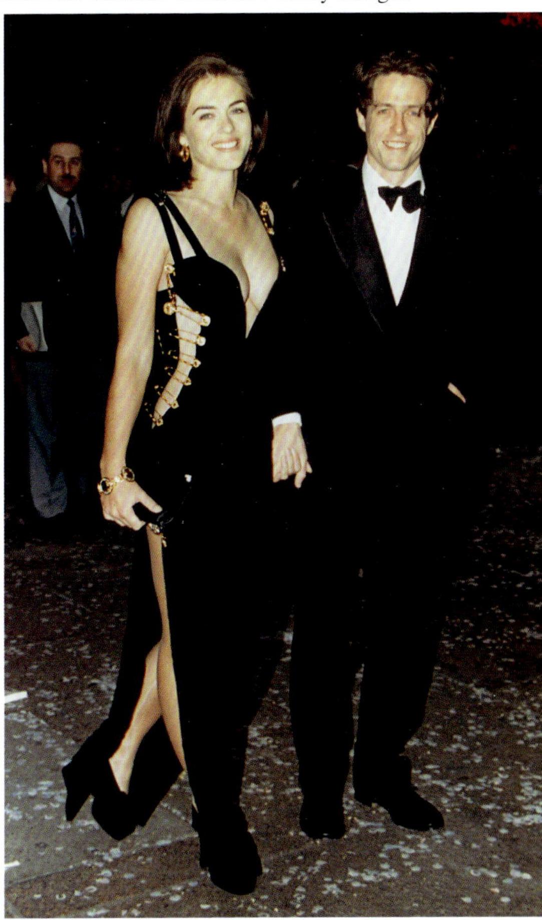

fig. 50 Elizabeth Hurley and Hugh Grant at the premiere of *Four Weddings and a Funeral*, May 11, 1994. Photo by Gareth Davies / Mission Pictures / Getty Images

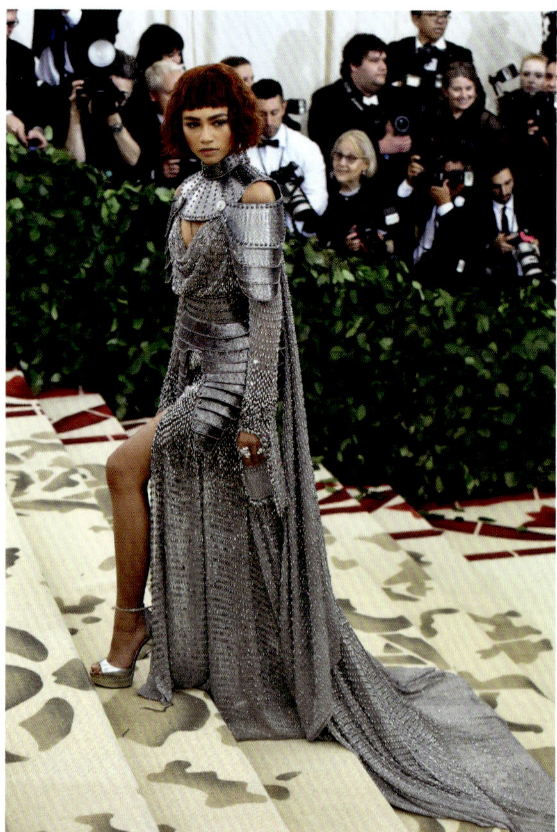

fig. 51 Zendaya entering *Heavenly Bodies: Fashion and the Catholic Imagination*, Met Gala, May 7, 2018. Photo by Sean Zanni / Patrick McMullan / Getty Images

and the performance environments: Italian fashion was always there, waiting in the wings. I think about someone like Beyoncé, who has always been wearing Versace, Pucci, Gucci, and Dolce & Gabbana custom and couture ensembles for her performances throughout her solo career.

LM: Definitely. A fun recent moment, especially since you mentioned the Grammys, was Sabrina Carpenter wearing the tailcoat that she ripped off to reveal the crystal-encrusted bodysuit by Dolce & Gabbana for her performance [**fig. 52**]. I think Italian fashion, style, and the respective houses represent an air of being unabashed, thrilling, and frenzy for beauty's sake.

D-JL: To build on that: In recent years, there has been a strategic alignment of Italian fashion houses through initiatives like celebrity endorsements and using social media in industry, leading to multilateral ways to bolster their impact in the pop-culture realm.

LM: There's no sea the Italian fashion realm will leave uncharted. Speaking from my personal experience: I've been running HauteLeMode for ten years now, and for a while, there was little care from the fashion industry for what I did from a communications standpoint. When the pandemic hit, social media and online fashion reporting became the way to go. Major Italian fashion brands took notice, and they were the first ones to welcome me to come in person once pandemic regulations were lifted. You mentioned the celebrity-endorsement standpoint; I think about Valentino having Zendaya as their ambassador. I grew up when Zendaya was a Disney Channel star, in which embracing a child actor who was still in the process of developing their adult professional career is miraculous, because Valentino is introducing itself to a completely younger and new generation.

When Gucci was headed by Alessandro Michele, the house had rapper Gucci Mane in ad campaigns. Instead of persecuting him for creating a career off their house's name, they knew that he would be the perfect conduit to permeate his audience. The same thing with A$AP Rocky and Bottega Veneta. This is also to say that, realistically, most people don't have the finances to consistently consume many of these brand's products, but, if persuaded by the right endorsement, a handful of people may go and buy something slightly more accessible from a brand's matrix like a fragrance because Sabrina Carpenter has her face next to it.

D-JL: Back to the point of Gucci Mane: There is this fascinating dichotomy between Italian houses and their association with hip-hop culture and R & B acts that dates back to the 1980s and that paved the way for a more synergetic relationship between the music and fashion worlds.

LM: I assume you're alluding to Dapper Dan.

D-JL: Absolutely. In the early '80s, Dapper Dan, a son of Harlem, New York, whose origin story many can read in his autobiography [*Dapper Dan: Made in Harlem*, 2019], began printing unsanctioned monograms on quality fabrics to pass off as official products from mostly Italian and French luxury houses. He would then take those fabrics and tailor them into commissioned designs for numerous clients, from street "wise guys" to major athletes like Mike Tyson and rappers like LL Cool J and Eric B. & Rakim. Even though his operations were shut down until recently, the stylistic impact of his designs reverberated for generations.

LM: You bring up a great point in thinking about the era when Alessandro Michele was leading Gucci. For the Resort 2018 collection, many audiences online noticed aesthetics very similar to a few of the looks that Dapper Dan produced decades ago. That moment was a big deal because after the collection, Gucci forged a partnership with Dapper Dan, which proved beneficial for both parties from a cultural and economic standpoint. This arc seems too good to be true, but Italian brands like Gucci are very keen to build cultural bridges, which has allowed them to maintain incredible staying power, unlike many of their counterparts.

D-JL: His story is quite incredible, and there is beauty in Gucci collaborating with Dapper Dan, setting precedent for many houses to consider an array of conventional and unconventional designs and marketing partnerships that expand our lexicon of fashion. That said, sewing a button on our dialogue: As a fashion critic, are there certain aesthetics that you're fancying?

LM: I'm really enjoying the "quiet luxury" trend that's happening. Houses like Brunello Cucinelli, Bottega, Max Mara, and Loro Piana have always stood at that intersection, but more of the Italian houses are embracing that approach to all aspects of their business. I also love that element of camp that is still at the heart of Italian fashion.

D-JL: These days, I'm also thinking about this realm of haute couture/*alta moda*, designs like Mr. Armani's timeless Privé collections [see **fig. 17**]. Absolutely flawless, and the organza creations give me so much thrill.

LM: It's true. Every single time I see one of those black velvet dresses, I just think I would like to glue them to my body for eternity.

D-JL: Well said. Luke, my friend, I had a blast. Thank you for joining me!

LM: Thank you so much for having me!

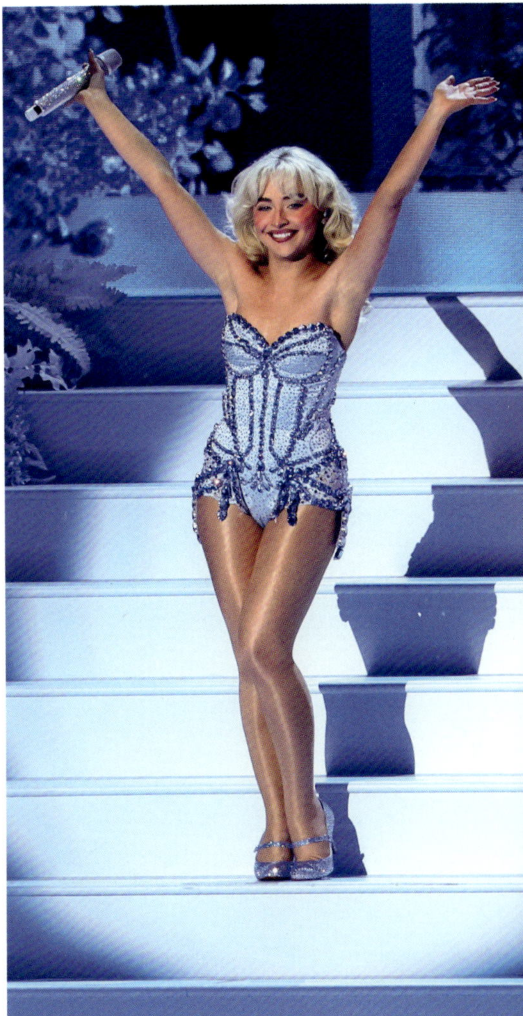

fig. 52 Sabrina Carpenter performing at the 67th Grammy Awards, February 2, 2025. Photo by Maya Dehlin Spach / Film Magic / Getty Images

CHAPTER 7

LIVING HERITAGE: ITALIAN FASHION ARCHIVES, THE DYNAMIC HEART OF CREATIVITY

by ALESSANDRA AREZZI BOZA

In recent years, the concept of heritage has dramatically evolved, making fashion archives more "in vogue" than ever before. No longer mere repositories for preservation or internal brand-identity tools, heritage has become a powerful narrative theme for fashion houses. It is now a crucial vehicle for communicating cultural, aesthetic, and formal values, occupying new spaces and forging unique languages.

At the heart of this transformation, since the late 1990s, lies the archive itself. Once a neglected, hidden receptacle accessible only to insiders, it consciously transitioned into a structured curatorial device. Today, it stands as content to be spectacularized, communicated, and even musealized (**fig. 53**).

Initially inaccessible, archives have become epicenters of storytelling, unexpected stages radiating brand identity with unprecedented force. They are inexhaustible reservoirs of history and cultural heritage to be proudly displayed and celebrated. This metamorphosis marks a pivotal shift in how major fashion brands conceive and leverage their past, turning preservation into a powerful communication strategy.

Several factors underpin this "rediscovery" of fashion archives. In an era

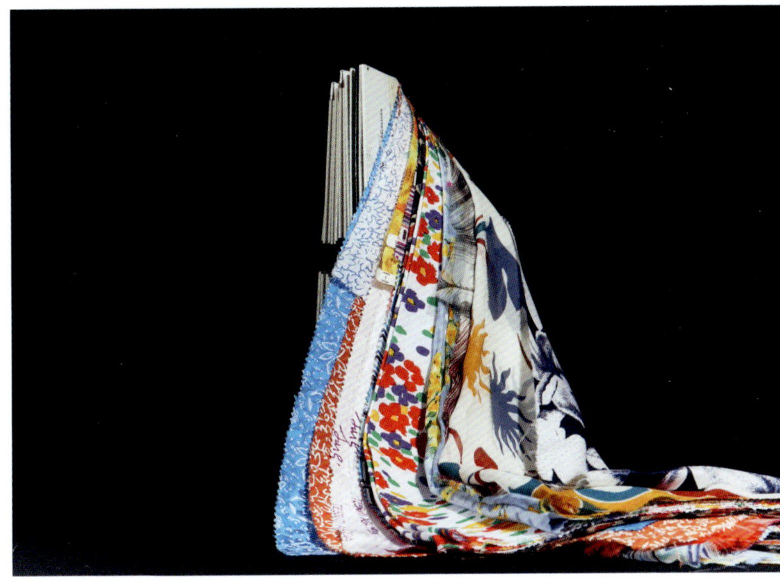

fig. 53 Textile samples, Archivio Mantero. © Mantero

characterized by a saturation of images and a frantic chase for trends, brands sought to differentiate themselves by grounding their identity in an authentic and recognizable history. The archive, in this context, has revealed itself to be an invaluable source of uniqueness, a reservoir of distinctive stylistic codes that define a brand's very essence, its brand identity.

Contemporary designers, often tasked with reinventing a maison's identity or projecting it toward new creative horizons, find an inexhaustible wellspring of inspiration in archives. This includes symbolic assets, transferable know-how, and, most importantly, codes and values for redefinition and differentiation. This is not a sterile representation of the past, but rather a fertile dialogue between a brand's legacy and current sensibilities.

65

Concurrently, the discerning modern consumer seeks authenticity and tangible values behind the products they purchase. A brand's history, its roots, and its founders' creative journey become a form of cultural legitimation. These elements are crucial in shaping perception and forging emotional connections. Showcasing the archive, revealing creative secrets, and sharing anecdotes about iconic pieces makes a brand more approachable and accessible, transforming mere consumption into a cultural experience (**fig. 54**).

From Runway to Museum: Expanding the Narrative

From the late 1990s into the twenty-first century, fashion's expressive spaces expanded beyond traditional runways and shop windows, embracing museum settings as venues for self-representation. Exhibitions became a vehicle for conveying messages, igniting a robust debate on fashion curation and the importance of fashion not just as a product but also as a language and aesthetic. The proliferation of monographic, often itinerant, exhibitions in recent decades underscores how the exhibition format, particularly for luxury brands, has become an integral part of a complex communication strategy, often coinciding with topical moments—an anniversary, a relaunch, or a change of guard in creative direction (with the consequent need to erase the recent past and redefine the present based on an iconicized narrative). By engaging with museum dynamics and spaces, brands intuitively grasped the immense narrative potential of heritage as a primary form of value creation. Shifting the focus from the object to the ideas and concepts that object expressed highlighted the need to "curate" history, defining the brand's territory and imagery to reach a broader, more complex audience than that of the consumer, with diverse methods and languages.

More recently and significantly, some brands have centered their heritage-based communication directly on the archive (Armani Silos, 2015; Dior, 2017; Ferragamo, 2020; Gucci Archivio, 2021). This involves dramatizing its dynamics and practices as a journey of discovery and engagement in the brand's rhetoric and mythopoiesis. Allowing even a fleeting glimpse inside the archive—the true "sanctum sanctorum" of brand history—showcasing the genesis of a new collection, or highlighting fascinating museum practices of restoration and conservation sparks new and multifaceted stories. For brand devotees, it is an immersion in an "authenticity" that only the value of the past can guarantee. Moreover, the advent of digitization and social media has played a starring role in this evolution. Archives, once confined to physical spaces and accessible to a select few, have found a global showcase on the Web—a virtual stage to tell their story and reveal their treasures to a vast audience.

Brands have also accounted for this shift in designing archival spaces. They are no longer mere storage areas but multifunctional and aesthetically defined environments: laboratories for research, work, internal and external training, and, crucially, for communicating and representing brand values. In this light, the archive itself becomes a narrative, a nerve center, and a treasure trove of riches to be recounted in a distinct, yet parallel and integrated, context compared to that of traditional exhibitions and museums.

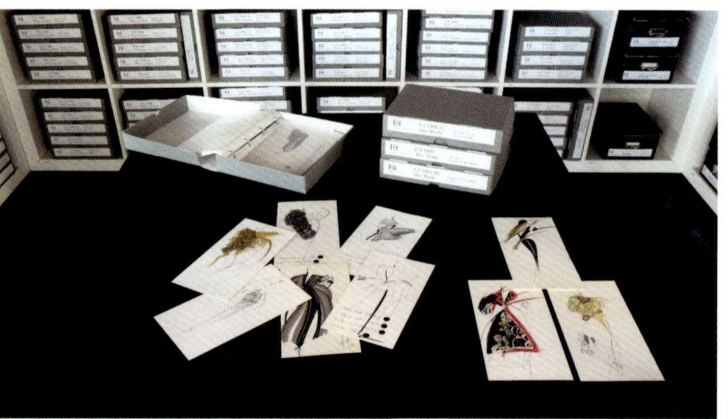

fig. 54 Sketches and drawings from the Archive, Centro di Ricerca Gianfranco Ferré. © Centro di Ricerca Gianfranco Ferrè, Politecnico di Milano

66

Gucci Archivio, Florence
In its current form, the Gucci Archivio exemplifies a strategic vision launched for the brand's 2021 centenary, aimed at preserving and enhancing its rich history (**fig. 55**). Its new home, the Palazzo Settimanni in Florence—a historic building acquired by Gucci in 1953, which was initially its first Florentine factory and later a show-room—was a deliberate choice. This connection to the firm's origins under-scores the desire to preserve and unveil objects in a place that bears wit-ness to the brand's roots. It also stages the archive itself, showcasing its prac-tices and conservation methods (com-pact shelving, archival boxes, acid-free containers, garments stored in breath-able organza bags made by the maison's seamstresses). The archive's complete online accessibility (virtualtourgucciarchive.gucci.com), facilitated by an immersive virtual tour, is no accident; it allows one to delve into the palace's rooms and discover its safe-guarded treasures. The curation reflects museum-level care but substantially differs from the Gucci Garden museum, emphasizing the archive's role as a strategic center for memory, inspiration, and internal training (it houses the Gucci Education hub), as well as an internal historical and creative laboratory, bridging Gucci's past, present, and future.

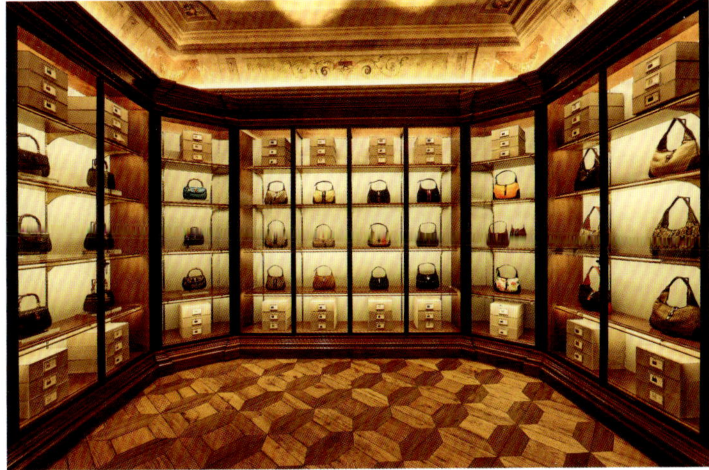

fig. 55   Swan Room, Gucci Archivio, Palazzo Settimanni. © Gucci

It was no coincidence that, amid the transition between designers, the latest Cruise collection (May 2025) was staged within the archive itself. This was a programmatic statement, asserting that the brand's future is firmly rooted in its heritage.

The Italian Anomaly: Archives as Living Heritage
While the evolution of the archive concept is globally evident, the Italian scenario is uniquely complex and varied. To fully grasp the profound importance of archives with-in Italian fashion and creativity, some crucial considerations are in order.

Unlike France, where couture has long been celebrated as an art form deserving dedicated museums (like the Musée des Arts Décoratifs or the Musée Galliera), or Anglo-Saxon countries with institutions such as the Victoria and Albert Museum (V&A) and the Met's Costume Institute, Italy has yet to find institutional spaces and methods to fully valorize one of its most vital contemporary expressions and sectors of excellence.

A Delayed Recognition
Despite Italy's undeniable status as a global fashion powerhouse universally acknowl-edged for its creativity, excellence, and incredible know-how in shaping contemporary fashion, institutional recognition of its strategic and, more importantly, cultural signif-icance has been belated. A systematic historical mapping and enhancement of Italy's fashion landscape is still lacking, even with projects such as the Portale degli Archivi della Moda (part of the Sistema Archivistico Nazionale; SAN) emerging in the last decade to promote Italian fashion archives and map their sources.

Paradoxically, the majority of the critical reflection and foundational exhibitions on Italian fashion and its creators have originated from foreign institutions and scholars. Notable examples include Valerie Steele's *Fashion, Italian Style* at the Fashion Institute of Technology (FIT) in 2004, Sonnet Stanfill's *The Glamour of Italian Fashion* at the V&A in 2014, *Moda, e Made in Italy* at the Modemuseum in Hasselt in 2013, and currently Darnell-Jamal Lisby's *Renaissance to Runway: The Enduring Italian Houses* at the Cleveland Museum of Art.

Furthermore, it is anomalous that despite years of debate, Italy still lacks a dedicated fashion museum on a par with international institutions. Such a museum would systematically and critically narrate Italian fashion, fostering dialogue between the many worlds that constitute Italian fashion through research and the curating of exhibitions, continual engagement with brands, production districts, and universities, and an acquisition policy that shifts focus from costume history to contemporary fashion.

Corporate Archives: Beyond Heritage
In this landscape, the critical importance of corporate archives becomes strikingly clear. Whether from major luxury brands or diverse textile and manufacturing companies, these are now far more than organized repositories. They are inexhaustible wellsprings of inspiration, guarantors of authenticity, and narrators of tales of excellence. They have transformed into dynamic mechanisms that constantly reactivate and circulate a unique cultural heritage: a wealth of testimonies, specialized expertise, supply chain and district specificities, artisanal traditions, and manufacturing know-how—precisely what renders Italian fashion unique.

My two decades consulting in this field have revealed to me the rich, diverse approaches to preserving and researching this heritage, and notably, the dedication of many Italian fashion firms, which organize and elevate an invaluable material and immaterial legacy. This asset is vital not just for individual companies but also for their regions and the entire "Made in Italy" ecosystem. Thus, Italian fashion archives are a living heritage: a strategic and competitive edge as well as a cultural value.

Each company's independent, practicality-driven approach to its archive project—rather than theoretical dictates—resulted in diverse strategies, goals, and outcomes. Despite this variety, a shared aim unites them: to re-energize corporate heritage and, indirectly, the entire Italian fashion industry. Some archives have even blossomed into institutions or museums, like Armani Silos, Museo Ferragamo, or the Gucci Garden.

A comprehensive analysis of these realities would require volumes; a definitive mapping of their presence and activities in Italy remains elusive. Here, we can only delve into a few exemplary cases, examining both their formation and evolving objectives.

Centro di Ricerca Gianfranco Ferré, Milan
"The stages of a process that is already complete can also demarcate the routes for a new journey, where suggestions and impressions are reshuffled and point to new horizons. . . . And this is another reason why I have always nourished the desire that the most tangible evidence of my work should not remain inexorably locked up in a safe to which I alone had access."[1]

With this mission, the Centro di Ricerca Gianfranco Ferré stands out, particularly for its commitment to education (**fig. 56**). In 2008, the Ferré family established the Gianfranco Ferré Foundation to share knowledge, forming an institution unlike any other in the sector. As the organization noted, "The Ferrè Foundation's archive started from this heritage of materials. The anomaly or the paradox is that the archive did not survive its founder, but was actually created when he passed away. It was not born to fuel the production of new consumer goods as with many business archives, but rather as a tool for the transmission and deepening of knowledge and education."[2]

Over the years, this objective of sharing knowledge and leveraging heritage for "new journeys" has driven various activities: digitalization, conservation, thematic exhibitions, publications, and collaborations with museums and institutions. This culminated in the donation of the archive and all Foundation assets to Politecnico di Milano, leading to the creation of the Centro di Ricerca Gianfranco Ferré. Integrated within Politecnico's Design Department, the center is not merely a place of preservation but a laboratory for research, training, and creative activities. It focuses on applying digital technologies to make heritage accessible and interactive, aiming to explore and experiment with advanced techniques for visualizing, representing, and utilizing high-cultural-content artifacts typical of creative industries.

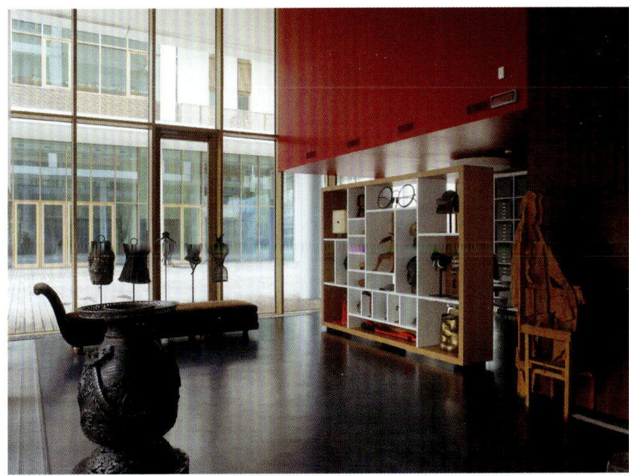

fig. 56   Lobby display, Centro di Ricerca Gianfranco Ferré. © Courtesy of Centro di Ricerca Gianfranco Ferrè, Politecnico di Milano

BAI Max Mara, Reggio Emilia

BAI Max Mara—Corporate Archive and Library (BAI) presents a different, yet equally compelling, story. Born from the passion of Laura Lusuardi, Max Mara's fashion director, who meticulously preserved garments and documents, collection after collection, and tirelessly sought out and acquired pieces globally, the BAI was established in 2003. Its purpose was to consolidate an already significant collection of garments, textiles, yarns, historical documents, magazines, and books. Since 2015, the collection has been housed in Reggio Emilia, within the Art Nouveau premises of a

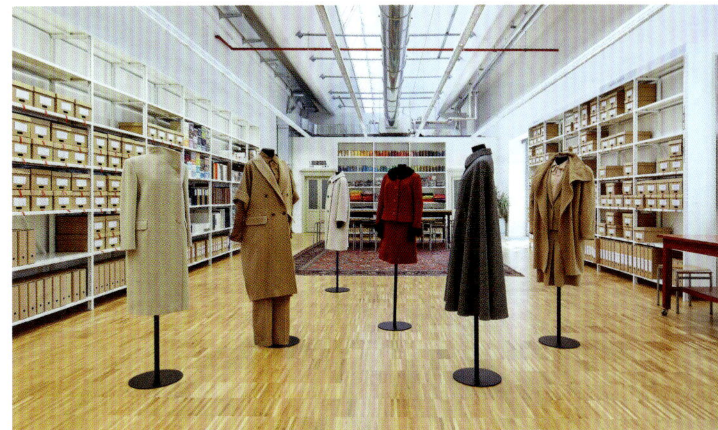

fig. 57   Heritage garment display, BAI Max Mara— Corporate Archive and Library. © Courtesy of Max Mara

former hosiery factory, now safeguarding approximately 300,000 items. Beyond the Max Mara and Sportmax collections, BAI boasts more than 8,000 vintage garments and accessories whose importance, beauty, and quality compare with those of fashion museums (**fig. 57**). BAI also includes a library and a periodical archive, among the richest and most comprehensive in Italy.

Since the beginning, BAI's primary objective has been to support the company's style offices and designers, sometimes through curated thematic selections displayed as small, internal exhibitions. As Federica Fornaciari, director and chief curator, explains, "Referring to the garments, being able to touch them, study them, arrange them on a mannequin freely without any binding conservative protocol, is indispensable for a designer to develop that research and ideation activity that is not possible in any other production department. . . . Creative design requires free access, and the tactile

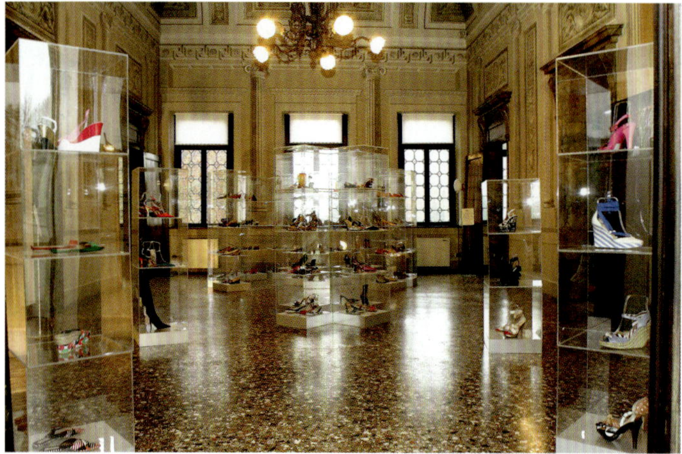

fig. 58 Gallery, Museo della Calzatura di Villa Rossi Foscarini. © Museo della Calzatura di Villa Rossi Foscarini

fig. 59 Shoe display, Museo della Calzatura di Villa Rossi Foscarini. © Museo della Calzatura di Villa Rossi Foscarini

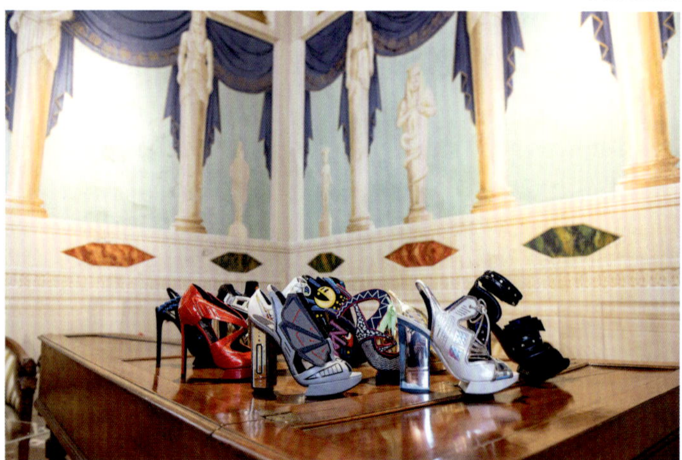

component is not yet surpassable, despite the digitalization that has completely revolutionized the approach and the reinvention of existing fashion archives, or perhaps it will be in the metaverse."[3] While not open to the public, the BAI, accessible to researchers, scholars, and company teams, has become a true fashion hub, "an innovative example of the contemporary use of corporate heritage, in which the history of the brand Max Mara acts as a continual source of creative inspiration for the present and as an opportunity for training and raising awareness on the values of expertise."[4]

Museo della Calzatura di Villa Rossi Foscarini, Strà

Another important example of the role corporate collections can play, not just for the company and its future but as a testament to the know-how and expertise of an entire district, is the Museo della Calzatura di Villa Foscarini Rossi. This is a unique institution in Italy, entirely dedicated to the history and evolution of luxury women's footwear, with a particular focus on the synergy between the footwear industry and major fashion houses. Situated within the splendid seventeenth-century Venetian Villa Foscarini Rossi in Strà, along the Brenta Riviera (in the province of Venezia), the museum is more than a repository of historical and contemporary footwear; it is a true journey through Italian costume, design, and savoir faire (**fig. 58**).

The museum's core comprises more than 1,700 models of women's footwear, testifying to the historical collaboration between the Rossimoda footwear factory, founded by the Rossi family and now part of the LVMH group, and some of the most prestigious international haute couture houses (Dior, Christian Lacroix, FENDI, Emilio Pucci, and Yves Saint Laurent, of which original sketches are also preserved; **fig. 59**). The Museum is a cultural institution that documents a fundamental aspect of Italian fashion and footwear history: the strong link between the manufacturing industry of the Brenta Riviera footwear district (historically, a significant region for quality footwear production) and artisanal excellence and the creativity of great designers. While a private, rather than public, museum, the Museo della Calzatura underscores its deep roots in the local productive fabric. Its mission is not only to preserve memory and enhance artisanal skills but to transfer the knowledge of "beauty and well-made" to new generations. Through exhibitions, workshops, and especially its historical collaboration with Politecnico Calzaturiero—the Footwear Design and Technique School, a benchmark for professional footwear training in the Brenta Riviera—the Museo della Calzatura has become an essential reference point for anyone wishing to delve into the history and discover the secrets and evolution of this iconic accessory.

Last but not least, we turn to the backbone of the Italian fashion system: the archives of the Italian textile industry. Particularly since the post-war period, this industry has developed into specialized districts: silk in Como, wool in Biella and Prato, and cotton in Lombardia. This geographical concentration has fostered a unique blend of expertise, tradition, and innovation, making these districts places where world-class fashion raw materials (fabrics) are produced, as well as sites of creative experimentation.

Numerous textile companies, acting as vital collaborators with designers in creating collections, have gained a growing awareness of their archives' value as a springboard for new designs and ideas. This has led them to not only reorganize and digitize their "storerooms" but also actively seek out and invest in acquiring materials, sample books, or even complete archives of fabrics, prints, and samples from different periods and geographic areas. This preserves precious testimonies, even from companies no longer in operation, reactivating forgotten know-how and practices, becoming a significant strength and competitive advantage for clients who find countless ideas within these archives.

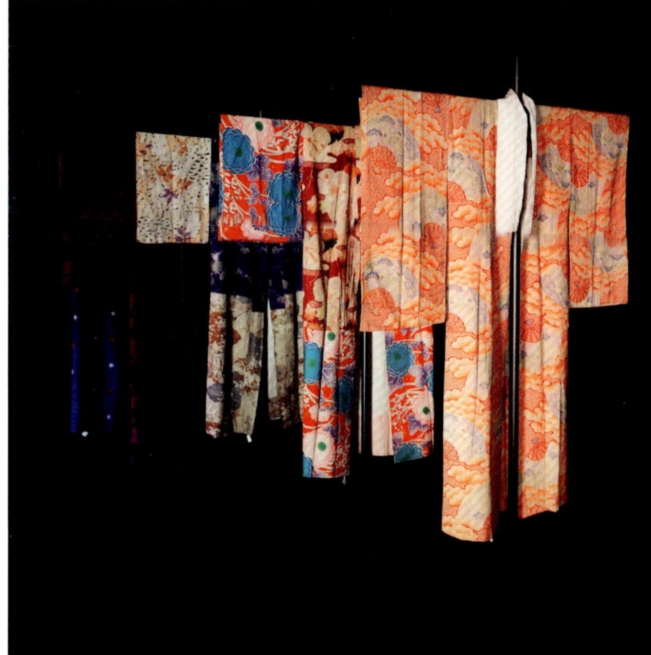

fig. 60   Kimonos from the Nancy Martin Stetson Collection, Archivio Mantero. © Mantero

Archivio Mantero, Como

A paradigmatic example is the Archivio Mantero, now considered one of the richest and most extraordinary textile archives and an indispensable reference point for everything related to silk production. It houses more than 10,000 volumes, 60,000 scarves from the leading fashion houses, thousands of hand-drawn designs archived by theme, test cards, fabric prints, and plain and jacquard fabrics (**fig. 60**). This incredible heritage has developed over the course of more than a century of the firm's creative production and through the acquisition of French, English, German, and American textile archives. It has recently expanded thanks to major bequests and acquisitions, such as the remarkable holdings of the Ken Scott Archive, which led Mantero to sign an exclusive agreement with Gucci in 2020 for the use of a selection of patterns from the archive and brand. Other notable acquisitions include the collection of over 300 Japanese kimonos, jackets, obis, and fabrics of rare and inestimable beauty from Nancy Martin Stetson and, finally, the Avantgard archive, a testament to meticulous research where craftsmanship and technology converged to create works of excellence.

A Legacy Reimagined: The Living Heritage of Italian Fashion
Thanks to the remarkable care and visionary foresight of countless Italian companies, this immense heritage has not merely been preserved; it is daily reignited and seamlessly woven back into the creative cycle. This continuous revitalization, fueled by fresh visions, new influences, and dynamic relationships, literally enriches the very fabric of global fashion. It is why Italian fashion archives are a vibrant, evolving living heritage—a testament to history's power to inspire the future.

[1] *Gianfranco Ferré: Archivi del contemporaneo alla Galleria del costume di Palazzo Pitti a Firenze / Contemporary Archives at the Costume Gallery of Palazzo Pitti in Florence* (Florence: Giunti, 2000), 24.
[2] "The Augmented Archive: The Gianfranco Ferré Research Center," *Archivio*, no. 9 (Torino, Promemoria Group, 2023): 63.
[3] Federica Fornaciari, *Archiviare la moda: Evoluzioni di inizio millennio* (Milan: Pearson, 2022), 32.
[4] Fornaciari, *Archiviare la moda*, 32.

CHAPTER 8

ITALIAN FASHION CURATION

DARNELL-JAMAL LISBY in conversation with DR. MATTEO AUGELLO

In this conversation, Dr. Matteo Augello, independent curator, lecturer, and author of *Curating Italian Fashion* (2022), and I discussed a range of topics emanating from his research on the foundations and elements of Italian fashion curation and exhibition practices (**fig. 61**). With museums around the world increasingly organizing fashion exhibitions, presentations often center Paris as the international capital of the fashion industry. Yet, as discussed below, Italian fashion curation as its own entity, alongside and in conjunction with the Italian fashion industry, has worked to mount exhibitions that focus on Italian creative contributions by building on their early modern legacy.

DARNELL-JAMAL LISBY: Hi Matteo, it's such a pleasure to be speaking with you on this subject, especially since you're the afficionado of this realm that I'm just visiting via *Renaissance to Runway*!

DR. MATTEO AUGELLO: It's my pleasure as well, and I'm excited to talk about everything!

D-JL: A great place to start is identifying how you define an Italian fashion exhibition within your curatorial practice?

DR. MA: That question was literally the starting point for my PhD: What is Italian fashion curation? And is there such a thing as Italian fashion curation? After a few years of research, I realized that exhibitions on Italian fashion curated by domestic Italian institutions or scholars highlighted specific aspects such as designers' inspirations and the centrality of materials to explore "Italianness." I could clearly detect a way of reflecting on national identity with perspectives different from how foreigners [curate shows on Italian fashion].

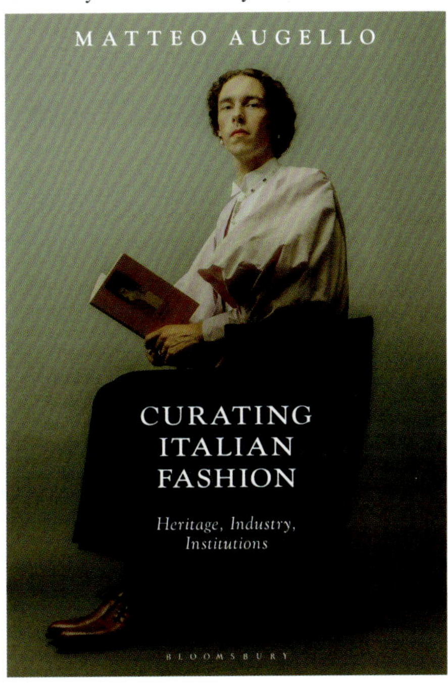

fig. 61   Dr. Matteo Augello on the cover of his book, *Curating Italian Fashion* (2022). Photography by Daniele Fummo; styling by Sofia Lai; makeup by Chantal Amari. Courtesy of Bloomsbury Visual Arts

D-JL: If there is a national-identity aspect of Italian fashion curation and exhibition-making, isn't this in line with the broader history of the Italian fashion industry, especially postwar?

DR. MA: Essentially, the Italian fashion industry had to justify itself against what was already being contributed to fashion globally during the twentieth century. Perpetuating fashion for fashion's sake wasn't an original concept. Moreover, instead of allowing other markets to lead the charge in defining what is or isn't fashion, the Italian fashion industry sold the idea of Italianness, or Italy's cultural and artistic heritage, supporting the framing of Italian fashion. Likewise, fashion exhibitions in Italy from the beginning of the twentieth century, however sporadic they may have been, were used as tools to articulate the connections between the garments and their art historical inspirations or by using context, like early modern architecture. For example, similar to the fashion shows that were staged in Florence's Palazzo Pitti in the 1950s, those types of locations would also have been used as exhibition spaces [**fig. 62**; see also **fig. 4**].

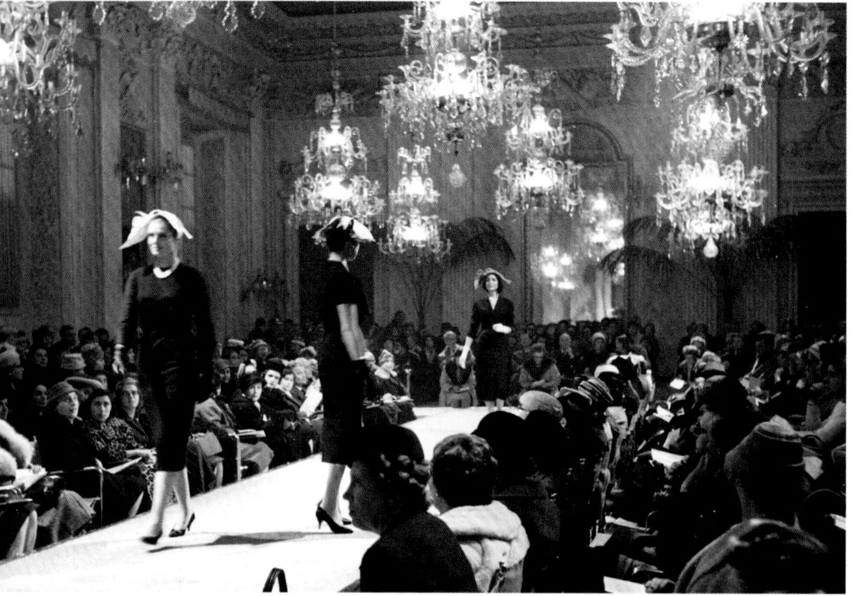

fig. 62   Fashion show, Sala Bianca, Palazzo Pitti, Florence, c. 1950s.
Photo: © Archivio Foto Locchi

D-JL: I think the correlations are very apparent even today when you see Italian fashion curatorial initiatives compared to how fashion industry organizations contextualize themselves, but I also see somewhat of an overlap where the two worlds between industry and academia are blurred, even more so than in other major fashion centers.

DR. MA: Certainly. Italian fashion curation has, in terms of content, explored on one side the identity of what Italian fashion is—it's sort of looking into Italianness. Then, another aspect crucial to Italian fashion curation from the 1980s is the relationship between scholarship and the industry, and having access to private fashion house archives, initiating a dialogue between scholars and companies.

D-JL: As you interpret the idea of Italianness, how was this area of study decentering the looming shadow of Paris fashion?

DR. MA: In one of the first examples: In 1906, feminist activist and designer Rosa Genoni [1867–1954] made the first clear attempt at Italian fashion by integrating references to old masters of Italian art into garments [**fig. 63**]. Meanwhile, the garments were not really deviating from Parisian style in terms of silhouette and construction, but the literal connection and the respective display made a loud statement. There is one type of concept of Italianness that developed domestically, between the world wars during the fascist regime, because it was a way of exploring Italian femininity and womanhood and defining it in opposition to France. Fashion during this period didn't really make an impact if you look at what came out. It was a more understated level of elegance.

However, the focus of Italianness shifted in the 1950s, when Italian fashion started to become commercialized more, or rather systematically, abroad, in particular in the

United States. Italianness especially makes sense in relation to a foreign gaze in the way in which it was framed; the target market was primarily American, amplifying their view of what they believed Italian history to be. Inspiration from early modern artistic creativity and the Renaissance propelled Italian fashion and mainstream cultural contributions. *Emily went to Rome* I will never get tired of saying that. There is a particular form of romanticization of Italianness in a traditional way of understanding the romantic plotline in films equivalent to understanding beauty in fashion. Some famous examples are *Under the Tuscan Sun* [2003], *All Roads Lead to Rome* [2015], and most recently, *La Dolce Villa* [2025]. To me, they are manifestations of the same approach to creativity.

D-JL: As I've been conducting research for *Renaissance to Runway*, what you're expressing is what I've been anecdotally observing. Whether it's my visits to the Museum of Costume and Fashion (a.k.a. the Costume Gallery) at the Palazzo Pitti or the Dolce & Gabbana exhibition at the Palazzo Reale [*From the Heart to the Hands*, 2024], through fashion there's this relentless convergence between past and present within this fantasy of fashion that translates between industry and academia.

DR. MA: This materialization, as you suggest, has been at the core of Italian fashion, in which brands have constantly used the historical reference. Pucci—they did that quite extensively in the 1950s, but many other brands did so in the 1960s. There was a bit of a void in using the early modern period in the '70s, but it returned in the '80s with Gianfranco Ferré. Recently, Dolce & Gabbana brought it back to the forefront, and Italian and foreign audiences never get tired of early modern referential imagery.

D-JL: It's funny you say this, because I know we definitely don't tire of it here on this side of the world. Switching gears: In the case of fashion exhibitions, what are foundational principles that created the trajectory for examining Italian fashion curation, which obviously culminated in your book *Curating Italian Fashion*?

DR. MA: I concluded that there are three main curatorial approaches. First, object-based study of dress, contextualizing the object based on art history, which derives from traditional academic training. In the early years of formulating the practice of Italian fashion curation, this approach derived from art historians because there wasn't much dress history readily available via an educational outlet. Many early dress historians studied decorative arts. As this institutional approach was being developed throughout the twentieth century, many of these dress historians worked with archives to create a framework for exploring techniques.

Second is object-based study via private brand archives. Italian brands were among the first in the industry at large to develop exhibitions about their respective organizations, in

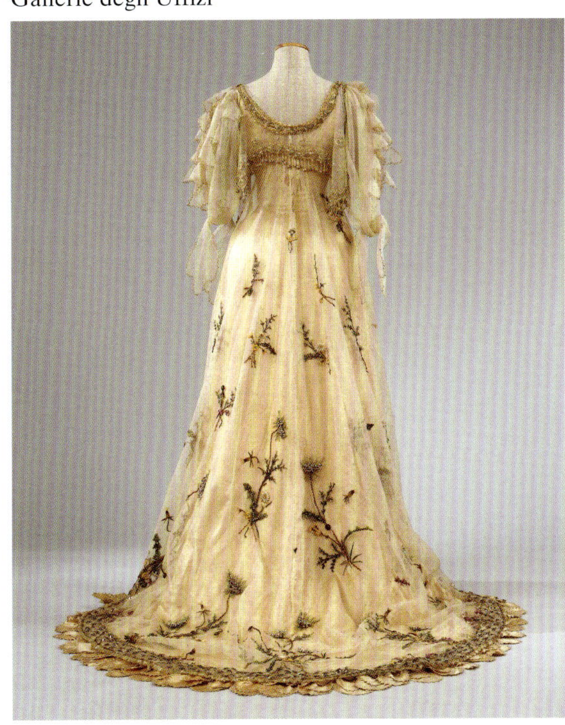

fig. 63 *Primavera* evening gown, 1906. Rosa Genoni (Italian, 1867–1954). Silk, metal thread, and mother-of-pearl. Museum of Costume and Fashion, Palazzo Pitti, TA 1719. Photo: © Gabinetto Fotografico delle Gallerie degli Uffizi

which they focused on techniques, archival content, and the sharing of knowledge that people might not otherwise have access to. In the late 1990s, after Gianni Versace passed away, there was the 1997 *Gianni Versace* exhibition at the Met's Costume Institute. In 1998, it traveled to Italy, where another section was added at the Fondazione Antonio Ratti in Como dedicated to the relationship between Gianni Versace and textiles. As vigorous as Versace's approach was to celebrity culture, he was marvelous about interpreting historical textiles. Very layered and complex.

The third approach, which evolved in the 1990s and which you can also find elsewhere, I would define as the editorial facet. This principle arrived alongside others among those who began studying contemporary art and journalism. During this period, the wave of Italian fashion exhibitions was less focused on the objects themselves and more on the narrative, similar to editorials rather than scholarly articles. They're not so much explanatory as suggestive of the respective themes.

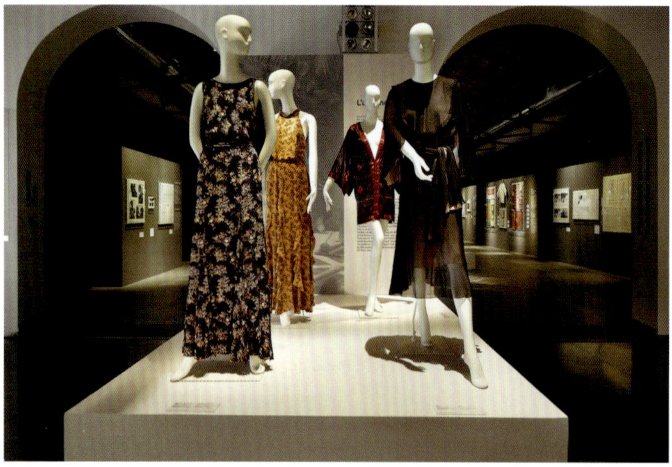

fig. 64   Installation view of *Walter Albini. The Talent, the Designer*, Museo del Tessuto, Prato, 2024. Photo: Andrea Gargalli. Courtesy of Museo del Tessuto, Prato

D-JL: Building on your points, I find there is a growing number of major fashion houses having their own archives and even their own museums, giving them the space to retrospectively elicit narratives that uphold the legacy of their houses. Thus, in Italy today, there's this blurred middle ground of industry carving out a slice of academia, and there is clearly a host of academics, as you mentioned, weaving contributions between public and private spaces. How have fashion curatorial processes been affected due to this relational model?

DR. MA: I always insert the disclaimer that there is still a binary division between public institutions and industry, although there are close ties between the two. Companies have been promoting the study of corporate heritage. In my book, I wrote a chapter that has nothing to do with fashion but with how companies, from energy to steel, led this area of study because they realized they could benefit from it.

There's no value judgment in this. It's a fact, and it doesn't diminish the cultural value of the operation. And so, companies then realize that if they take charge of this role rather than sponsoring an event that's created by others and decide whether or not it aligns with their goals, they can conceive exhibitions and other cultural activities that can perfectly align with their marketing goals. Thus, companies realized in the '90s to the 2000s that they could move from being cultural responders to cultural producers. For example, Stefania Ricci, director of the Ferragamo Museum, told me, "We want to do exhibitions in the same way that we make shoes," suggesting that the exhibition realm is a brand extension that can layer engagement with their customers or art aficionados. Because there aren't many consistent chances to celebrate each respective house, especially outside the V&A or the Met, in Italy they created more flexible types of institutions.

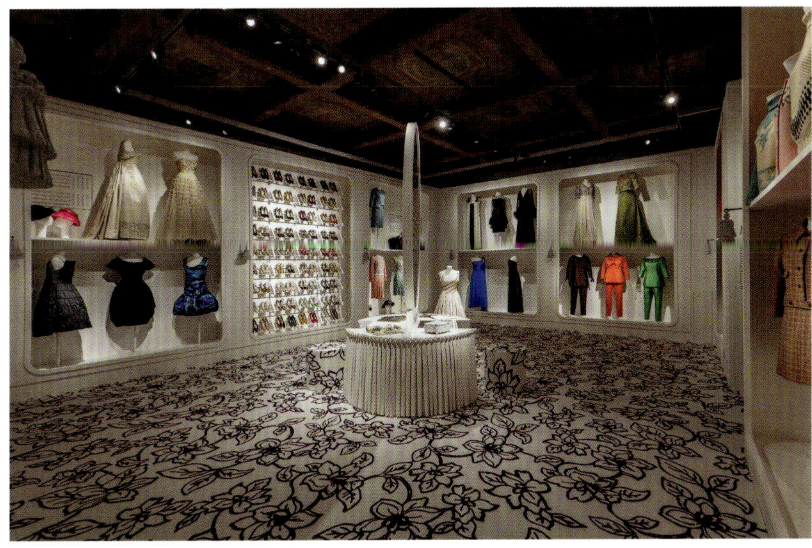

fig. 65 Installation view of *Women in Balance 1955/1965*, Museo Ferragamo, 2023. Courtesy of the Museo Ferragamo. Photo: Guglielmo De' Micheli

D-JL: As museum professionals, we know how difficult it can be to get an exhibition organized, which often limits the opportunities for these houses to work with museums on a consistent basis. Therefore, I completely understand filling this void by creating one's own museum if one has the resources. Where do some of these private house museums or even the monographic exhibitions have room to grow?

DR. MA: I think they can work on inserting additional cultural perspectives and self-criticism. Either won't detract from their gravitas; if anything, transparency results in having a more valuable relationship with audiences. In sum, in Italian fashion curation, there are the three principles, from the art historical to the brand-based, and then we move to the editorial framework. Now we're at a stage where these different approaches coexist, and we realize that we need them all.

D-JL: Have there been any exhibitions exemplifying your perspectives?

DR. MA: There have been a few exhibitions that I think were brilliant, one of which was the Walter Albini [Italian, 1941–1983] exhibition at the Museo del Tessuto [*Walter Albini. The Talent, the Designer*, 2024; **fig. 64**]. This was a good example of a fashion exhibition in a public museum. The curators examined a fashion designer who had been mythologized and where little had been written, and no one had previously studied what was researched about him in detail. So, the fashion scholars conducted rigorous, archival research to put together a seamless narrative and a fantastic catalogue.

In 2022, Ferragamo did one of the boldest exhibitions in Italy over the last twenty years. It was about women, the role of women in the Italian economic resurgence of the 1950s and '60s [*Women in Balance 1955/1965*, 2022–23; **fig. 65**]. I have never studied this subject or seen it prevalent in the curriculum during my days at university. I haven't really seen it explored much globally, especially thinking about women's role and agency being greatly challenged in Italy right now. Using the aura of the fantastic Wanda Ferragamo [Italian, 1921–2018], the wife of Salvatore, who was a complex woman with contradictions, an entrepreneur but also a housewife, the exhibition showcased how she wanted to be perceived, especially as a housewife first. The show addressed the complexities of womanhood and used fashion to celebrate this.

D-JL: There haven't been many exhibitions over the years devoted to celebrating design ingenuity from women. Even though it's not an Italian-focused fashion exhibition, the Costume Institute recently organized *Women Dressing Women* [2023], which decentered the male-designer perspective as arbiters of taste throughout the twentieth and twenty-first centuries and celebrated women designers creating fashion that meshed with, in your words, the complexities of being a woman. As we're putting a pin in this dynamic conversation, expanding on the aforementioned principles of Italian fashion curation and exhibition-making, can you walk me a little through your process and methodology in developing your research and book?

DR. MA: I started as a student of fashion design, but I knew I didn't want to be a fashion designer. I had a dear friend, Benedetta Barzini—she was a top model in the '60s and then became a lecturer. She told me to consider writing about fashion, and that's where I discovered the world of fashion criticism and museums. I did an internship at the Fondazione Antonio Ratti in 2010 in my second year of university, and I have been working with them ever since. When I began my master's in fashion curation at the London College of Fashion, I came across all of this fashion literature, mostly centered on Anglo-Saxon examples—US, UK—sometimes France, and I thought, Why is no one talking about Italy?

Through my work with corporate museums and archives, I began meeting and interviewing figures who trailblazed the realm of Italian fashion curation. These individuals, who are now in their seventies and eighties, told me so many anecdotes. From there, I began to research materials that haven't been translated into English from sources I sporadically found and then connected the dots, unpacking the relationship between scholarship and industry, because, as you know, this topic was very often discussed in binary opposition.

To the Renaissance point: In the first chapter, I centralized the period as the starting narrative, not only in reference to fashion, but also in terms of its imagery as mainstream inspiration and how people position themselves in relation to the arts. That's also why the cover of the book is my portrait styled as a tribute to Renaissance portraiture and the artist Giovanni Battista Moroni [see **fig. 25** and **fig. 61**]. There are these layers of meaning; you can't understand Italian fashion without understanding how the Renaissance can be reused, reinterpreted, and readapted as a concept to make sense both domestically and internationally.

D-JL: Being that you are the international expert on this subject, what is your hope for curating Italian fashion in the future?

DR. MA: I would say that my hope is that people realize there are specific conditions in Italy that need to be improved for fashion curation to profoundly persist. This is also why I wrote the book. We don't need to have large decorative arts museums as exist in other countries, and we should think of institutions or other forms of cultural management as responsive to the context of Italy and to its tradition rather than trying to import a model. I'm also hoping that we move away from fashion as purely an idea of industry.

D-JL: To your last point: There's this growing dialogue within the contemporary art world that is making space to examine fashion beyond industry and solely as a creative vehicle, but I'm also curious as to how the field at large moves away from the conventions of previous generations when analyzing fashion.

Thank you so very much for this time we shared talking about Italian fashion curation and thank you, also, for the work you do!

DR. MA: It was my great pleasure to be a part of this dialogue!

CHAPTER 9

BONAVERI AND THE ART OF MOUNTING FASHION

Over the years, a question I've always been asked after organizing an exhibition is: "Where do the mannequins come from?" That question is always followed by another that gives me a chuckle: "Are the mannequins from a retail store?" Understandably, fashion-exhibition practice is not as accessible and well known as many conventional professional spaces like a hospital, an elementary school, a law firm, or a Wall Street brokerage firm. Within fashion curatorial methodology, after choosing which fashions will be used to delineate an exhibition thesis, deliberation of how they will be presented occurs. Typically, fine art exhibitions displaying 2D objects are often framed and hung on walls, which aligns with the episteme of the artists who produced those works. In much the same way, fashion is often meant to be shown in motion but, to prevent long-term degradation to the objects on display—primarily clothing and accessories (hats, gloves, scarves)—using mannequins to mount fashion is most advisable, allowing audiences to examine an object as best as possible to connect with the intentions of the designer. There is a handful of mannequin manufacturers around the world that have impeccable molds; these include Bonaveri, among the only mannequin manufacturers in Italy to both survive and thrive.

Bonaveri's main factory is in Ferrara, and it has a showroom in Milan: an operational juxtaposition in the shadow of Renaissance fashion creation and textile production, as Ferrara and Milan were home to the stylish Este family as well as locales with flourishing luxury textile markets (**figs. 66**, **67**).[1] And no different from the Italian fashion houses with which they have worked closely over the years, Bonaveri is a multigenerational family business. It was founded in 1953 by Romano Bonaveri (1928–2017), who, with his wife, Adele (1929–2019), built an organization that has always prided itself on weaving sculptural artistic practice into their creation and production process, making Bonaveri mannequins more than just hollow fiberglass bodies but also works of art (**fig. 68**). In the early years of his business, after sculpting a mannequin design, Romano Bonaveri would show the design to local businesses, hoping to sell it.[2] From the 1950s to the 1970s, Romano grew the business to a sustainable level, but it was through his sons,

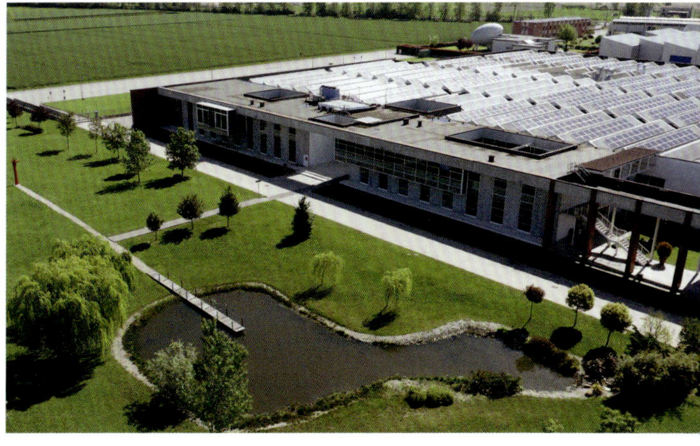

fig. 66   View of the Bonaveri headquarters, Ferrara, c. 2000s. © Bonaveri

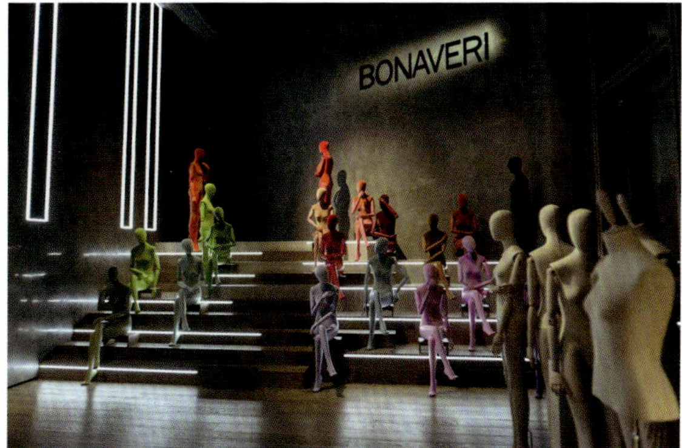

fig. 67   View of the Bonaveri showroom, Milan, c. 2000s. © Bonaveri

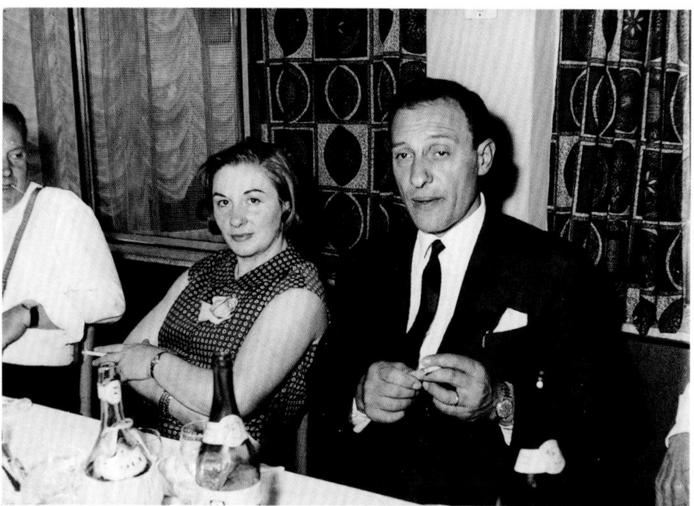

fig. 68   Romano and Adele Bonaveri, c. 1971.
© Bonaveri

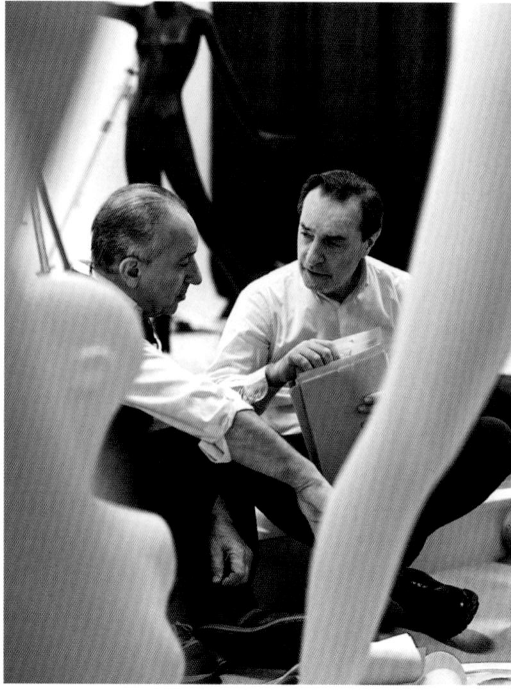

fig. 69   Andrea and Guido Bonaveri, c. 2000s.
Photo: Lapo Quagli, © Bonaveri

Andrea (b. 1961) and Guido (b. 1957), that Bonaveri made its leap, becoming a global brand precisely when the concept of "Made in Italy" was emerging, which led to collaborations with leading fashion designers such as Giorgio Armani and Gianfranco Ferré (**fig. 69**).

Over the years, with clients ranging from retailers to museums, Bonaveri has become the premier source for quality mannequins that bring fashion to life. The company produces approximately 15,000 mannequins annually, embracing a broad spectrum of styles and purposes. Their output ranges from the most evocative Schläppi-branded lines to the bespoke Sartorial mannequins, from the Classic collection to the more youthful B by Bonaveri offerings as well as the Rootstein line—renowned for its mannequins' naturalistic features—acquired in 2019 (**figs. 70, 71**).

The company's ability to merge manufacturing expertise with creative vision enabled it to witness and support the birth, definition, and establishment of the modern Italian and global fashion industry. Furthermore, the collaborations between Bonaveri and prestigious museums, luxury brands, and cultural initiatives demonstrate the brand's capacity to adapt to diverse scenarios, serving as a visual narrator for fashion, art, and sustainability. In addition to the Cleveland Museum of Art, it has formed notable partnerships with the Savannah College of Art and Design Museum and the Metropolitan Museum of Art's Costume Institute in New York, along with exhibitions and initiatives at the Musée des Arts Décoratifs in Paris, the Victoria and Albert Museum in London, MoMu in Antwerp, and the Palazzo Pitti in Florence. Bonaveri also plays a starring role in high-impact window displays and installations in prestigious retailers worldwide, especially in some of the world's most famous department stores, such as Bergdorf Goodman and Harrods. Brands such as Armani, Christian Dior, Dolce & Gabbana, Givenchy, Hermès, Valentino, and Louis Vuitton choose Bonaveri mannequins to execute their visual merchandising.

As mentioned earlier, a Bonaveri mannequin is a work of art. Sticking to the traditions of its founder, the process of creating a mannequin is as follows: Initially, ideas for different mannequin silhouettes are discussed and sketched, and mood boards developed with archival and contemporary images to define a collection—very similar to what a fashion house does when creating a collection.[3] Then, a miniature clay model is made, allowing artisans to experiment with various forms and poses. Next, a life-size version of the model is created using metal frameworks covered in clay (**fig. 72**).[4] Finally, plaster is layered on the life-size version and smoothed out, and the model is then sent to the factories to produce the mold.

In the early stages of a mannequin's design, distinct features are determined, marking the differences between each category of mannequin. For example, the firm's Schläppi mannequin has elongated fingers

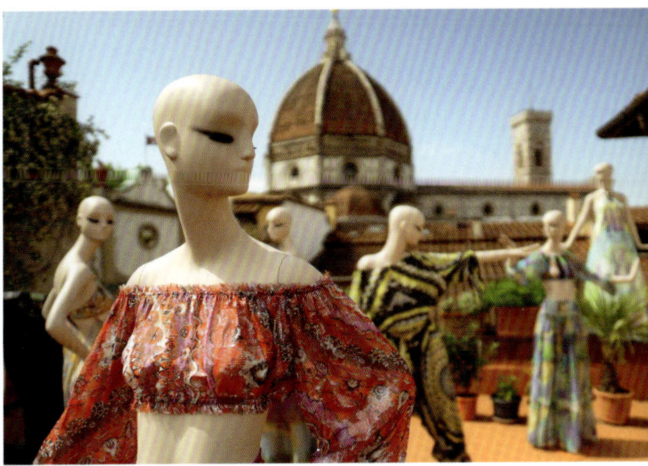

fig. 70 *Bonaveri: A Fan of Pucci* exhibition marketing photography, staged by Emma Davidge on the rooftop of the Palazzo Pucci, using the Schläppi 2200, Florence, 2018. Photo: Lapo Quagli, © Bonaveri

fig. 71 Schläppi Aloof collection, staged by Emma Davidge, 2014. Photo: Melvyn Vincent, © Bonaveri

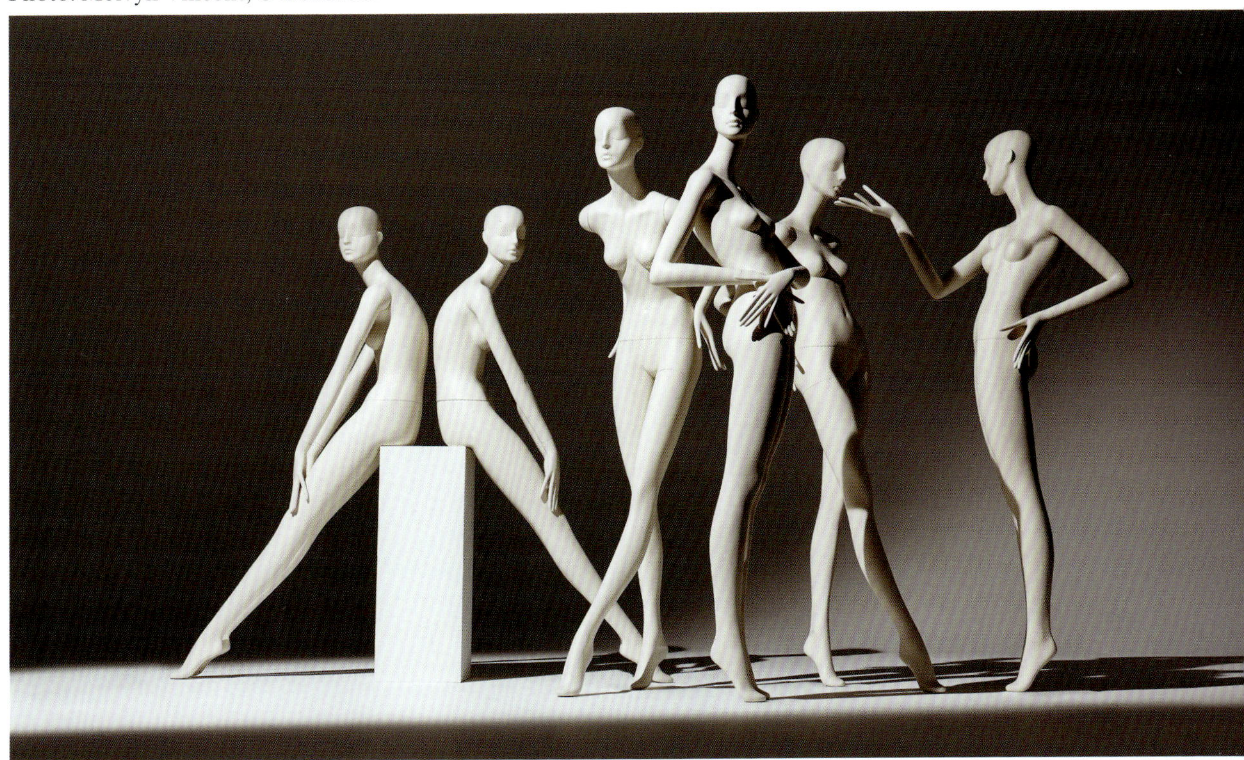

and torsos (see **fig. 71**), whereas the Classic collection mannequin has facial and bodily features that are more lifelike. Because of the more nondescript nature of the Schläppi mannequin, it has become the go-to model for fashion exhibitions worldwide. For the illustrations in the following section, Bonaveri's Sartorial Haute Couture mannequin

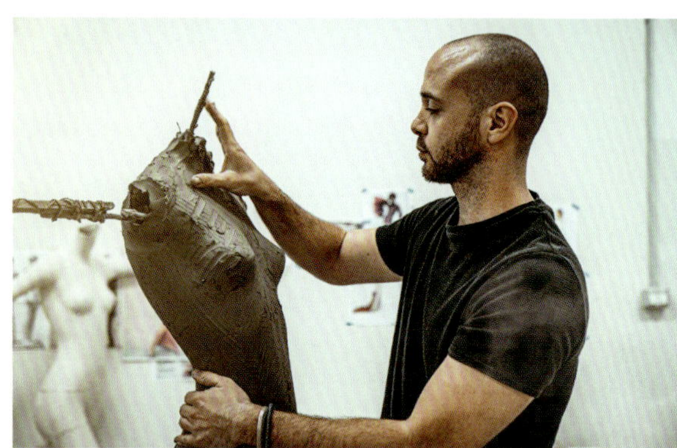
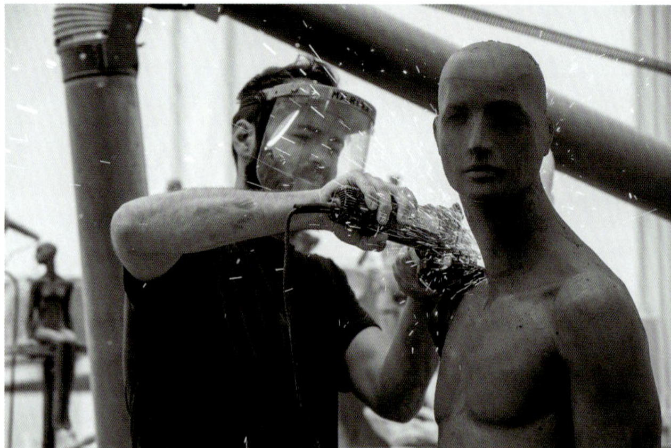
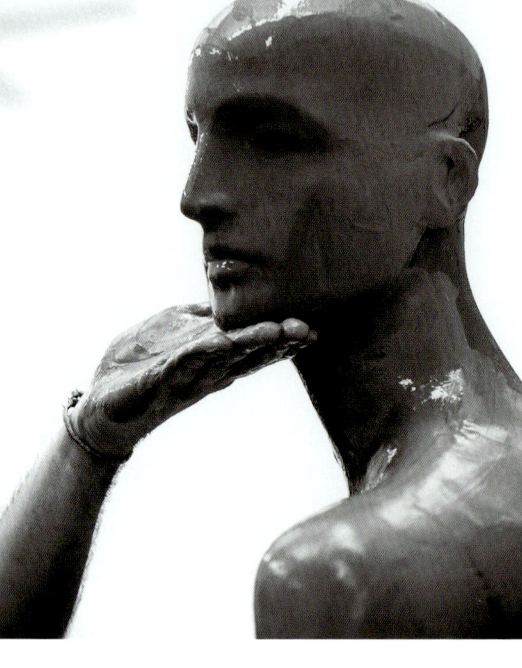

fig. 72   The making of a mannequin from clay in the
Bonaveri Sculpting Atelier, c. 2000s. © Bonaveri

was selected for its avant-garde visual appeal, which meshes with the gravitas of the fashions dressed on them (see **pl. 8**). Unlike the typical full fiberglass form, the Haute Couture mannequins have a fabric cover over the torso and face as well as wooden articulated, marionette-like arms; the arms are so mobile, they can be positioned and posed in various ways to create a sense of dynamism—and visual drama is at the heart of *Renaissance to Runway*.

In the southern section of Milan in March 2025, right at the end of the Fashion Week hoopla, three large boxes from Bonaveri arrived on the set of *Renaissance to Runway*'s exhibition-catalogue photo shoot. Unpacking them like a kid on Christmas Day, I found the potential for the way we could move the arms incredibly inspiring, enabling us to begin experimenting with how each fashion would be photographed. The artistic director for this catalogue, Luca Stoppini, who for thirty years served as the creative director of *Vogue Italia*, came over, looked the mannequins up and down, and said to me: "This is going to be good."

Bonaveri mannequins represent the epitome of simplicity and elegance. As seen in the images in the following section, such simplicity can elicit a remarkable level of decadence to contextualize the imagination that drives our attraction to fashion.

1   Caterina Lunghi, "The House of Mannequins," Bonaveri, last updated April 14, 2020, https://bonaveri.com
    /publications/the-house-of-mannequins/.
2   Lunghi, "House of Mannequins."
3   Caterina Lunghi, "The Sculpting Atelier," Bonaveri, last updated April 21, 2020, https://bonaveri.com
    /publications/the-sculpting-atelier/.
4   Lunghi, "Sculpting Atelier."

MIRRORING

Fashion is integral to my life. I was born and grew up in this autonomous universe, governed by rhythms that do not coincide with the seasons of nature, where the language of a few must, in the span of a season, become the language of all. Here, tomorrow is not the future but the present; and the present has meaning only in becoming history. The same is true of art: The artist's gaze exceeds the present moment, and what takes shape becomes a testament to time's swift passage, both in private life and in public memory. It is within the tension between what vanishes and what endures that fashion and art meet, recognize one another, and tarnish one another — finding in that encounter their natural completion. My path — beginning in graphic design, developing in art direction, and reaching maturity in photography — has allowed me to move between these two worlds, close and yet remote. Along this journey, the mirror has assumed a central role: not merely functional but conceptual. In the studio, it is the stylist's indispensable companion, the place where the gaze confronts its own projection. In photography, it both reflects and multiplies, destabilizing any single vision, opening it to other perspectives and meanings. The mirror is sign and threshold: at once separation and connection.

In my images, it is never just a surface but a device of revelation — source of inspiration, witness, and accomplice to that enigmatic act we call the creative process.

fashion photos and text by LUCA STOPPINI

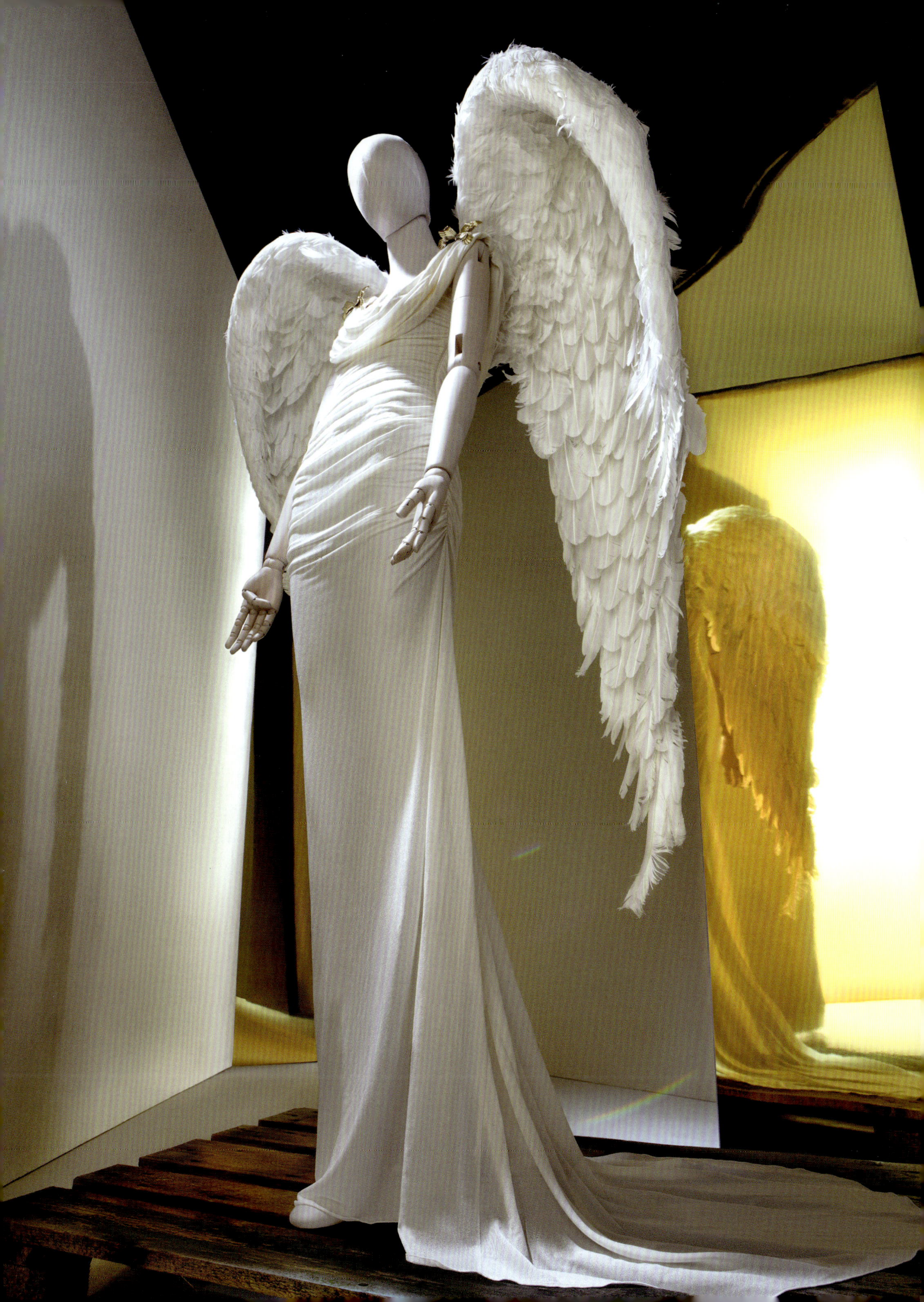

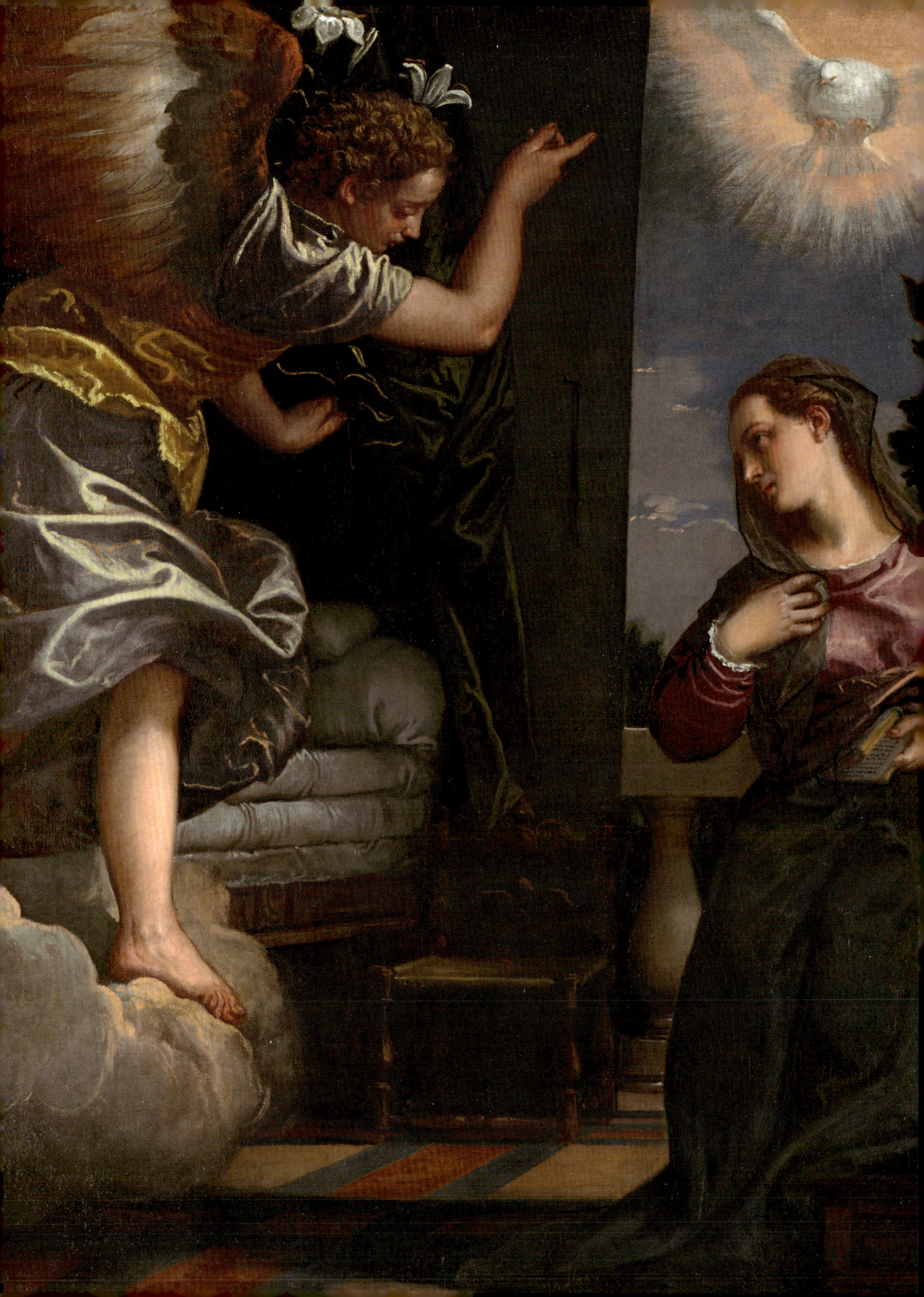

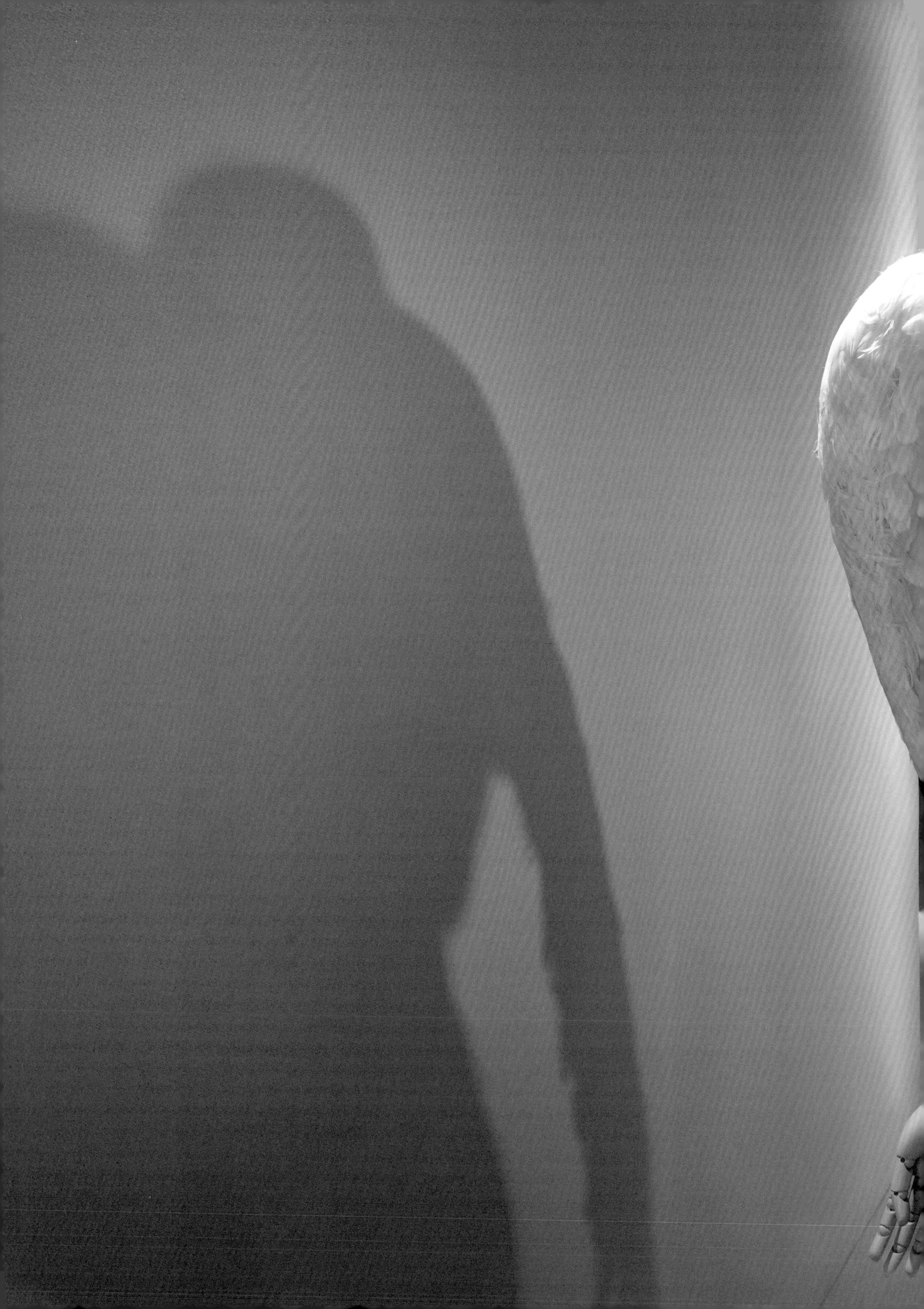

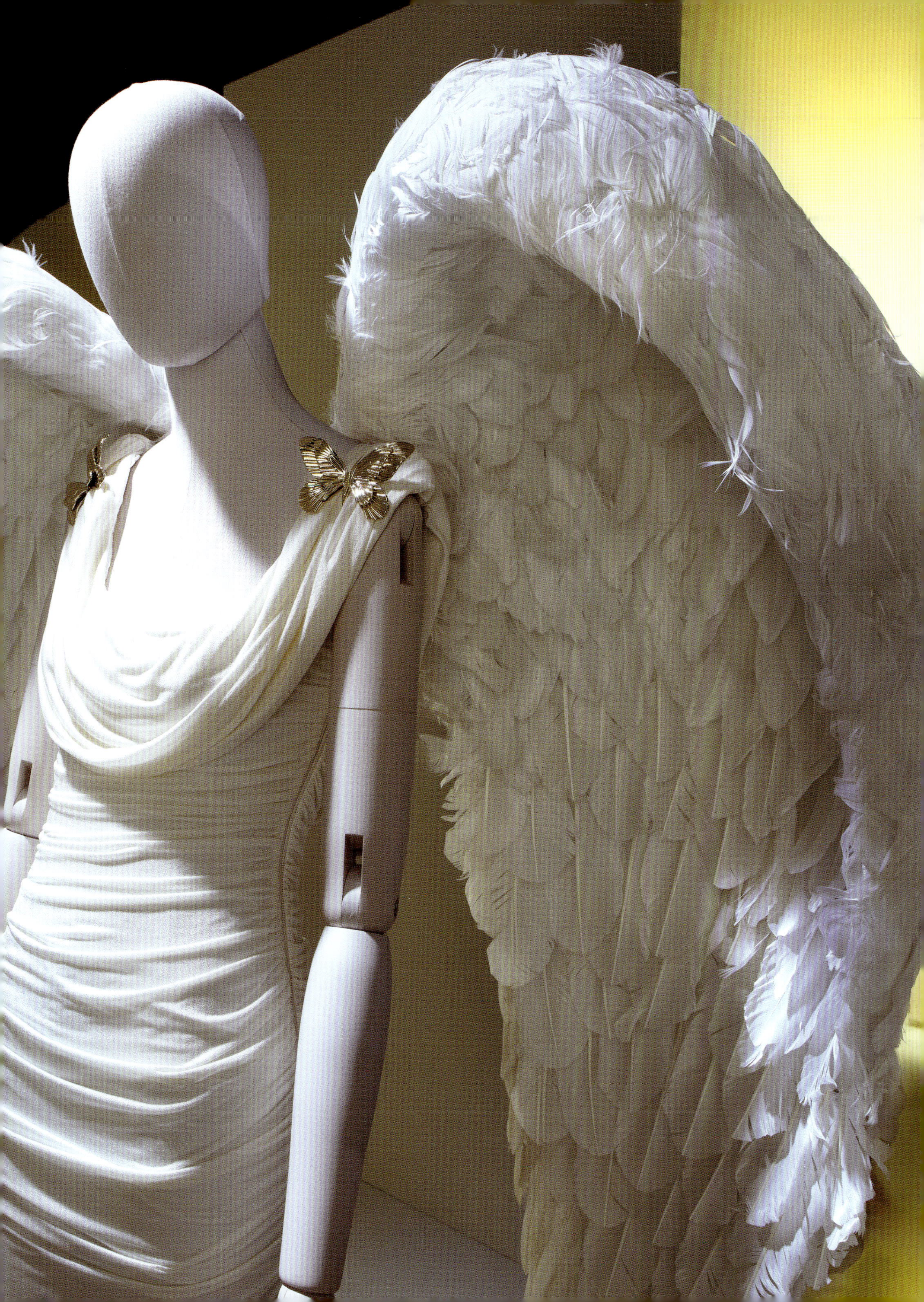

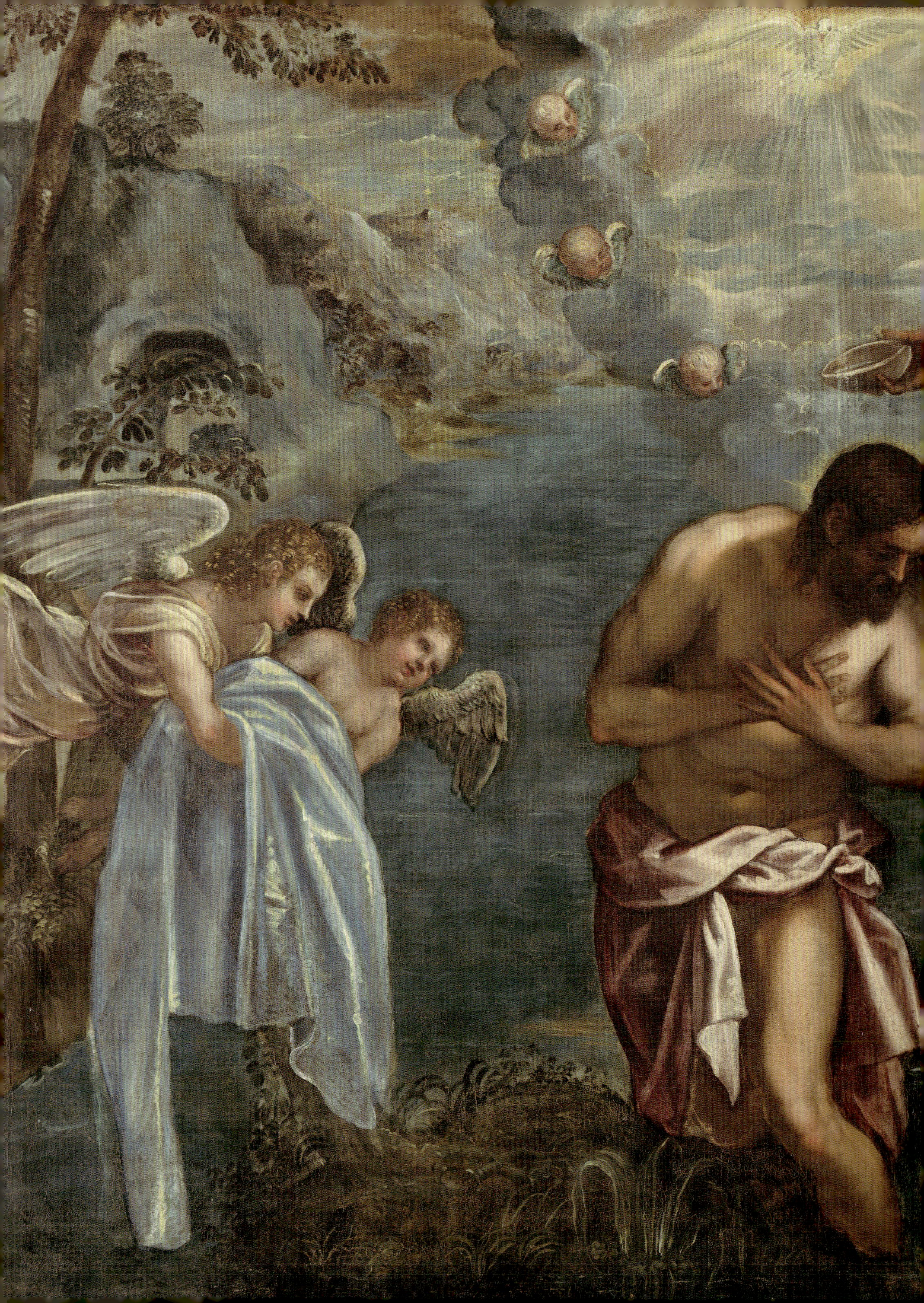

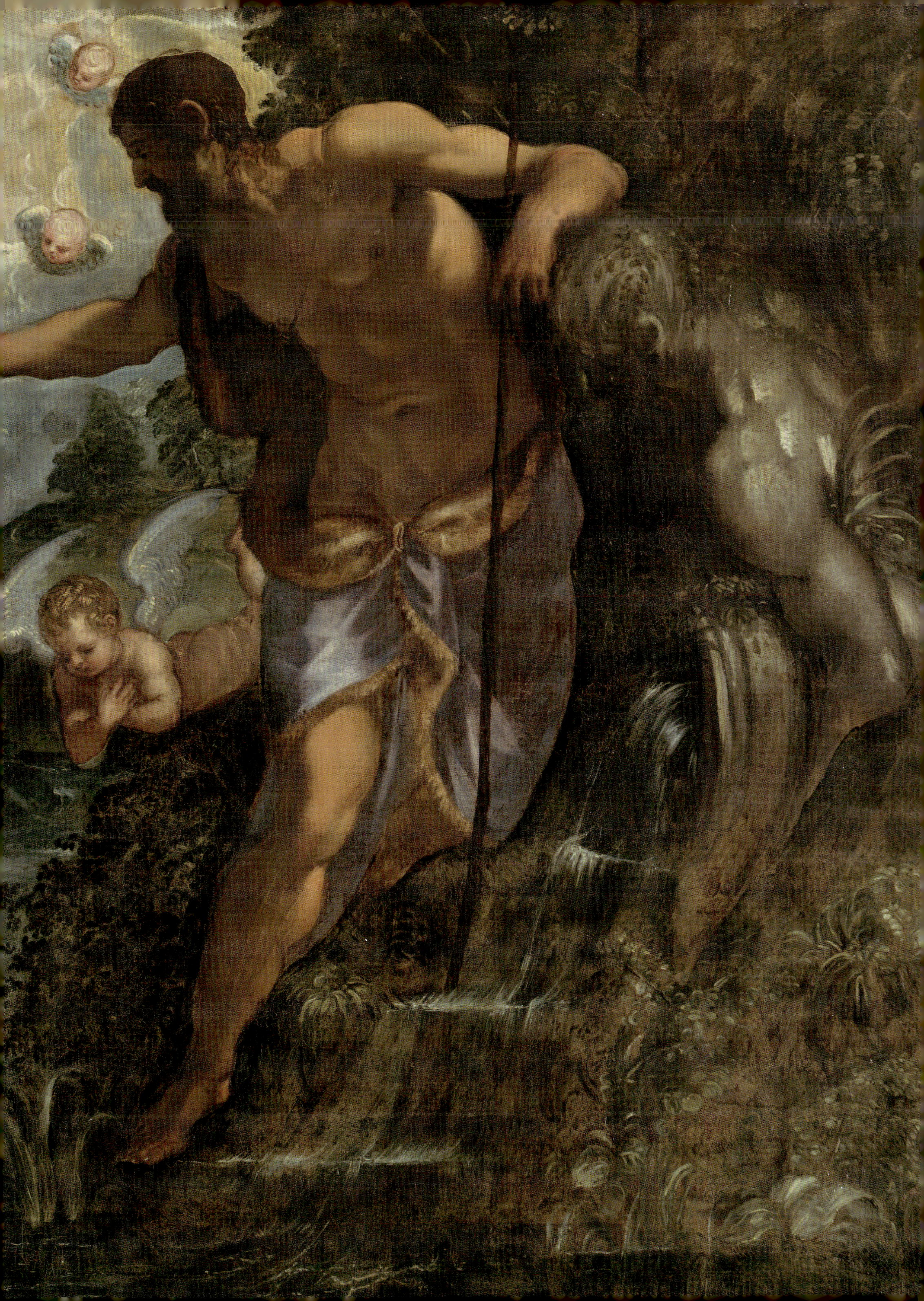

Plate 4: *Baptism of Christ*, c. 1580s. Workshop of Jacopo Tintoretto (Italian, 1518–1594). Oil on canvas; 169 x 251.4 cm. The Cleveland Museum of Art, Gift of the Hanna Fund, 1950.400

Plate 5: Evening Dress, Fall 2023. Maximilian Davis (British, b. 1995) for Ferragamo (Italian, est. 1927). Viscose. Courtesy of Ferragmo

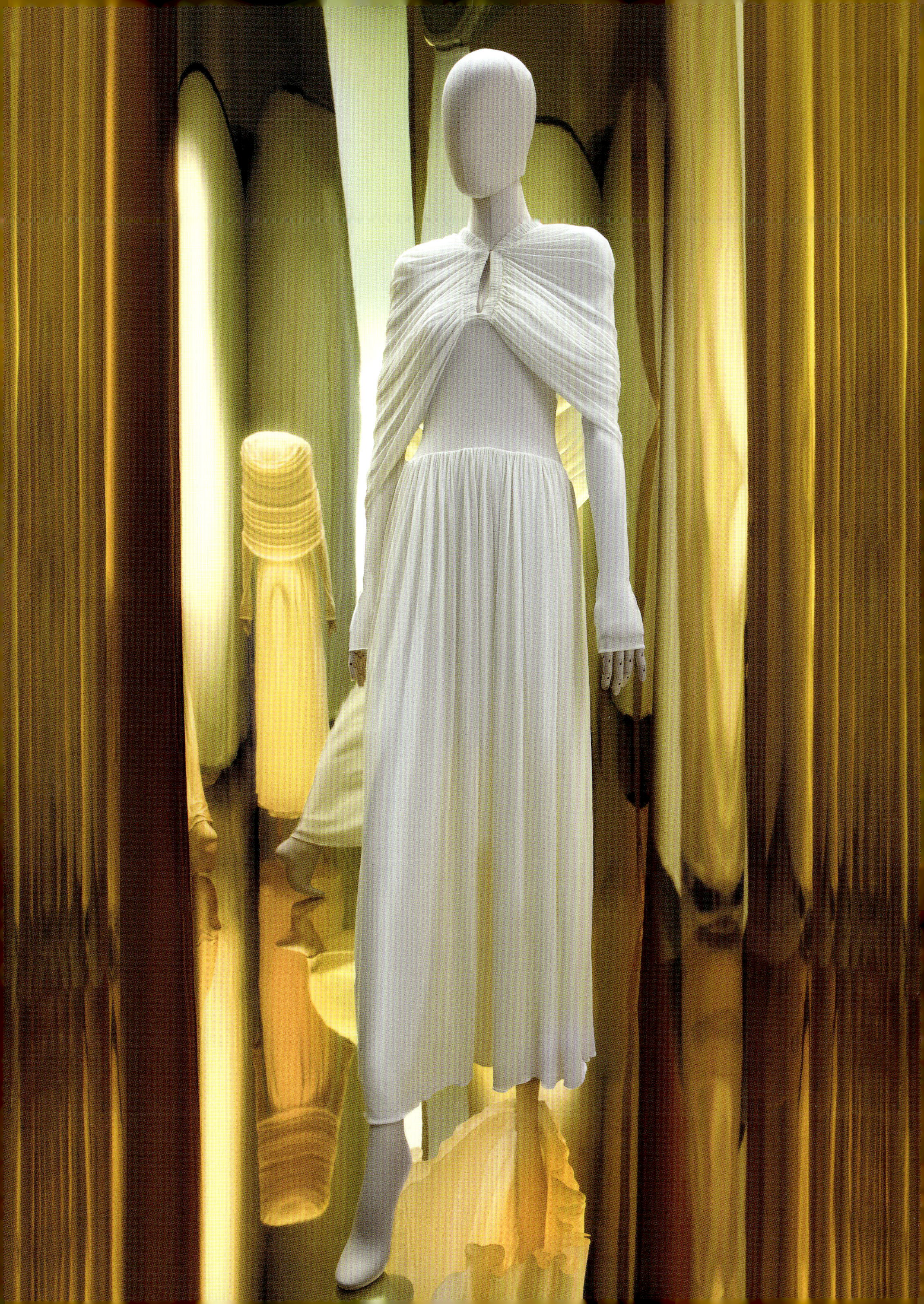

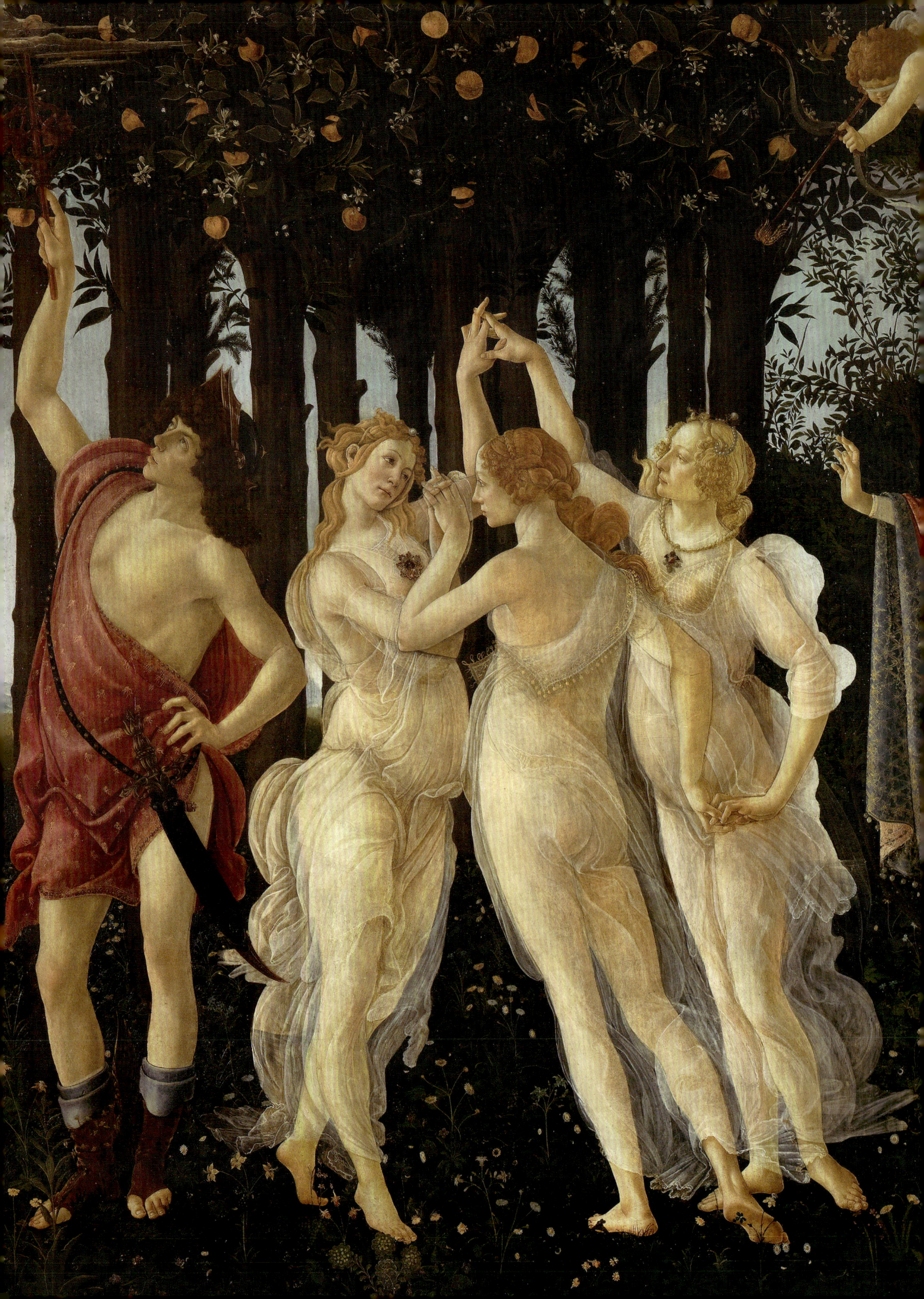

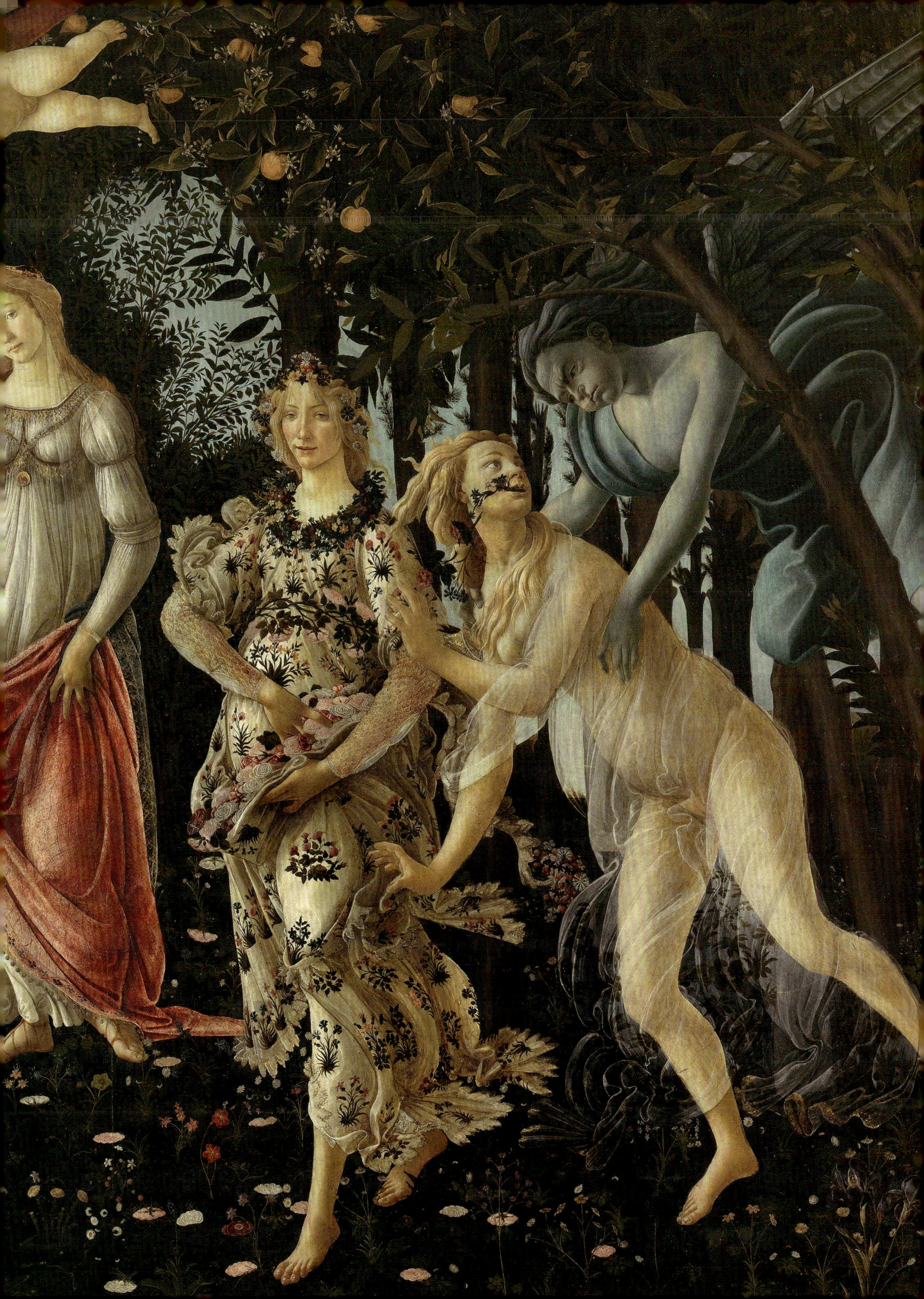

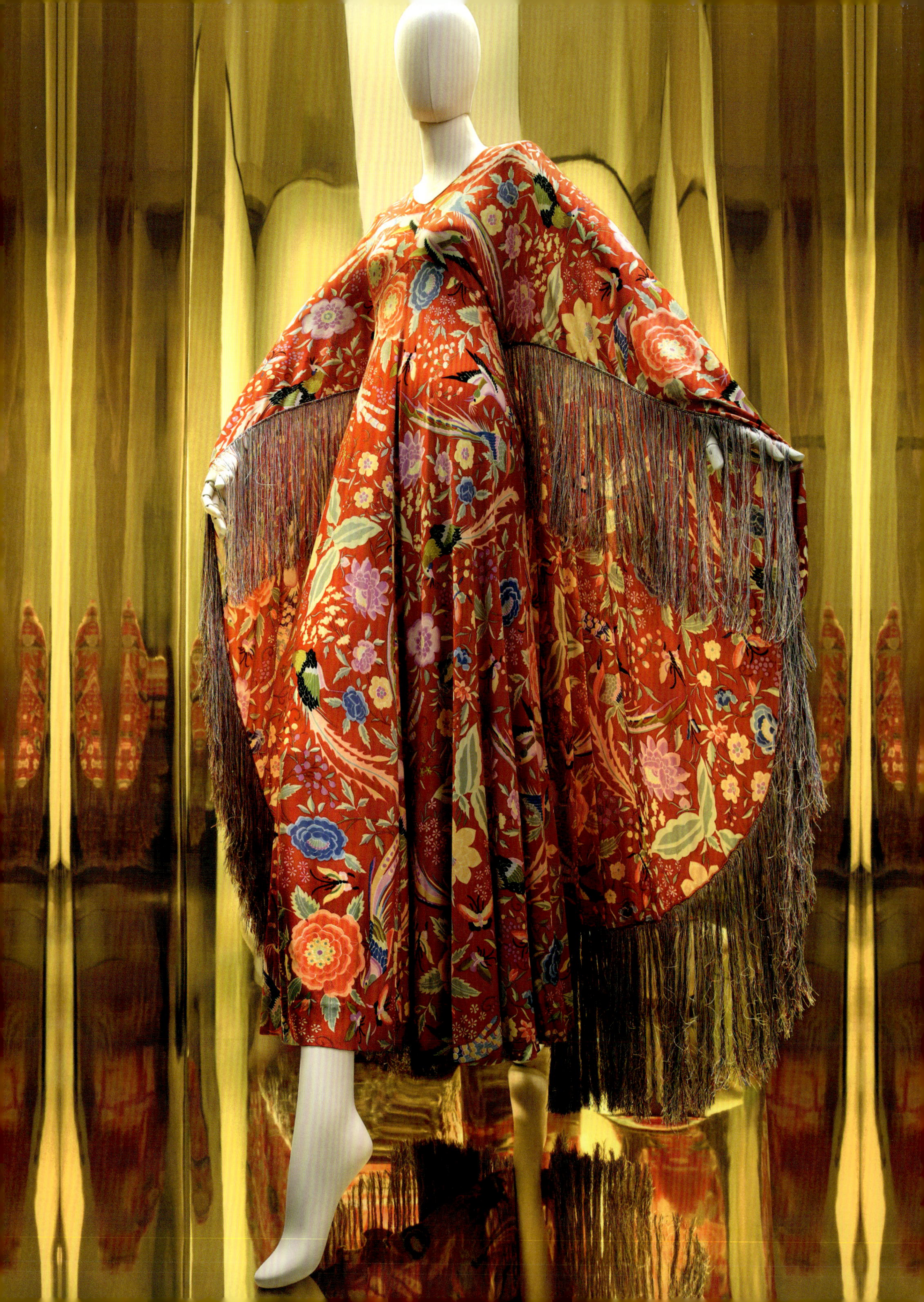

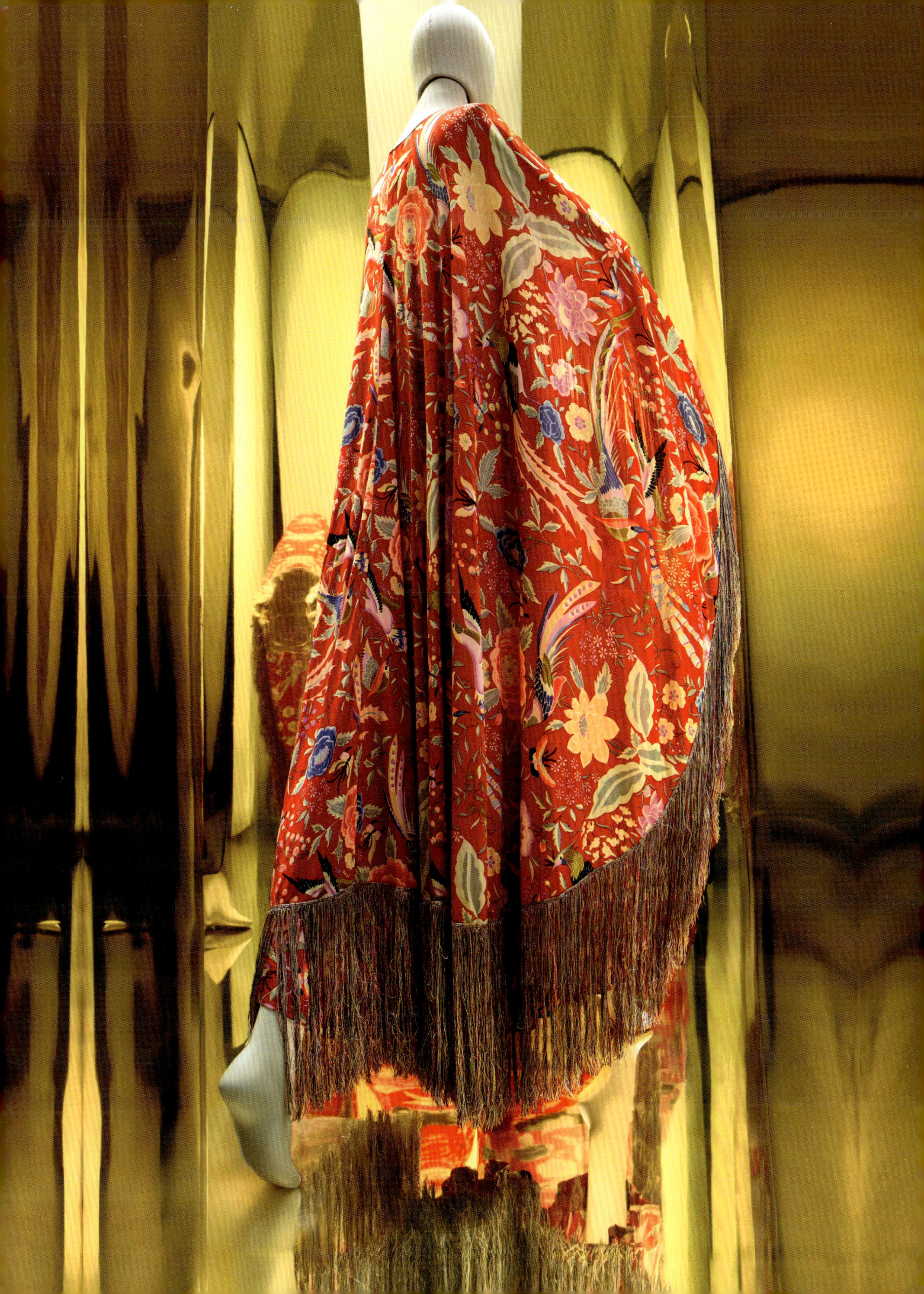

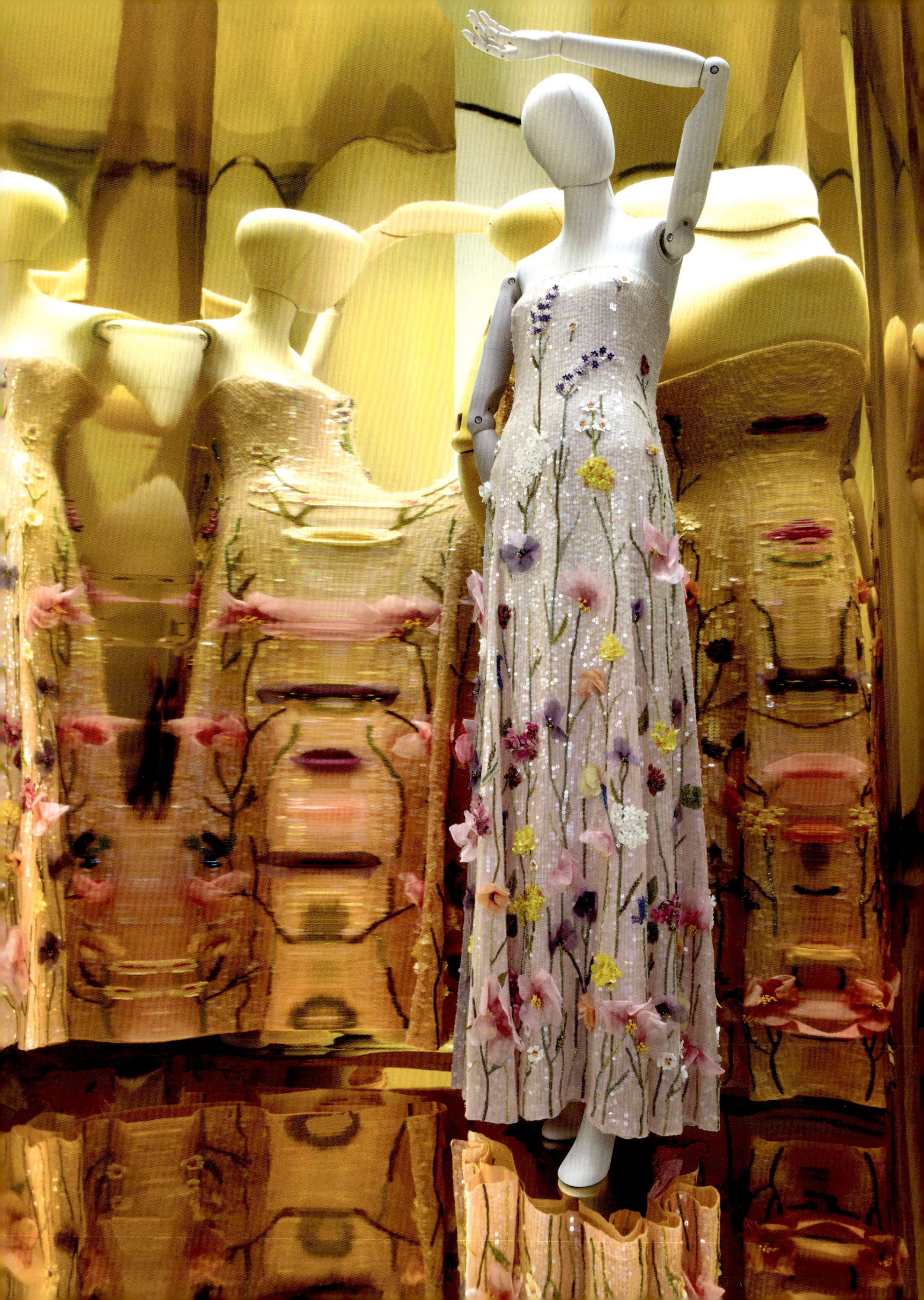

Plate 9: Gown, 1989. Roberto Capucci (Italian, b. 1930) for Roberto Capucci (Italian, est. 1950). Silk taffeta. Courtesy of the Fondazione Roberto Capucci

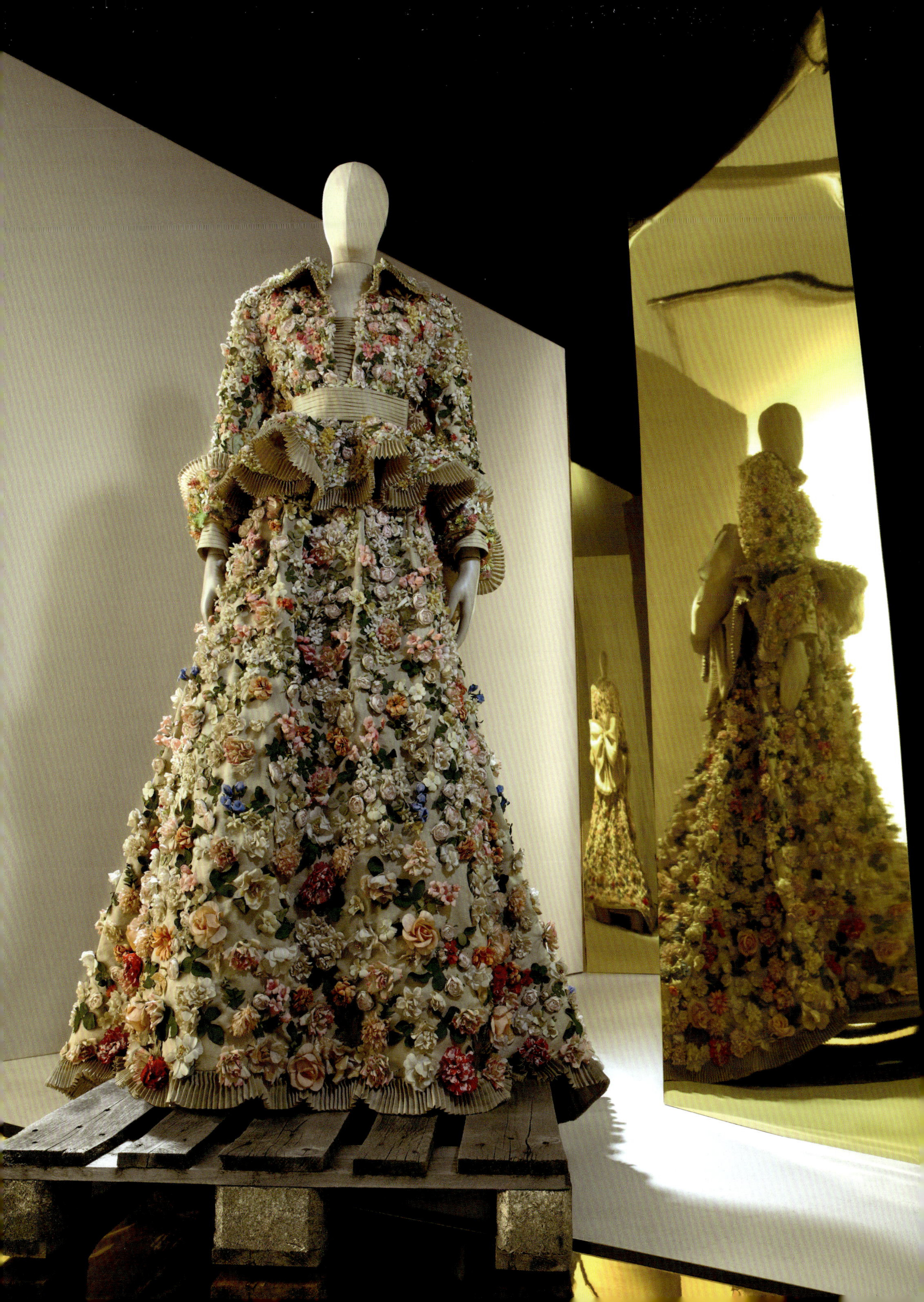

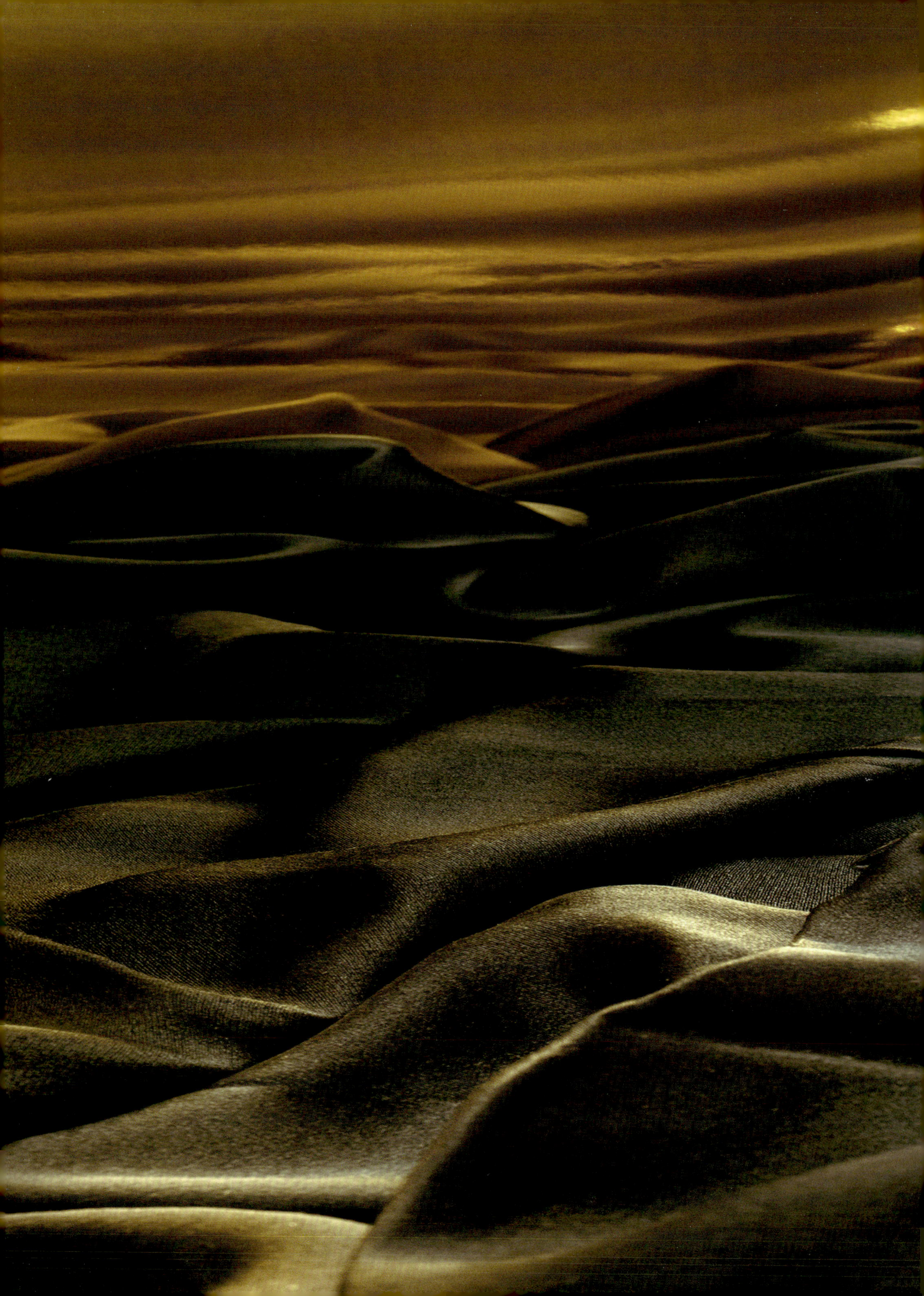

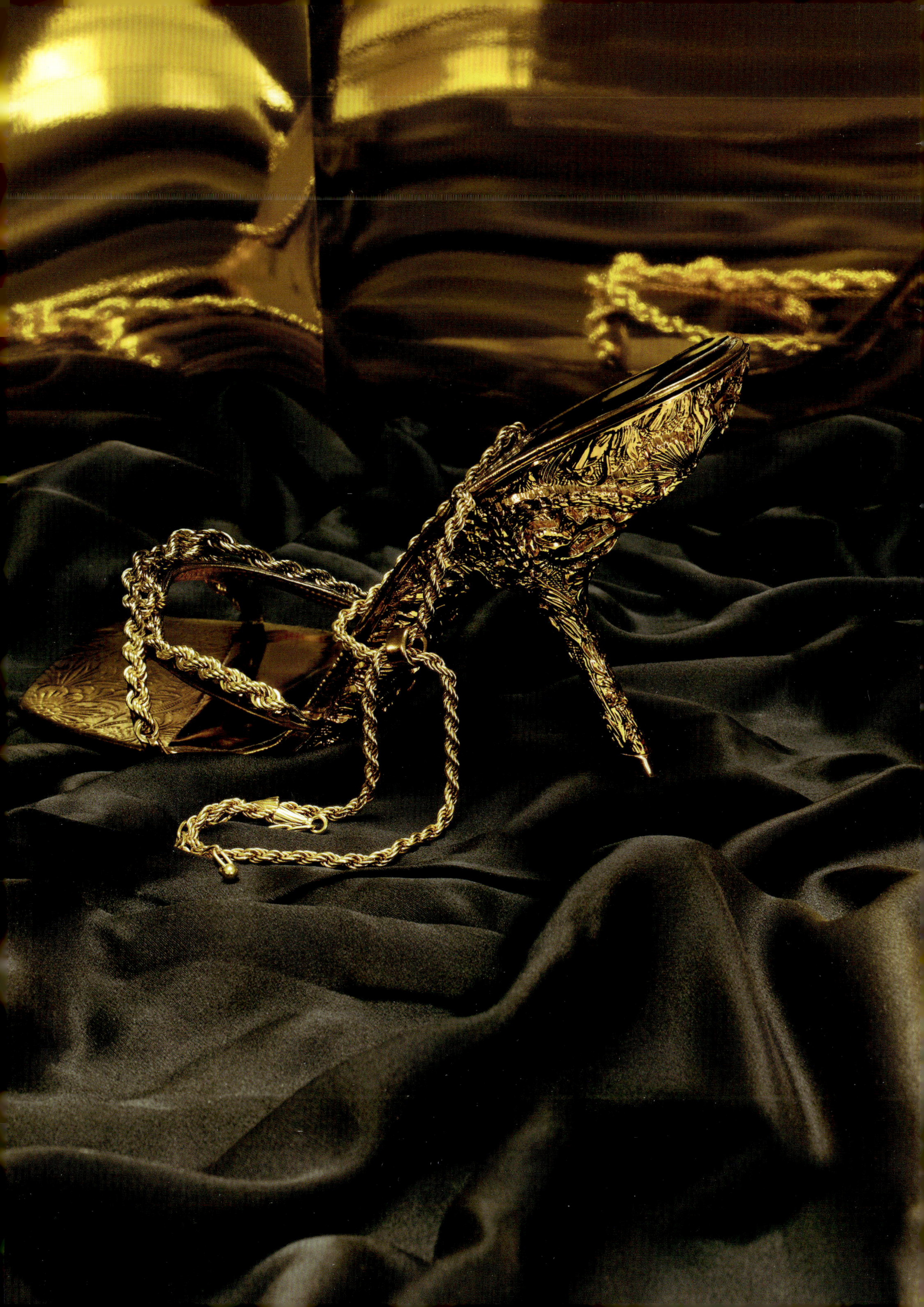

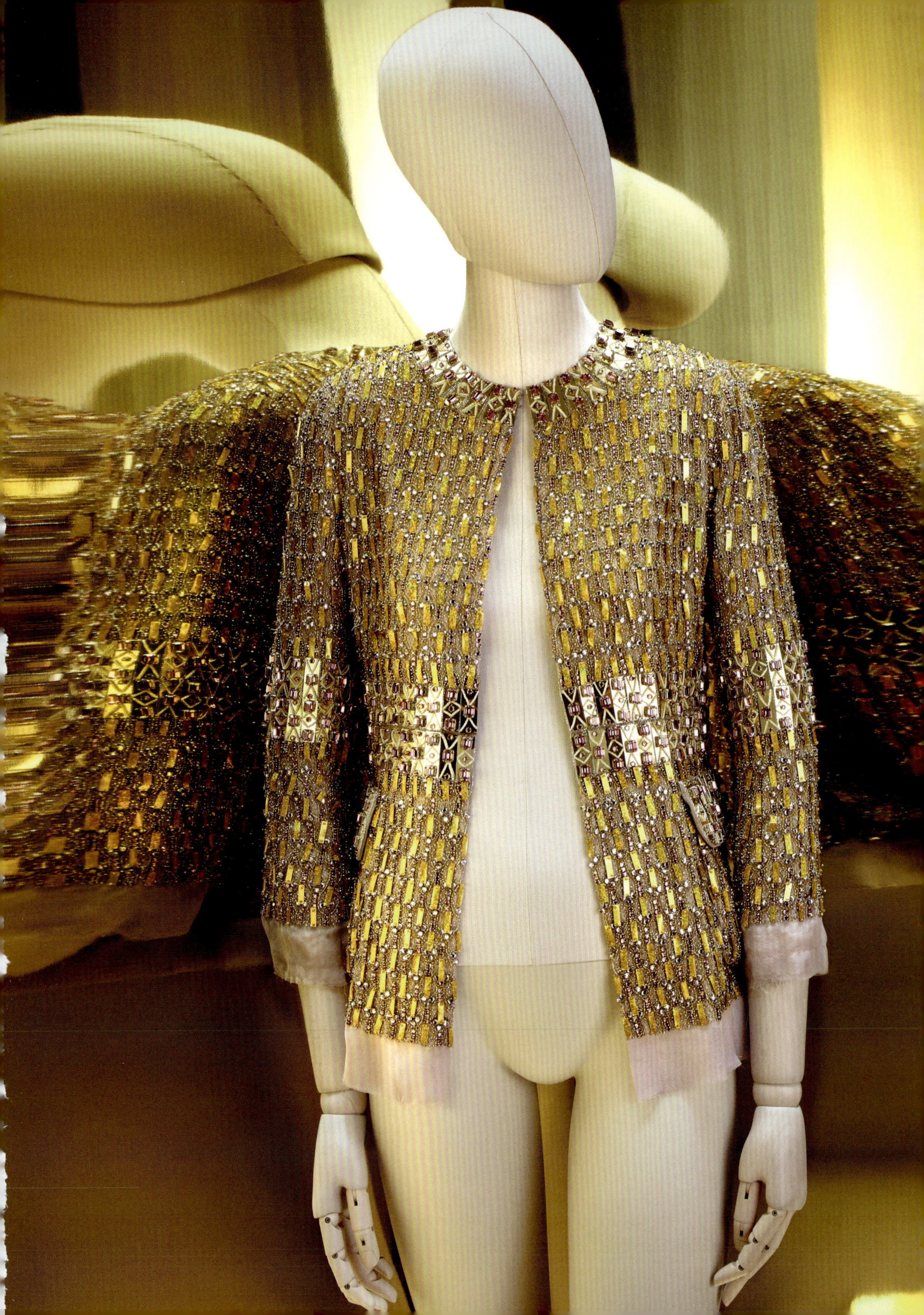

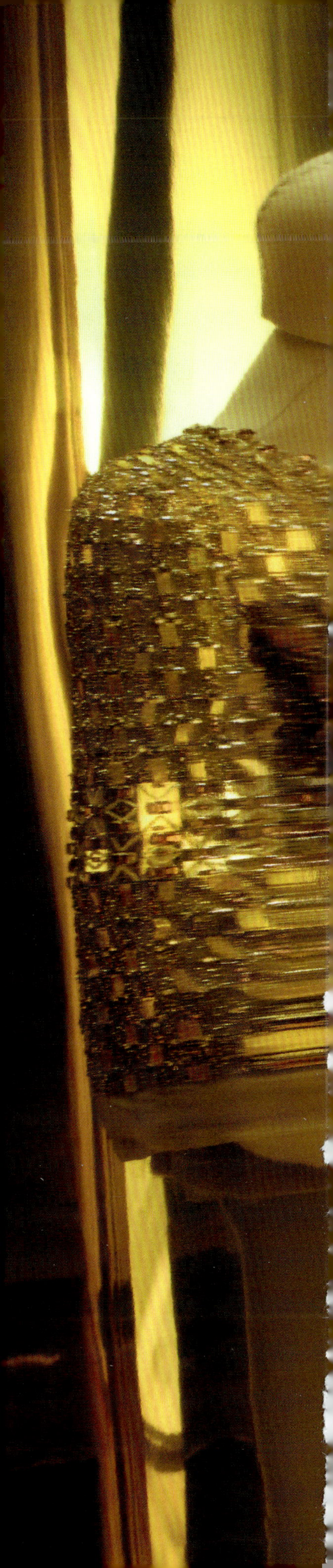

Pages 108–9

Plate 10: Jewel Sandal, Fall 2023. Maximilian Davis
(British, b. 1995) for Ferragamo (Italian, est. 1927).
Laminated leather. Courtesy of the Salvatore Ferragamo
Museum Archives

Pages 111–13

Plate 11: Jacket, c. 1990s. Domenico Dolce (Italian,
b. 1958) and Stefano Gabbana (Italian, b. 1962) for
Dolce & Gabbana (Italian, est. 1985). Silk, crystals,
beading, and mirror laminate. Private Collection

Page 114

Plate 12: *Idealized Portrait of a Lady (Portrait of
Simonetta Vespucci as Nymph)*, c. 1875–1923. Samuel
Arlent-Edwards (American, 1862–1938) after Sandro
Botticelli (Italian, 1444/45–1510). Mezzotint; platemark:
38 x 30.2 cm; sheet: 56.7 x 41.4 cm. The Cleveland
Museum of Art, Gift of the Artist, 1923.384

Pages 116–17

Plate 13: Ensemble, Fall 1987. Gianfranco Ferré (Italian,
1944–2007) for Gianfranco Ferré (Italian, est. 1978).
Wool, leather, and plastic. Courtesy of Centro di Ricerca
Gianfranco Ferré, Politecnico di Milano

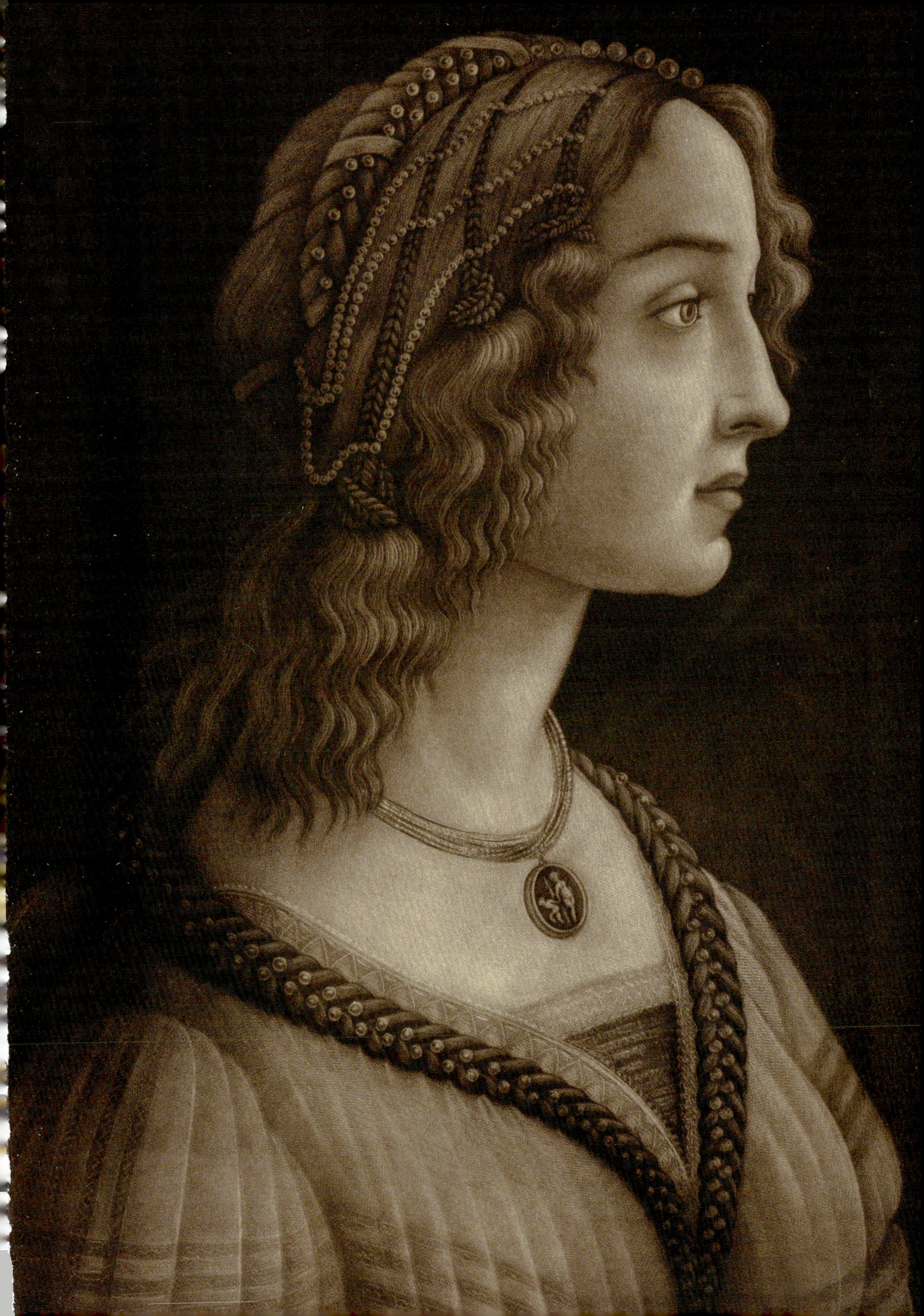

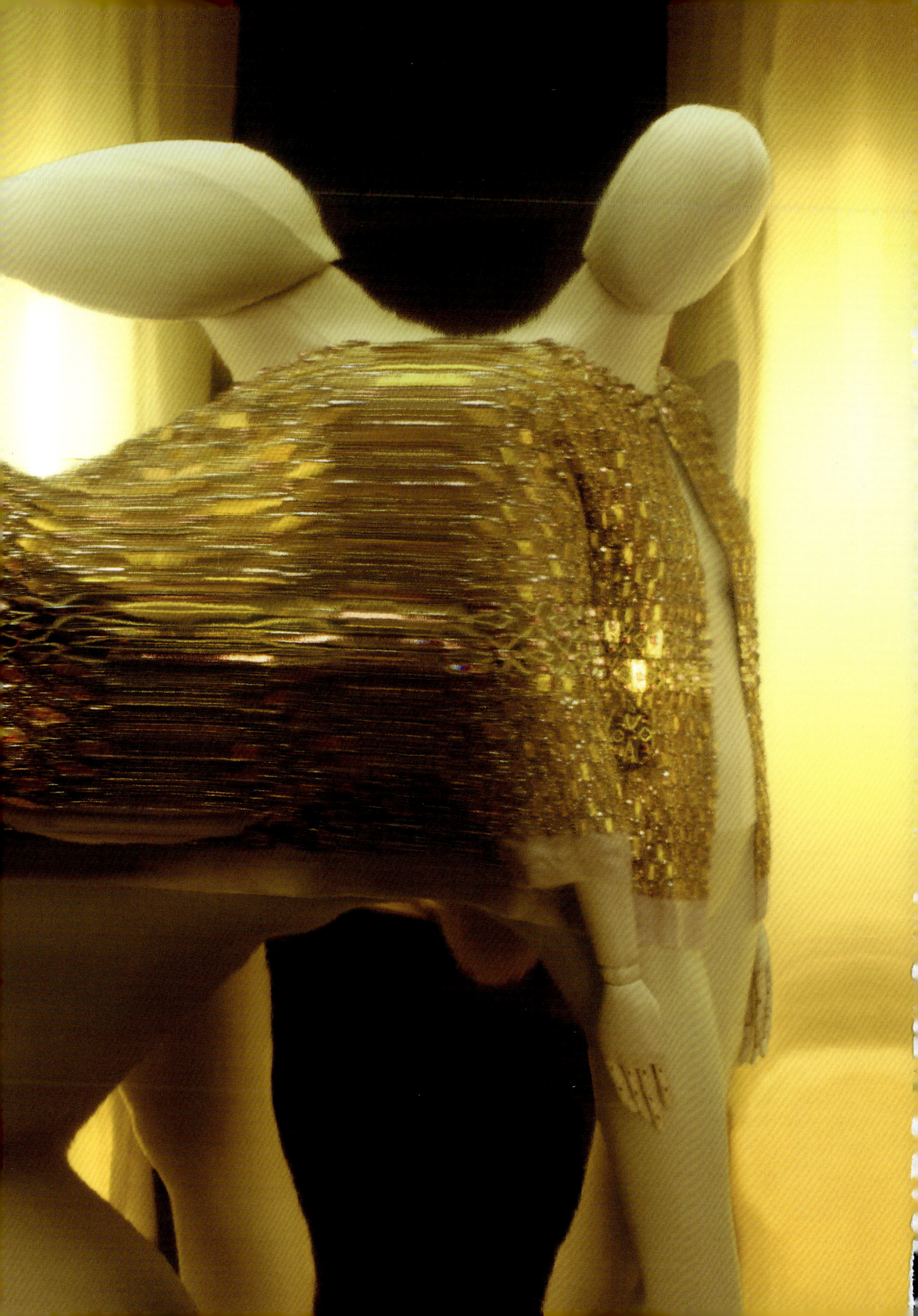

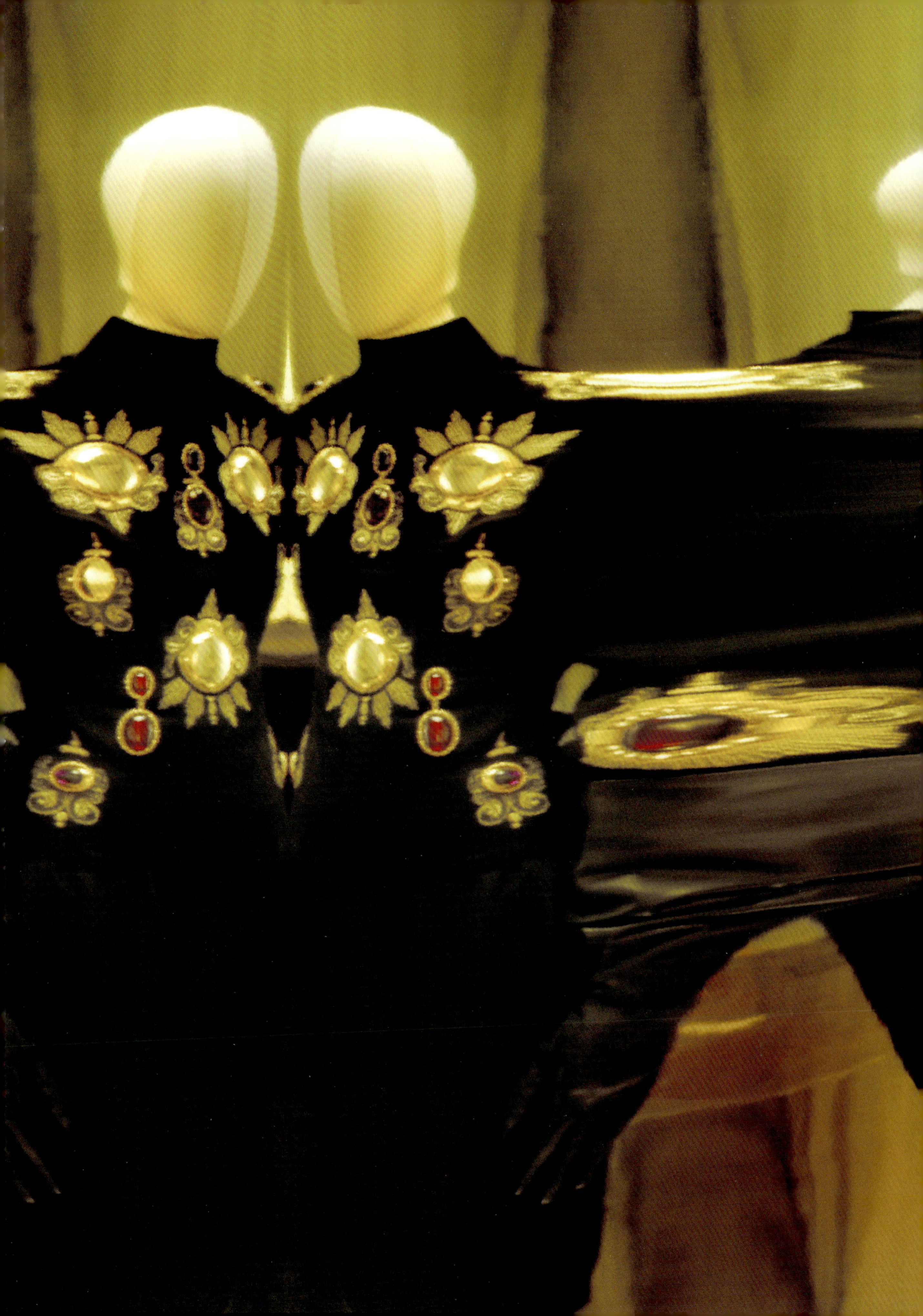

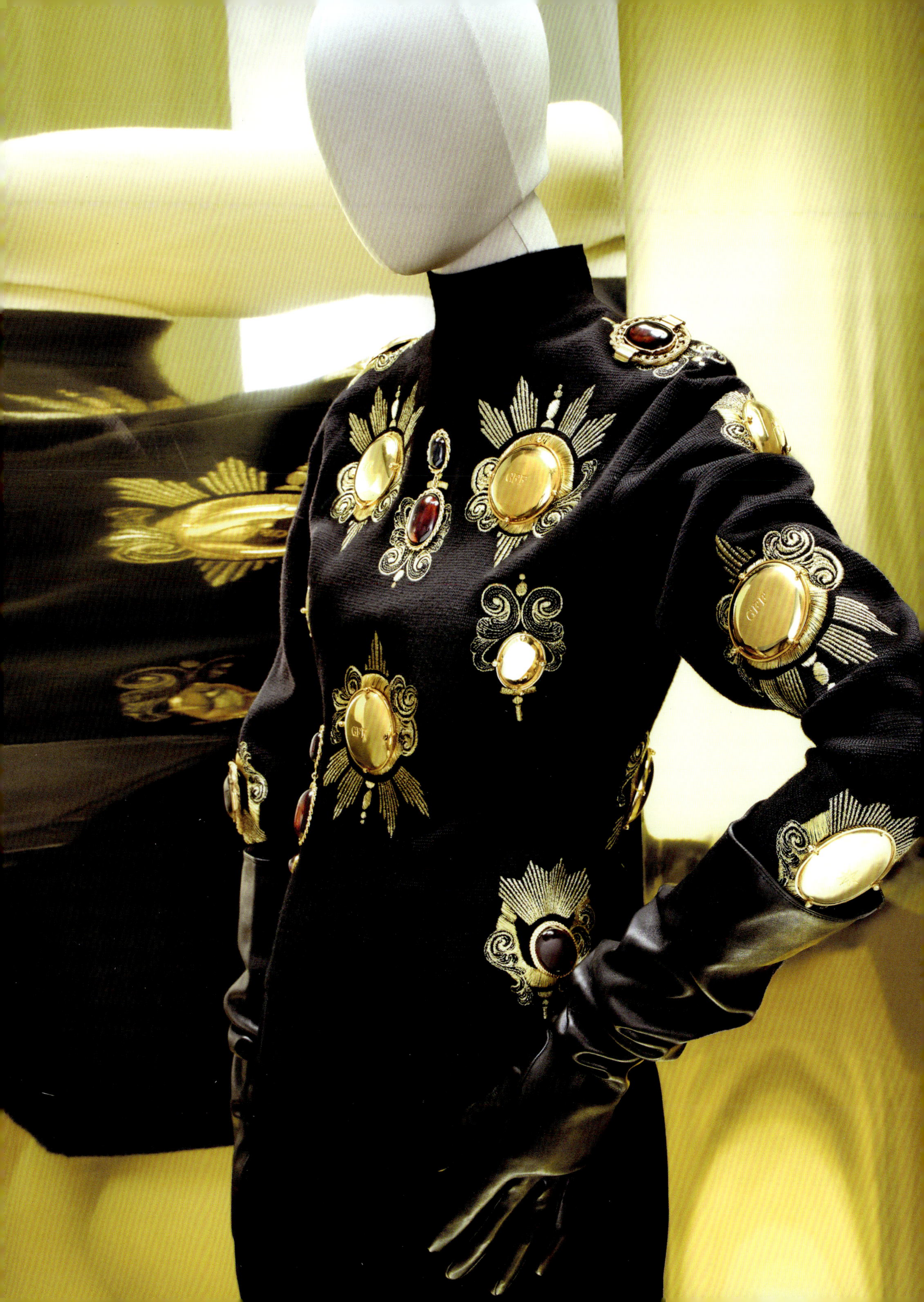

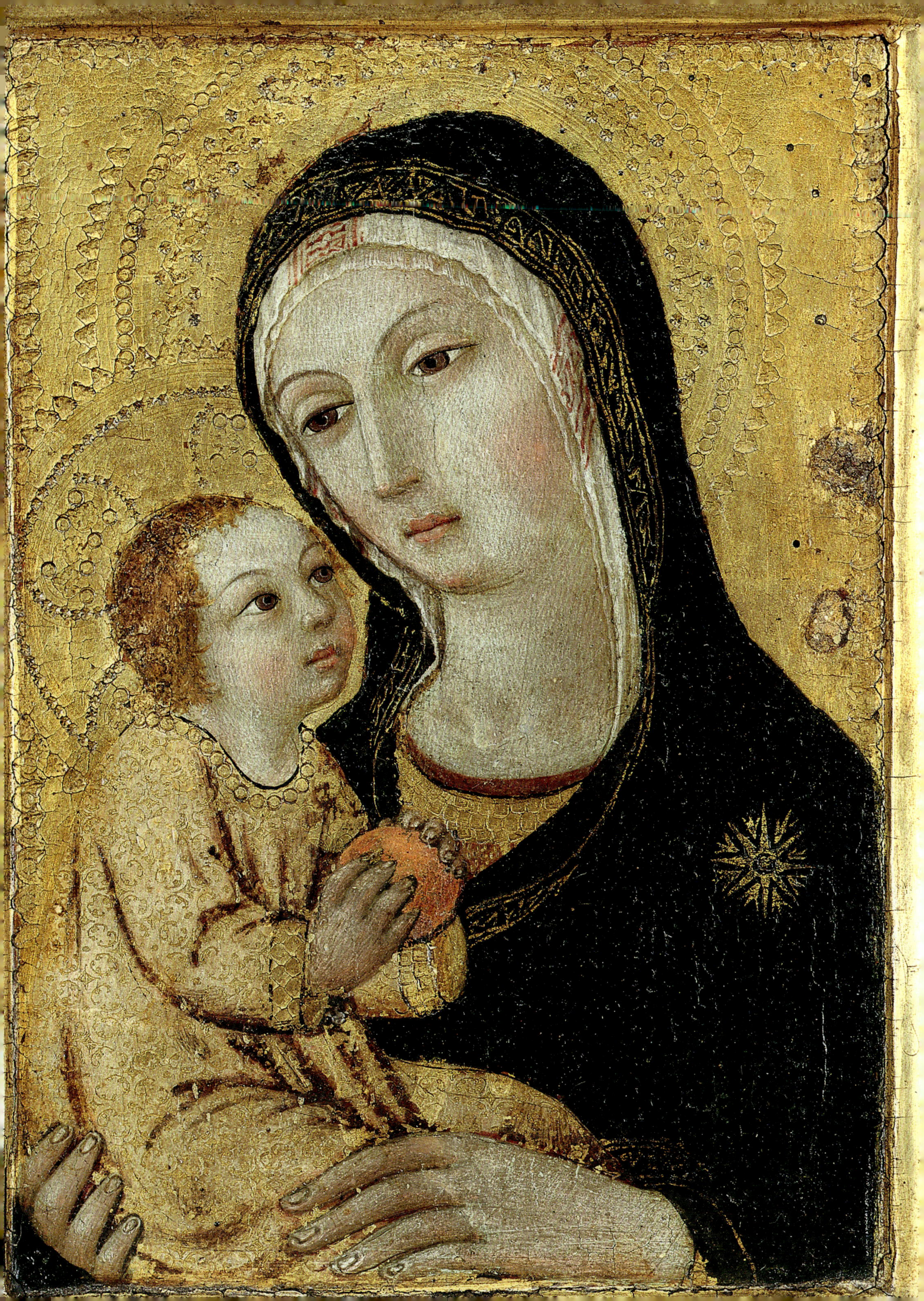

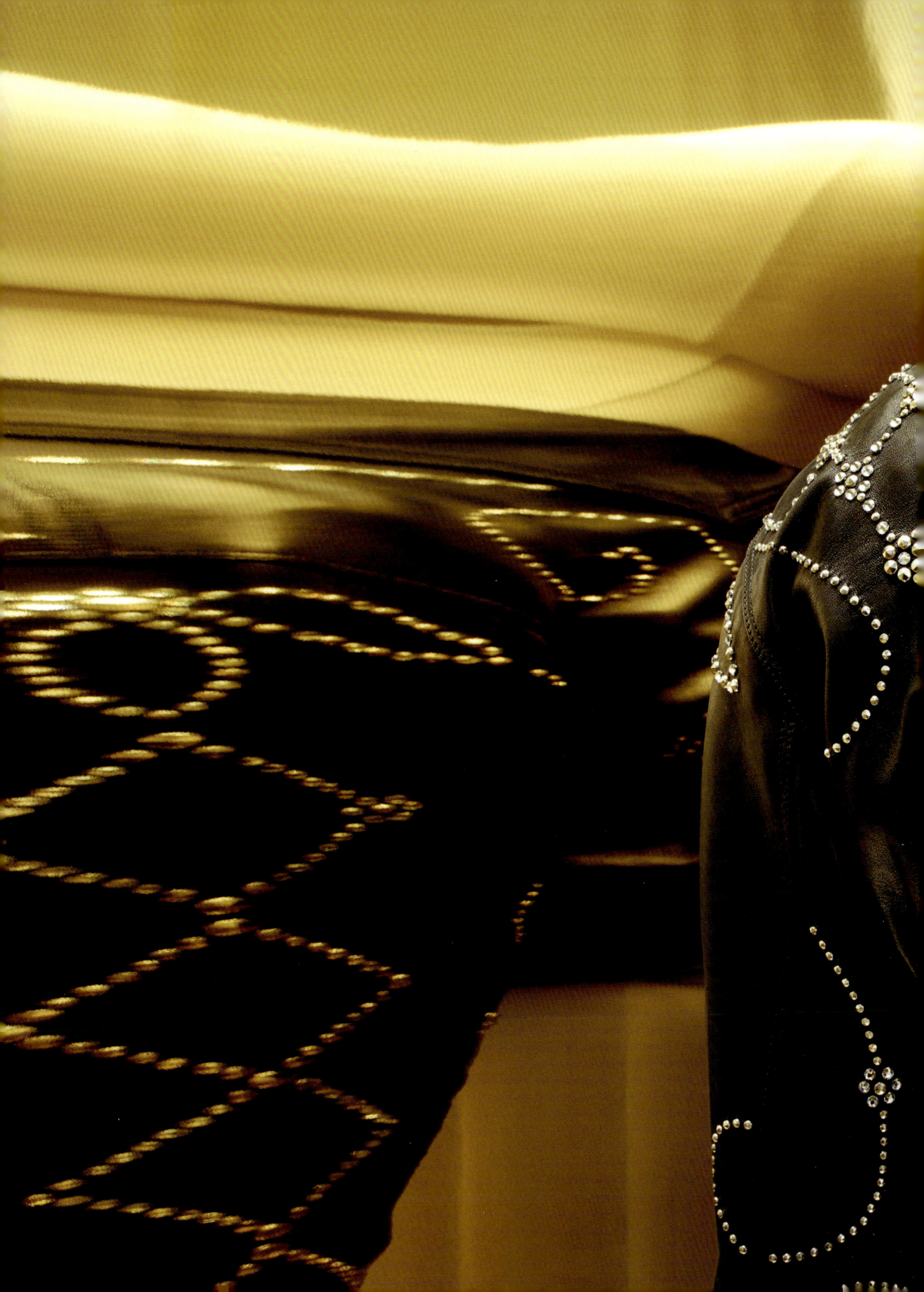

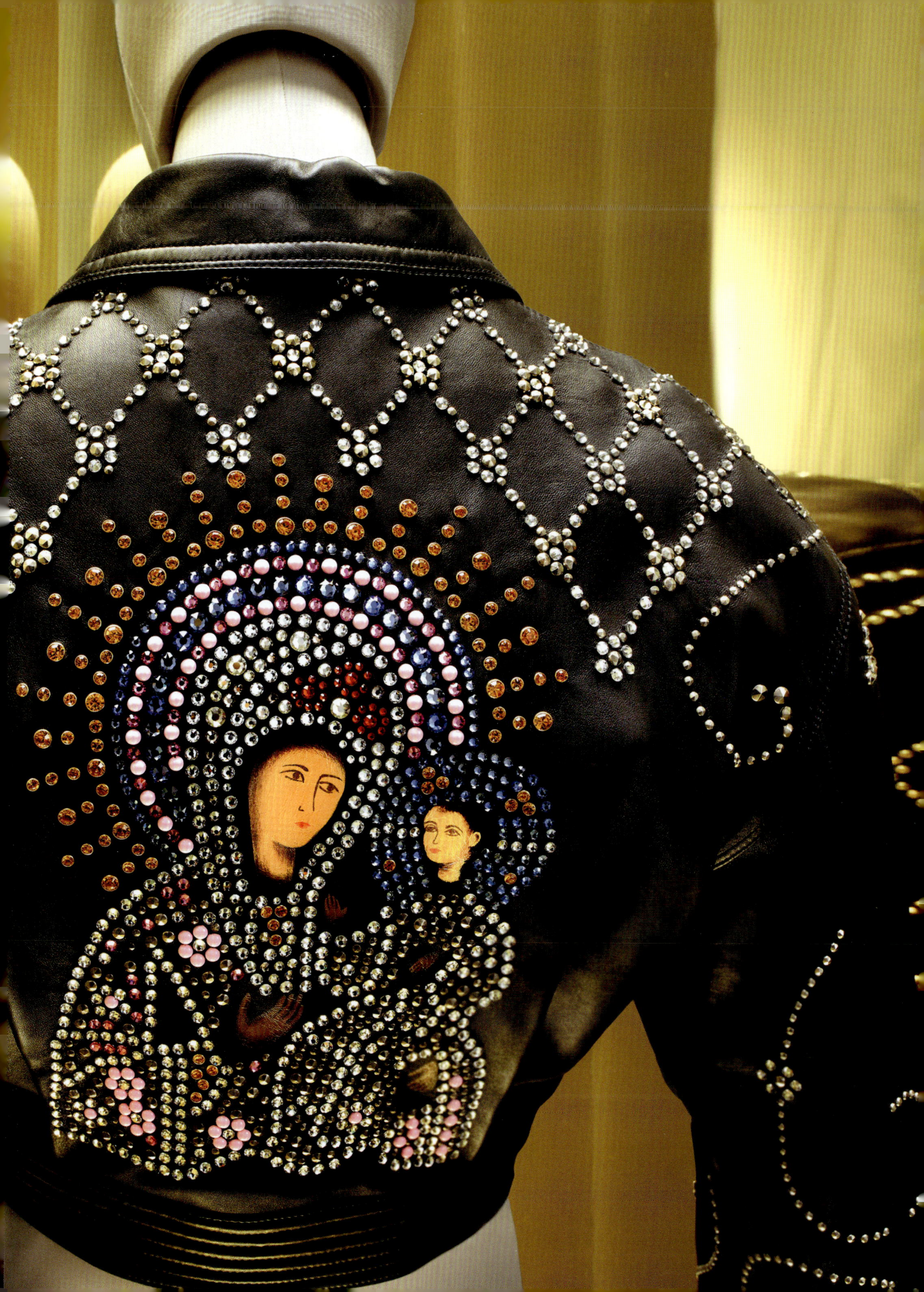

122

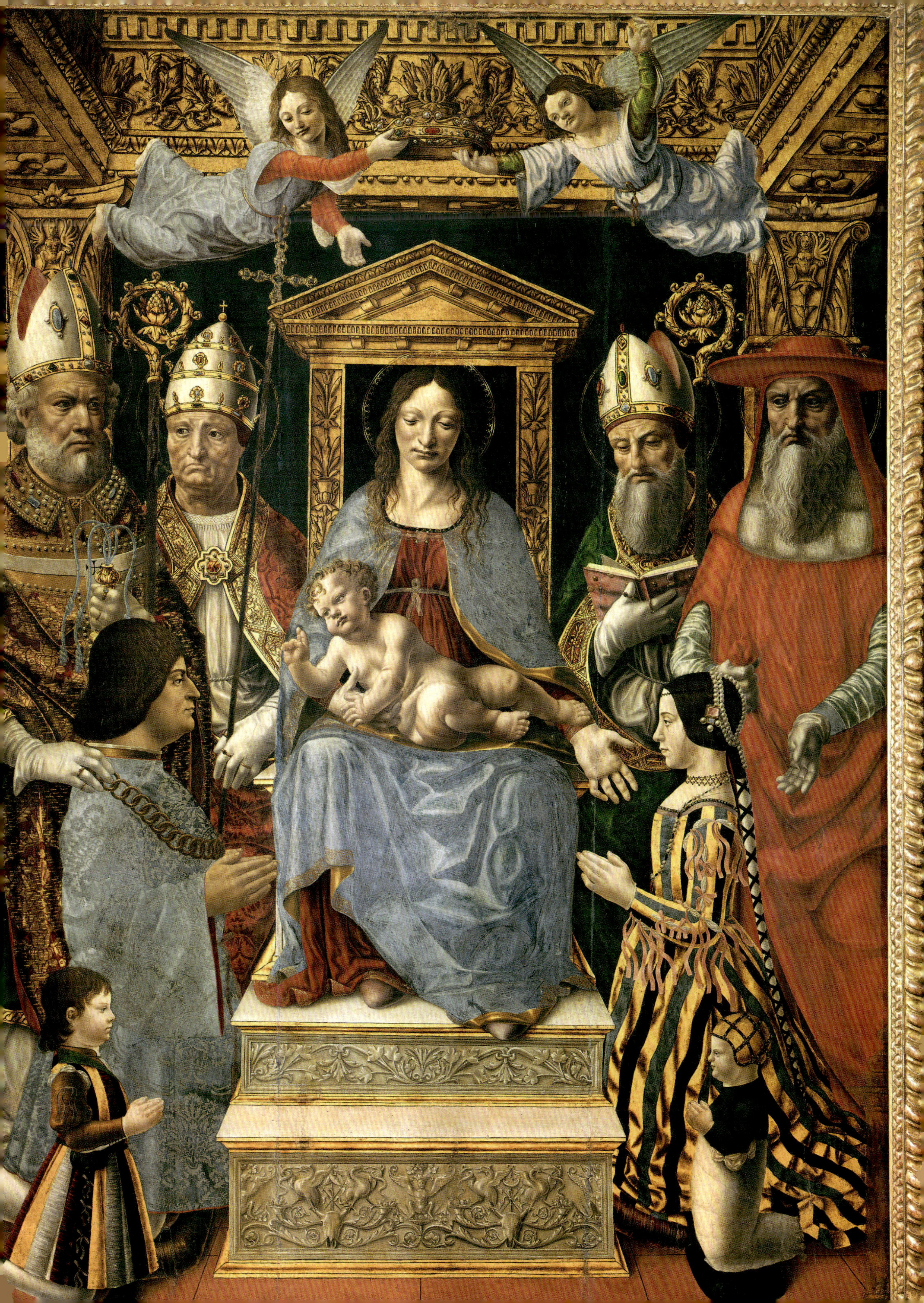

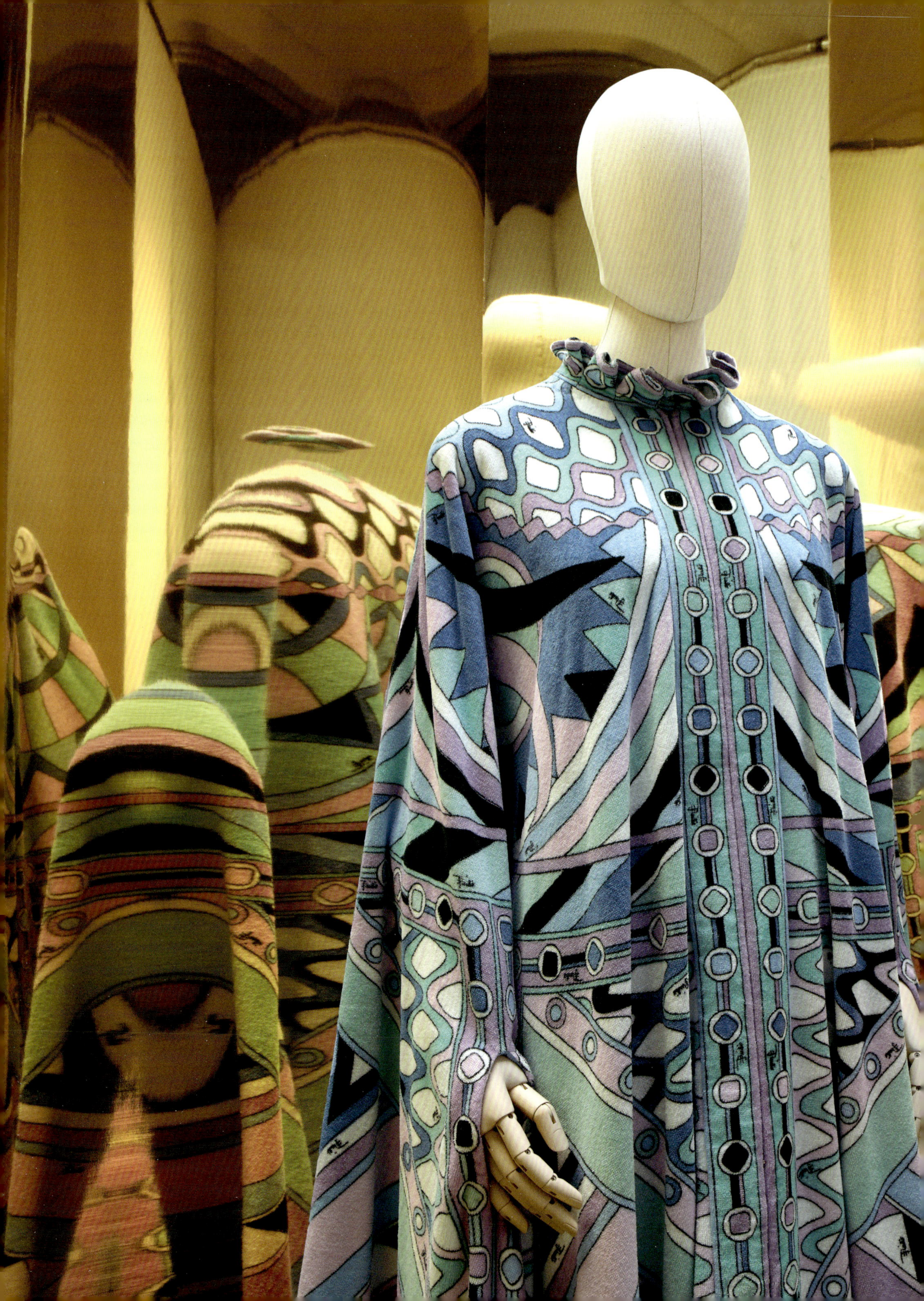

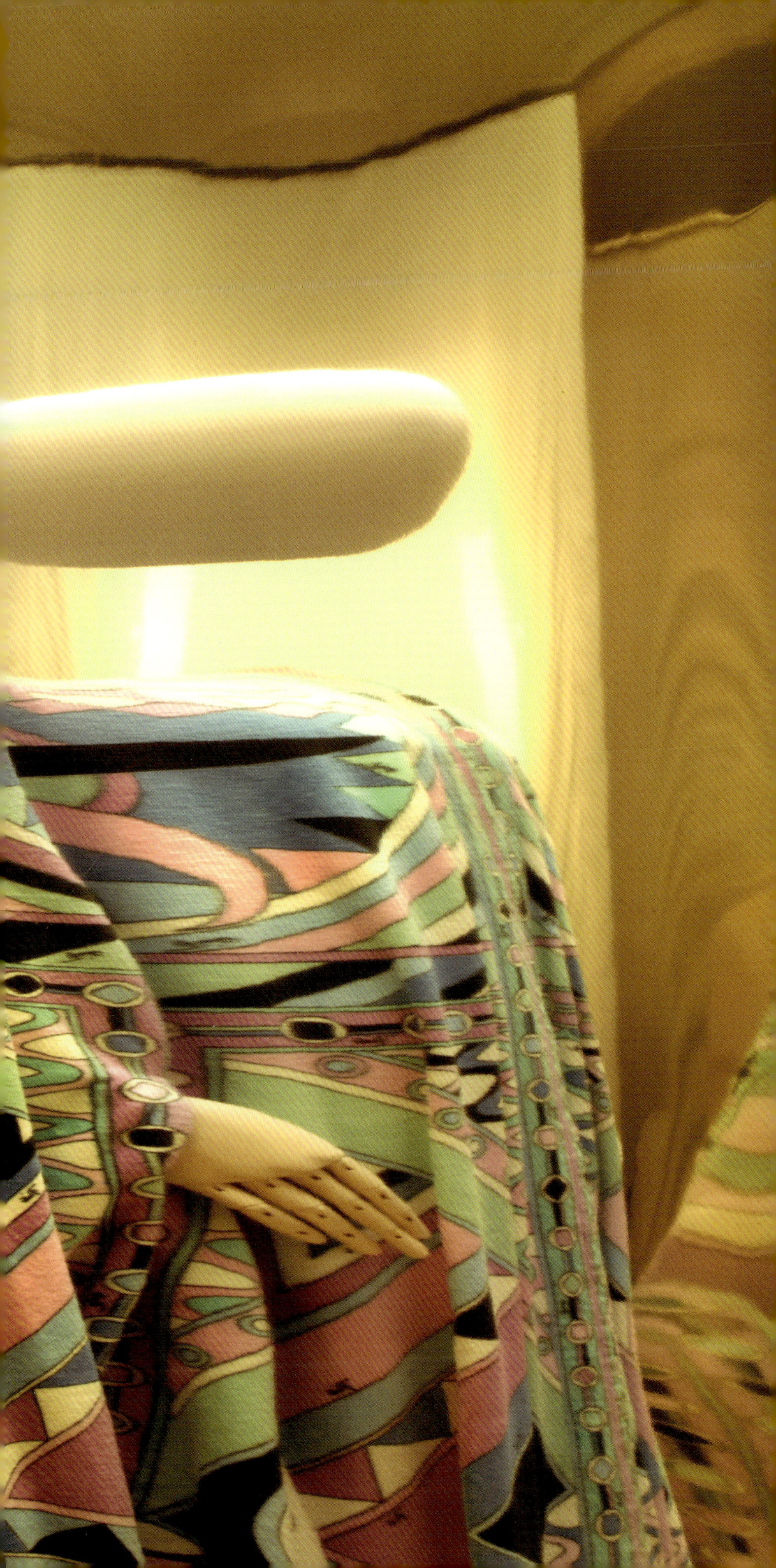

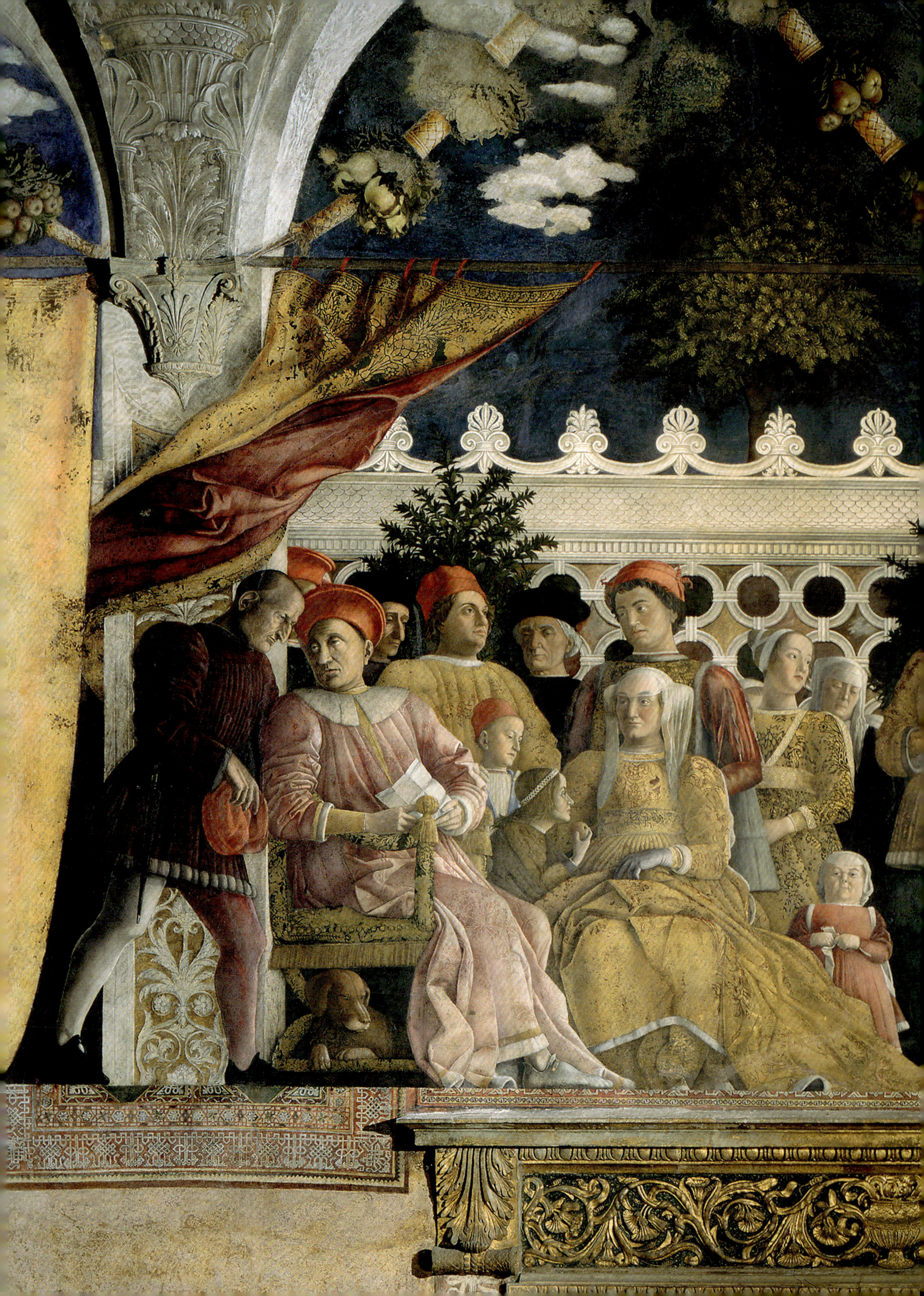

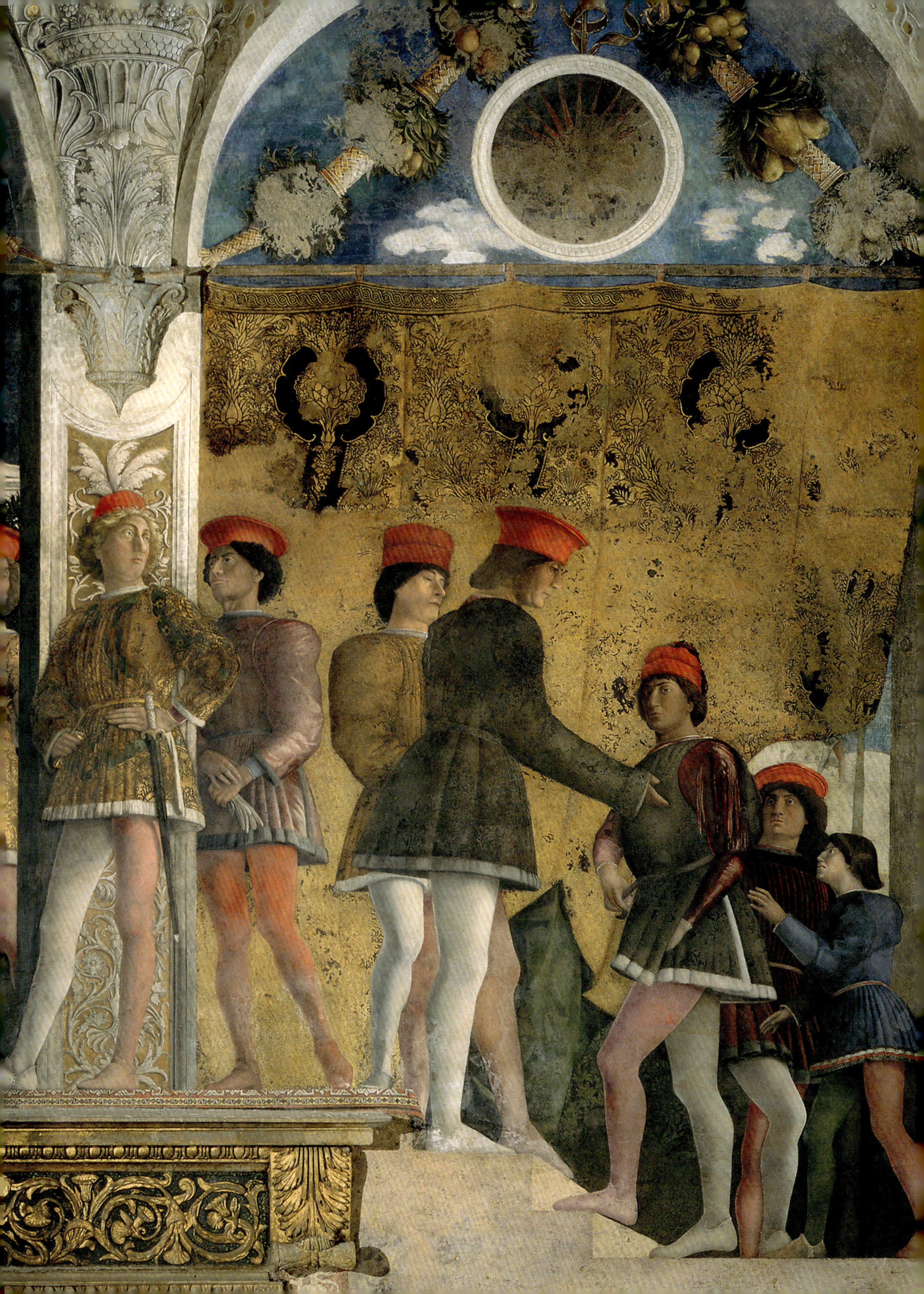

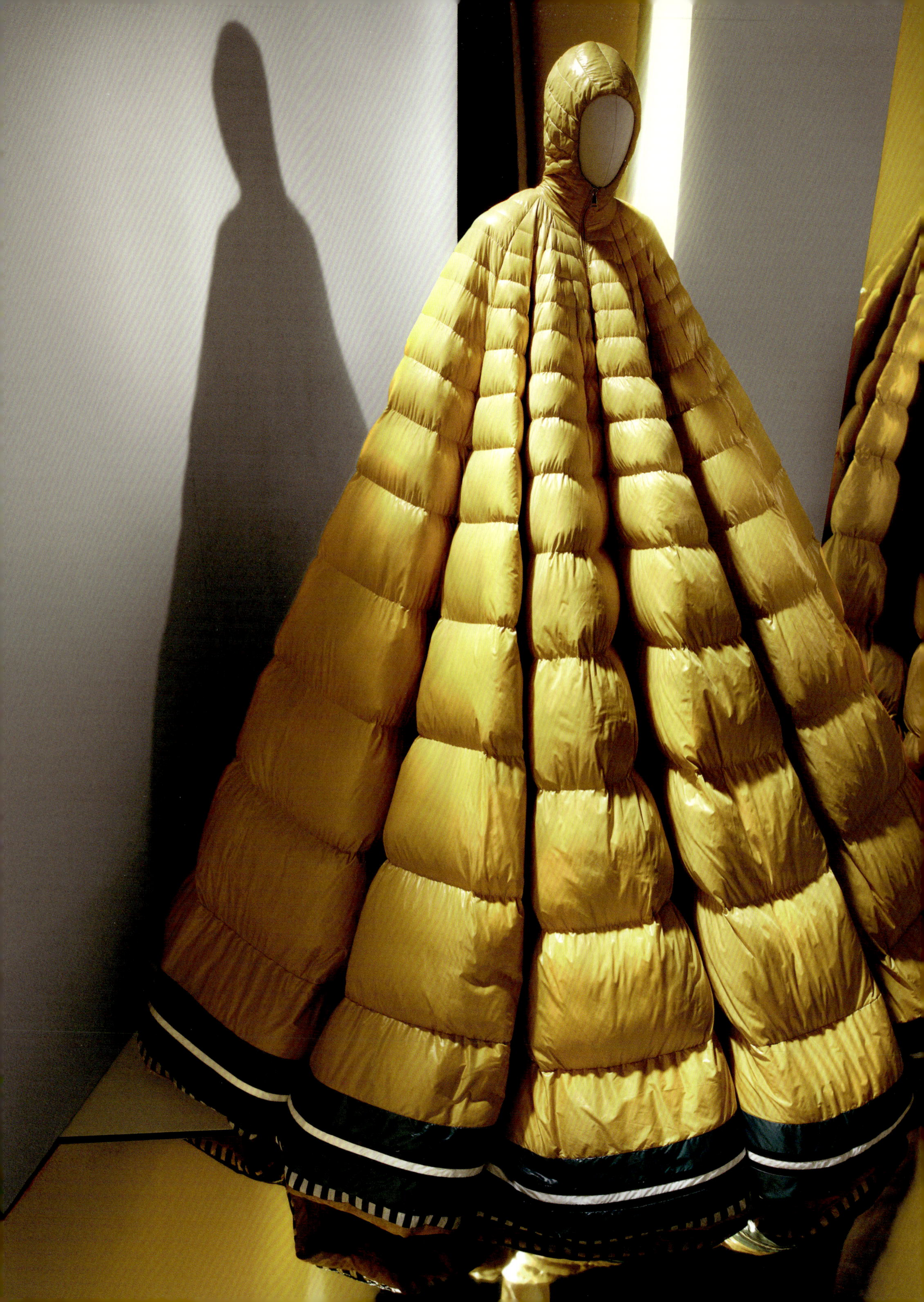

Pages 126–27

Plate 18: *The Court of the Gonzaga* 1474.
Andrea Mantegna (Italian, c. 1431–1506).
Walnut oil on plaster; 805 x 807 cm.
Camera degli Sposi, Palazzo Ducale, Mantua.
Photo: Scala / Art Resource, NY

Opposite

Plate 19: Coatdress, Fall 2019. Pierpaolo Piccioli
(Italian, b. 1967) for Moncler (French, Italian, est.
1952). Nylon laqué. Courtesy of 1 Moncler

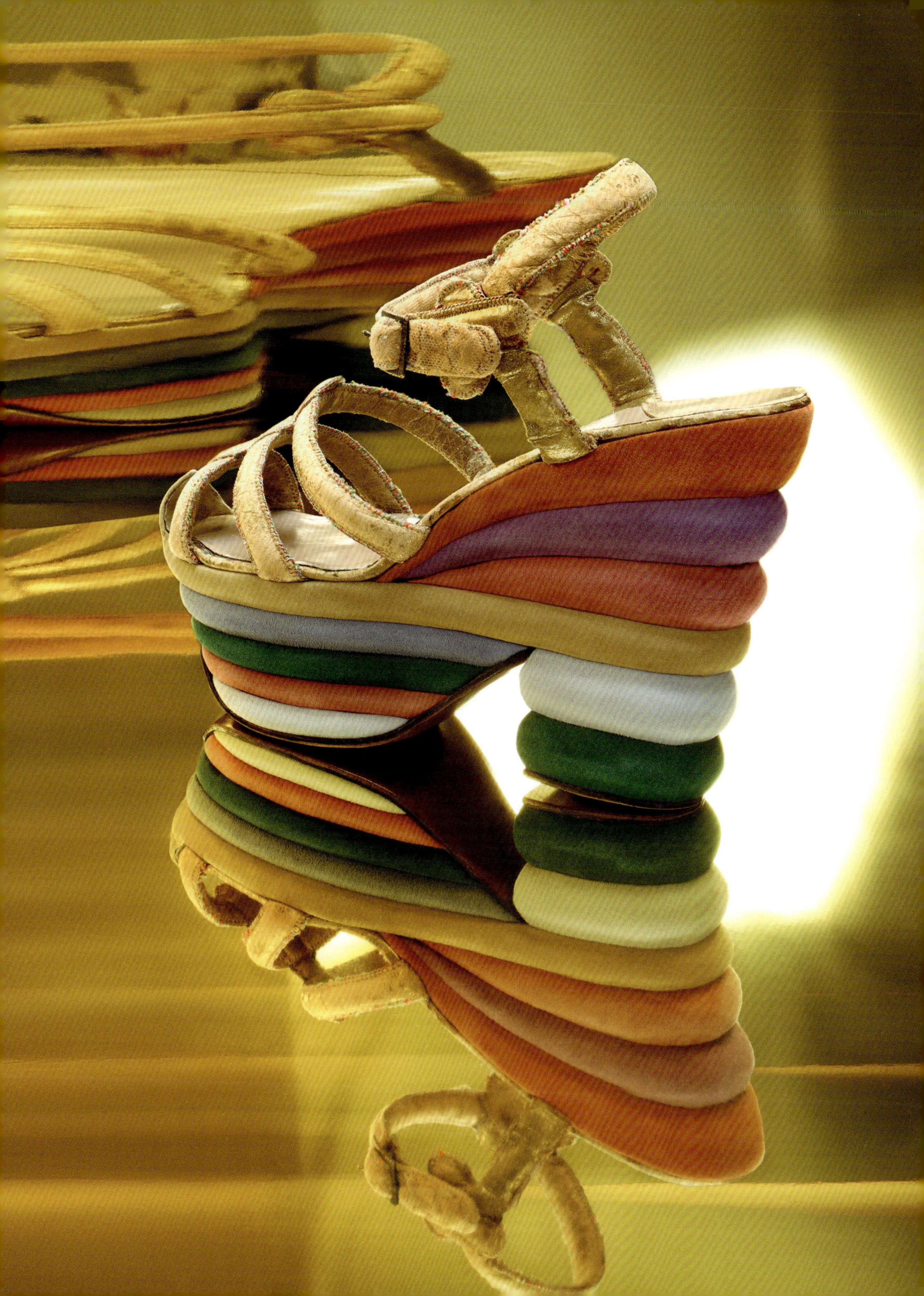

Pages 130–31

Plate 20: *Rainbow*, 1938. Salvatore Ferragamo (Italian, 1898–1960) for Ferragamo (Italian, est. 1927). Leather and cork.
Courtesy of the Salvatore Ferragamo Museum Archives

Opposite

Plate 21: *Two Venetian Ladies (The Courtesans)*, c. 1510. Vittore Carpaccio (Italian, c. 1460/65–1523/26). Tempera and oil on panel; 94.5 x 63.5 cm. Correr Museum, Venice, Class I No. 0046.
Photo: © Francesco Turio Bohm / Bridgeman Images

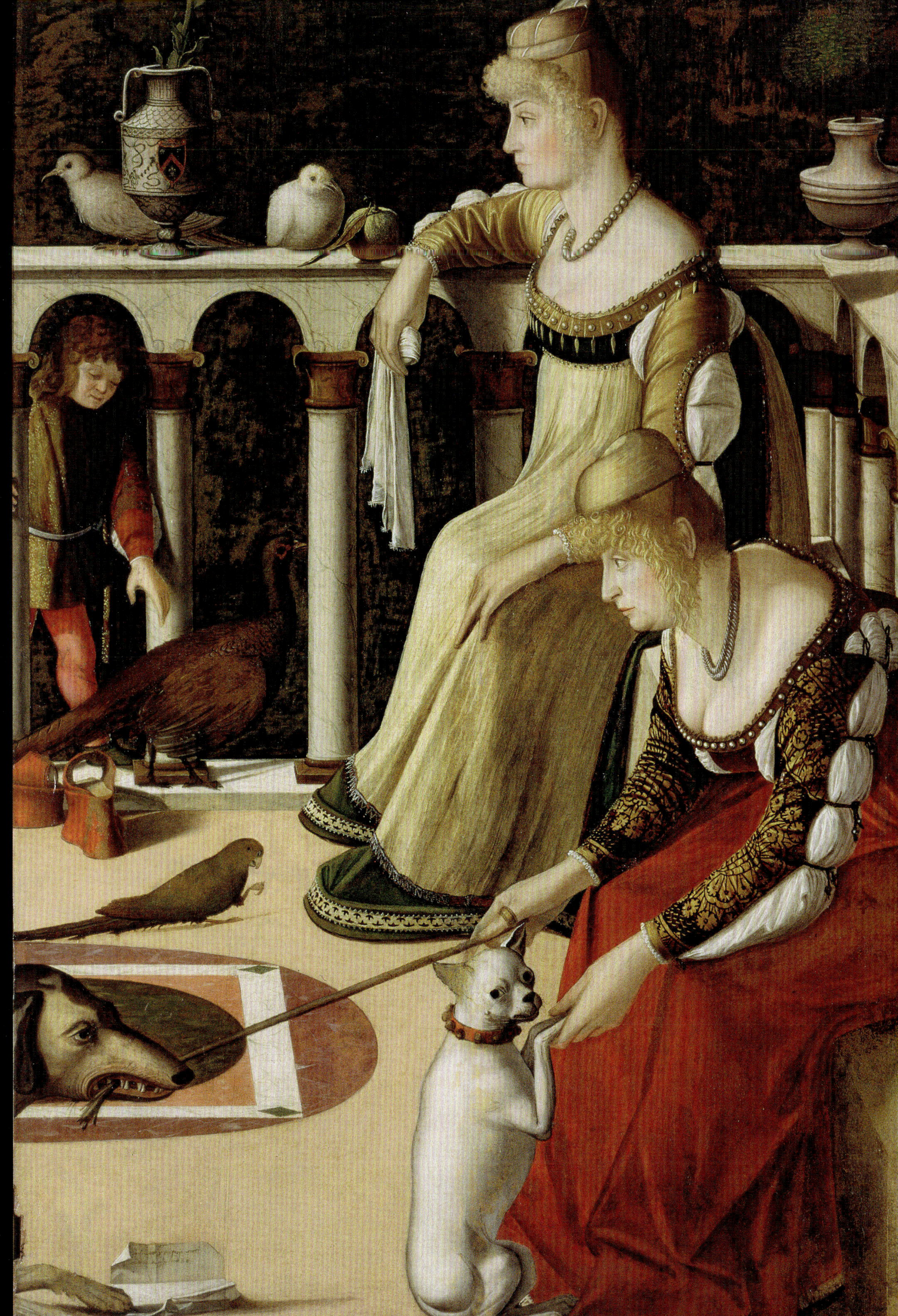

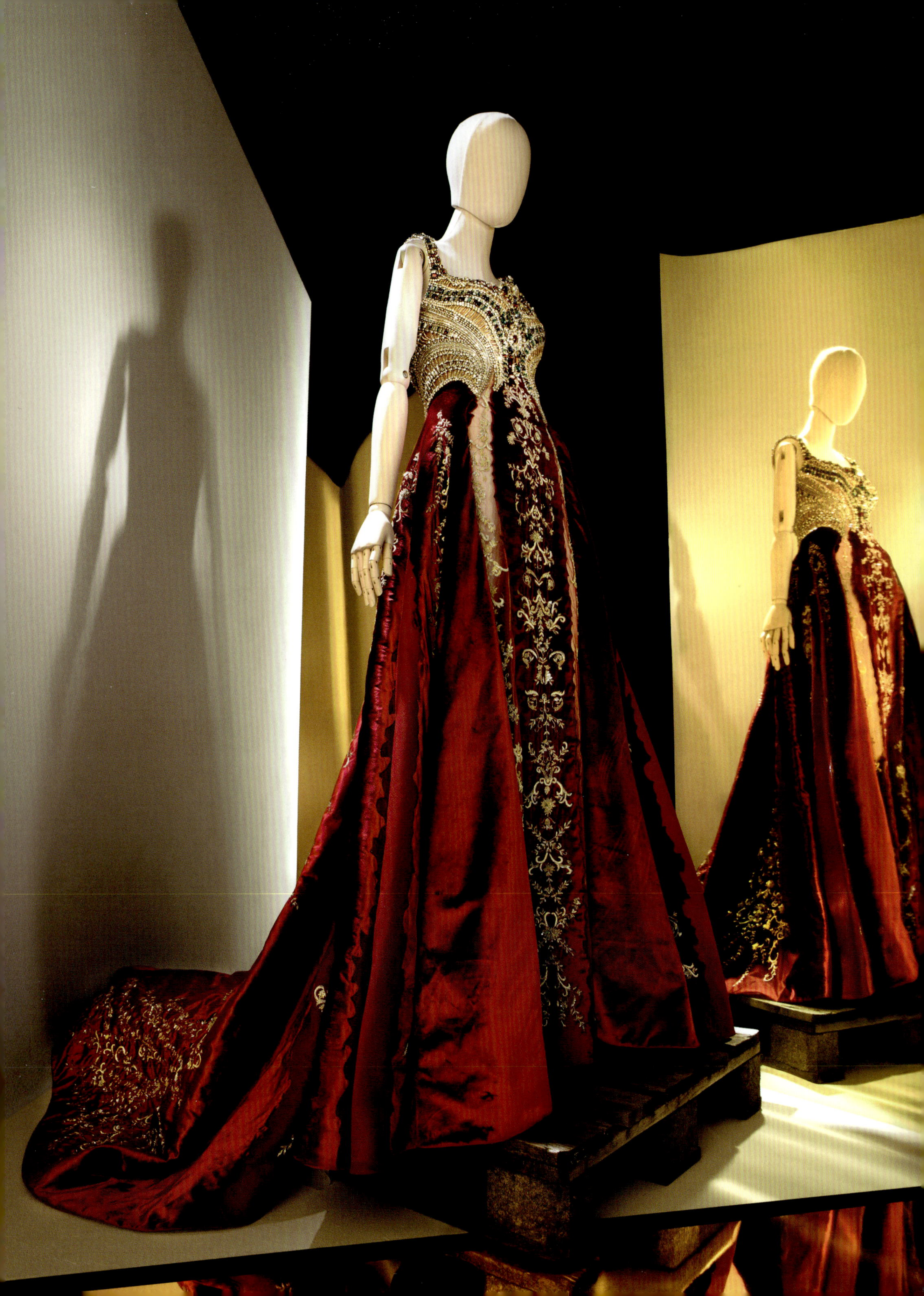

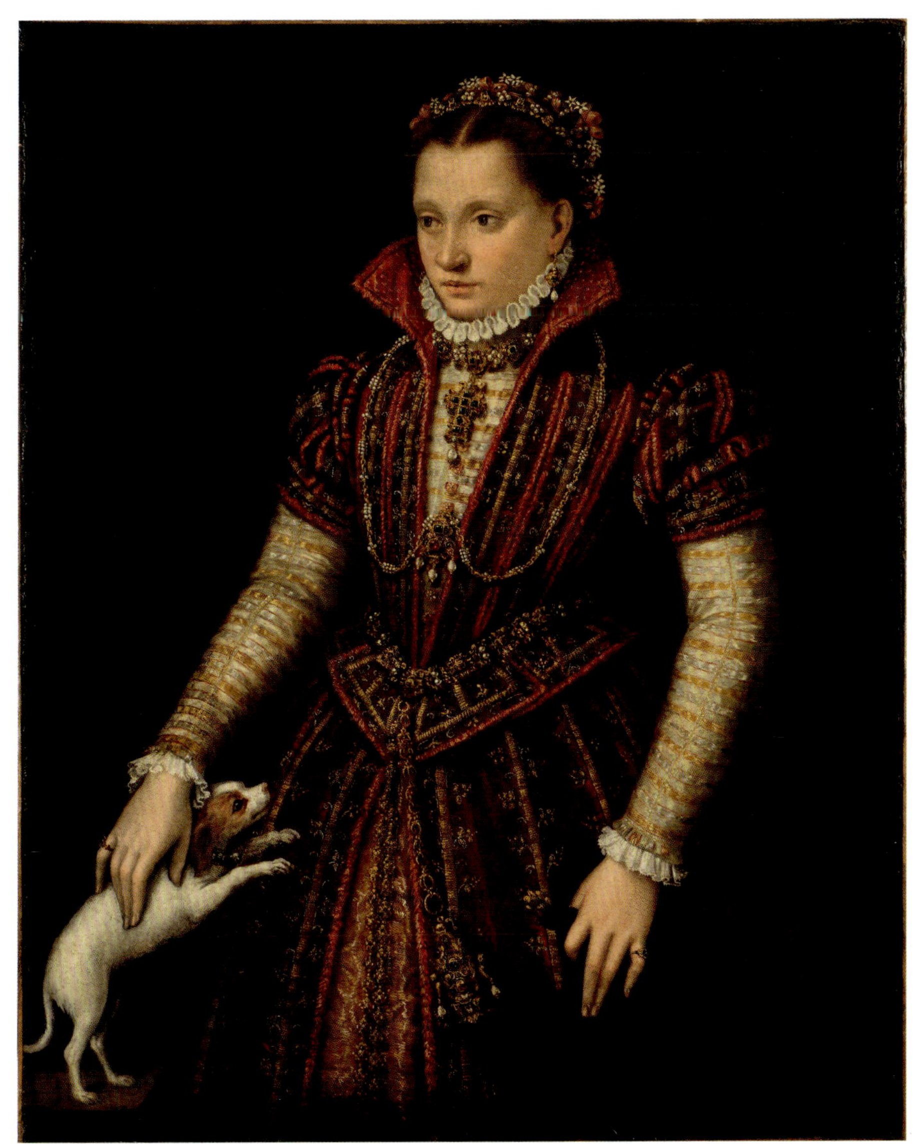

Opposite

Plate 22: Gown, Spring 2018 Atelier. Donatella Versace (Italian, b. 1955) for Versace (Italian, est. 1978). Silk velvet, tulle, multicolored gems, beading, sequins, Swarovski crystals, and gold- and silver-colored metal thread. Courtesy of Versace

Above

Plate 23: *Marriage Portrait of a Bolognese Noblewoman (Livia de' Medici Bandini?)*, c. 1589. Lavinia Fontana (Italian, 1552–1614). Oil on canvas; 115 x 89.5 cm. National Museum of Women in the Arts, Washington, DC, Gift of Wallace and Wilhelmina Holladay. Funding for the frame generously provided by the Texas State Committee. Photo: Lee Stalsworth

135

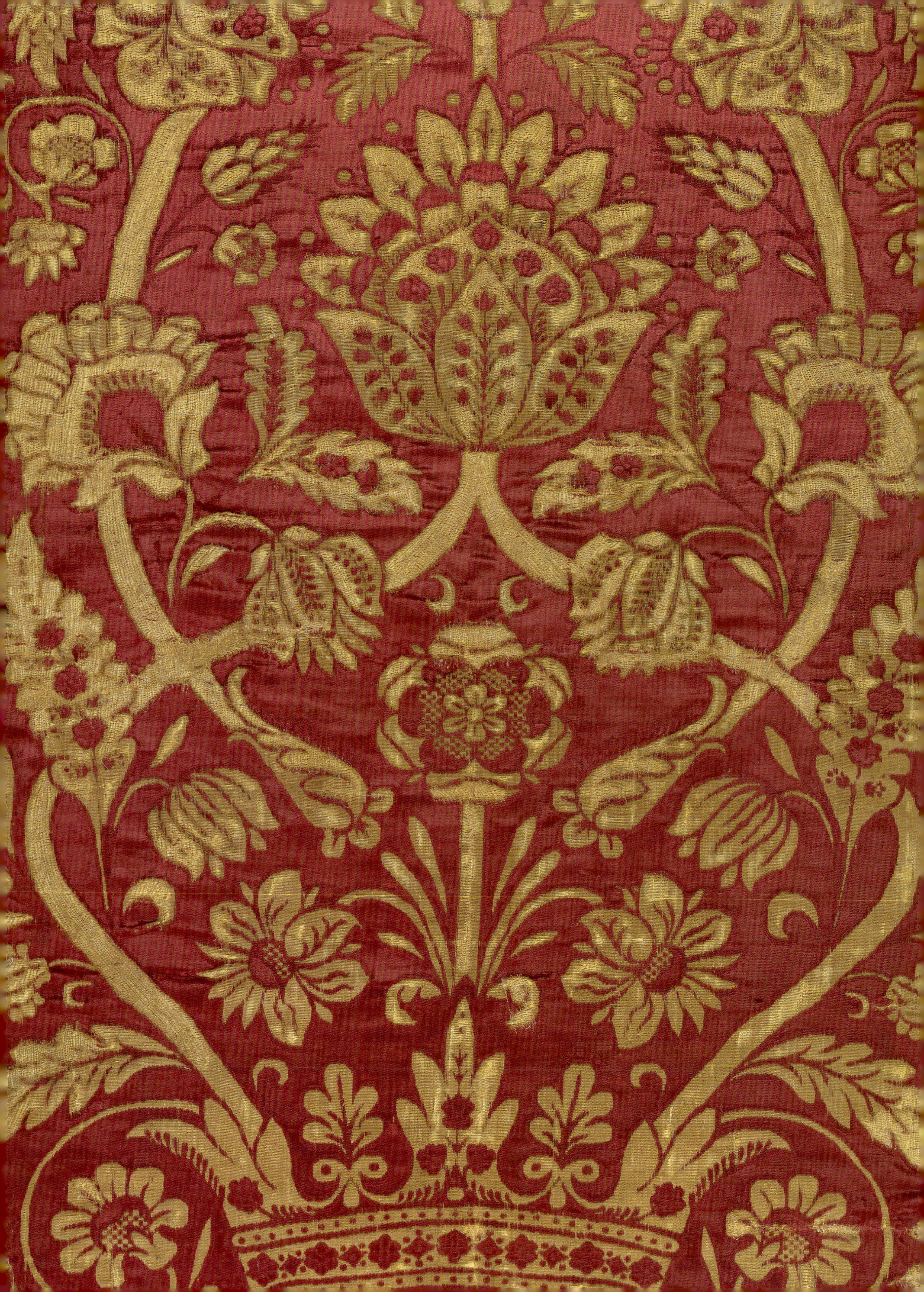

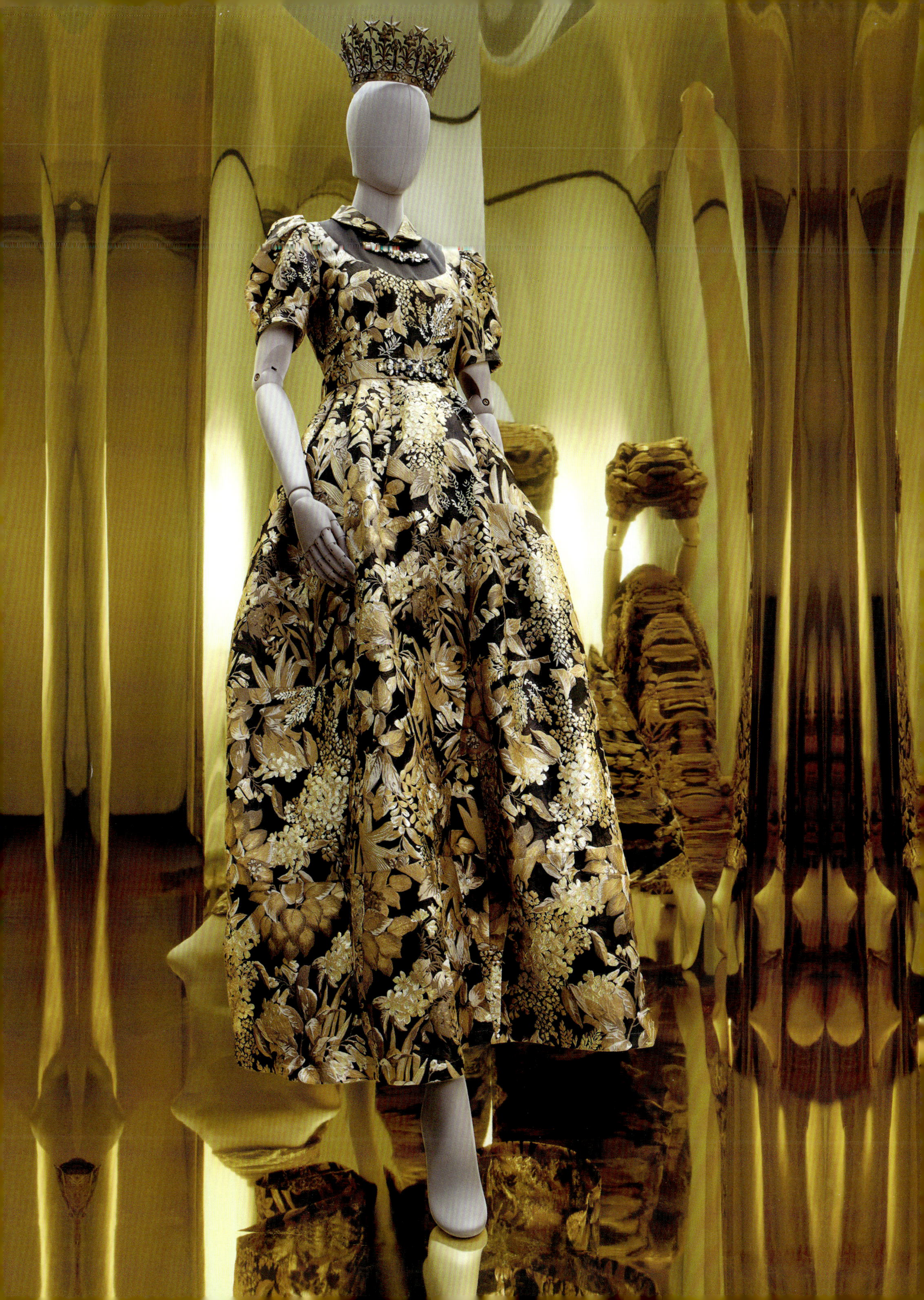

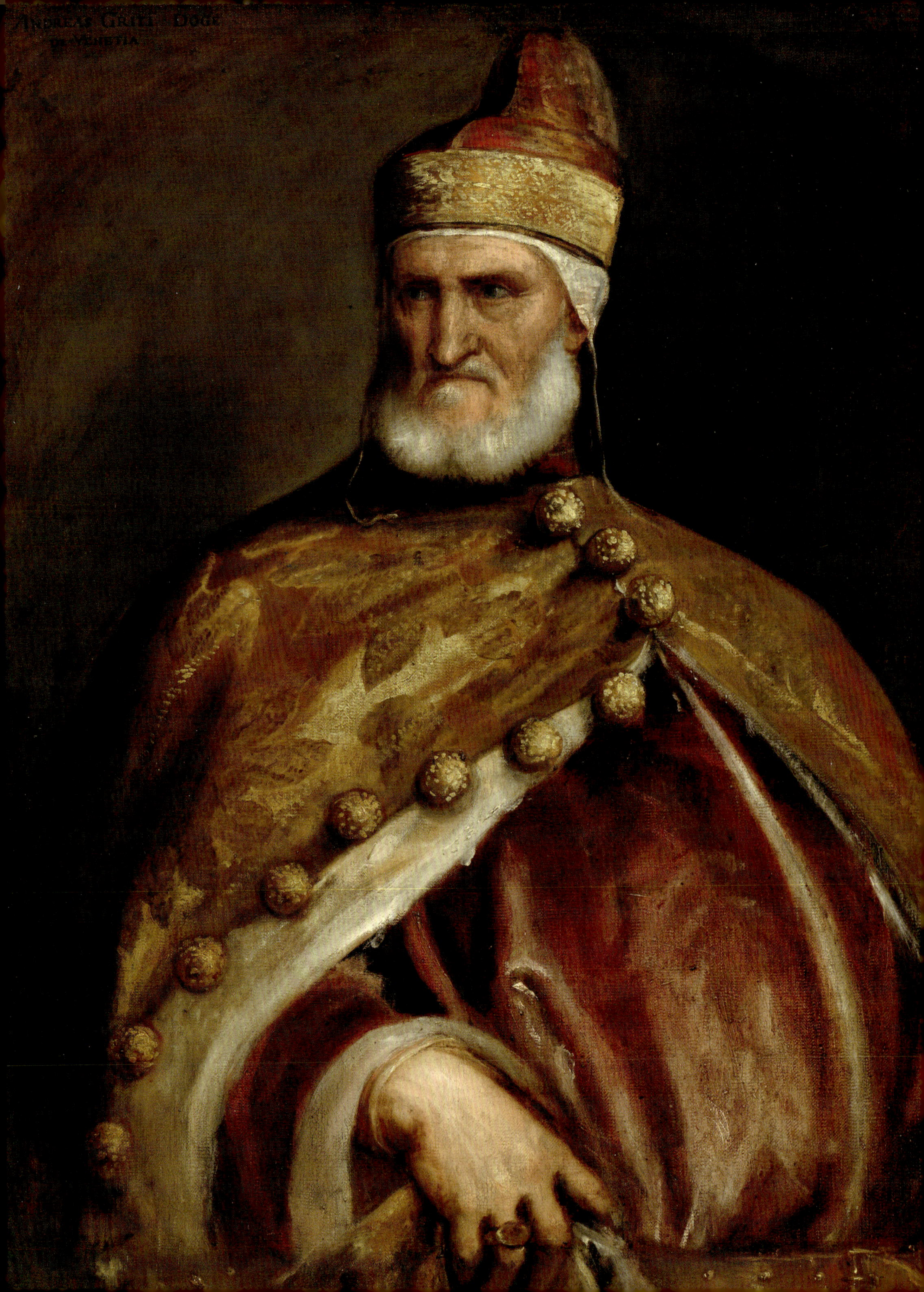
ANDREAS GRITI DOGE
DE VENETIA

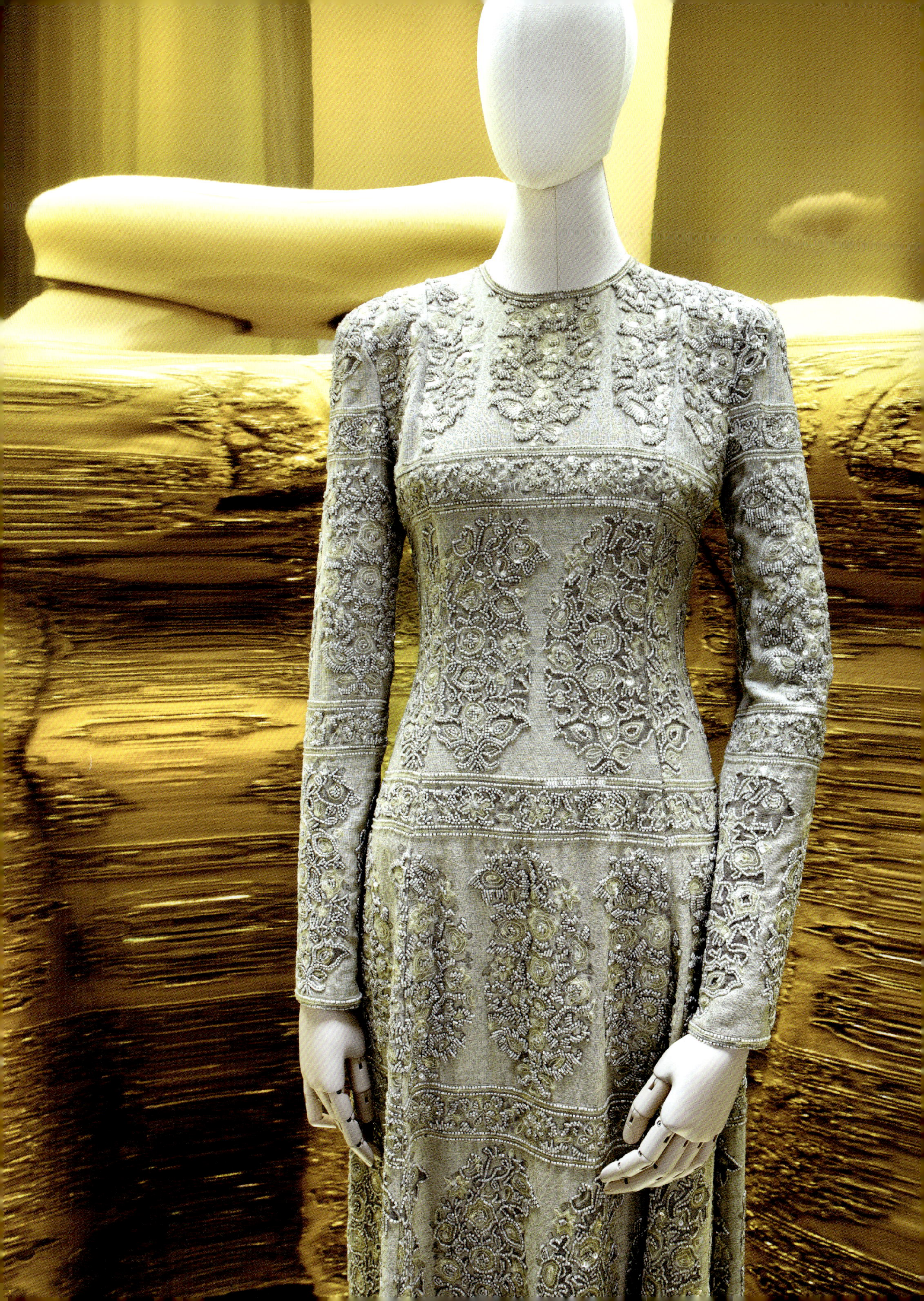

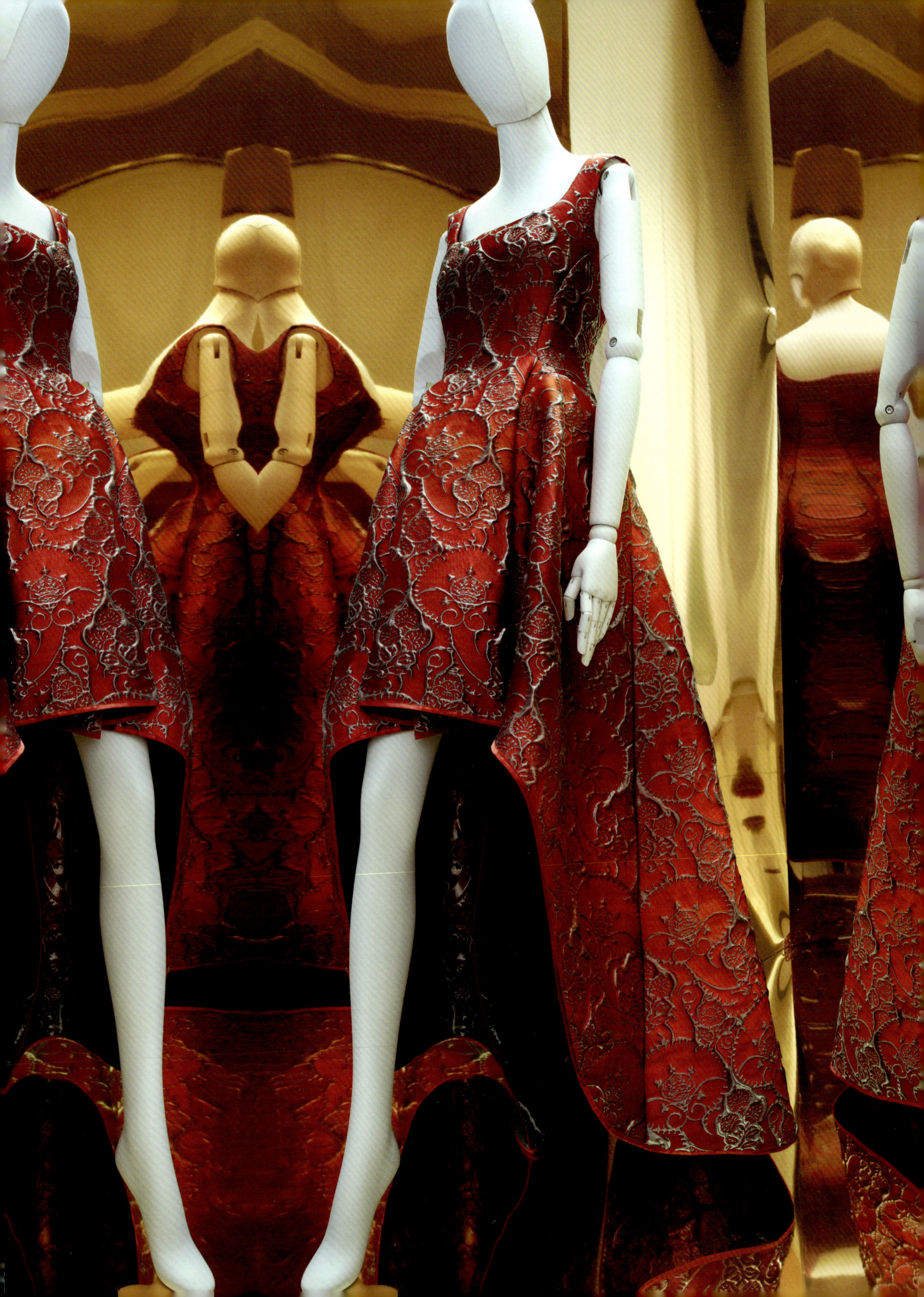

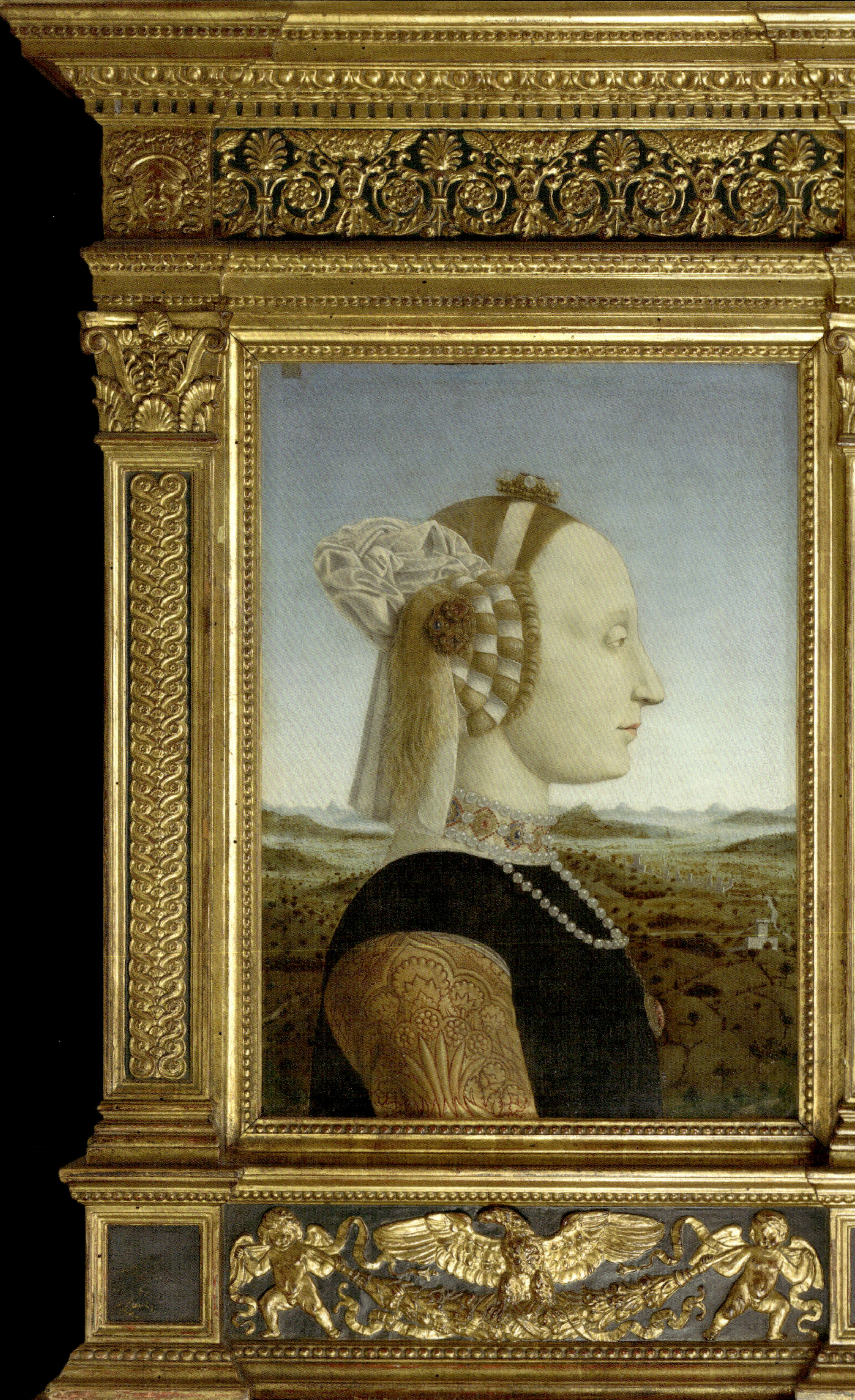

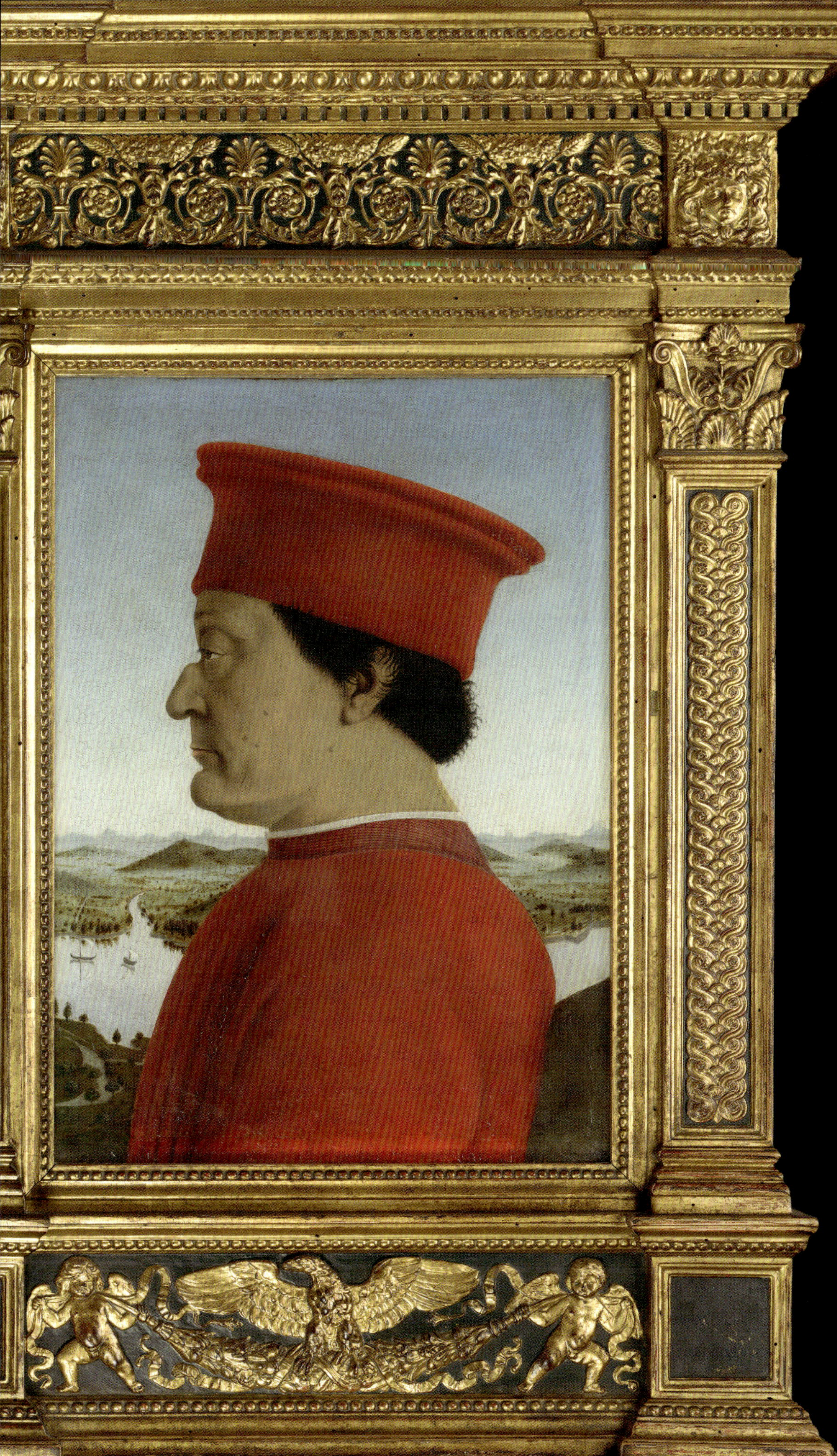

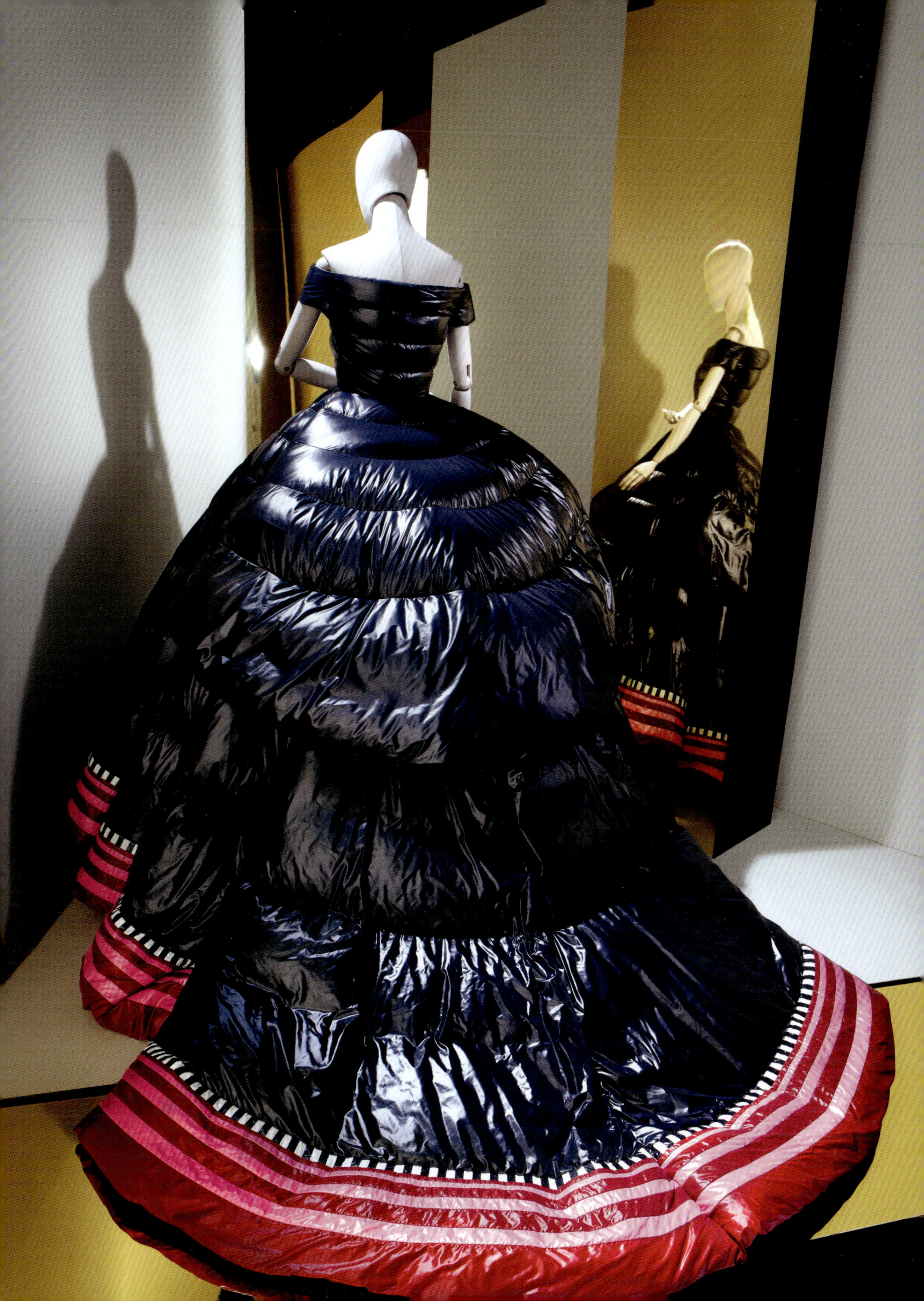

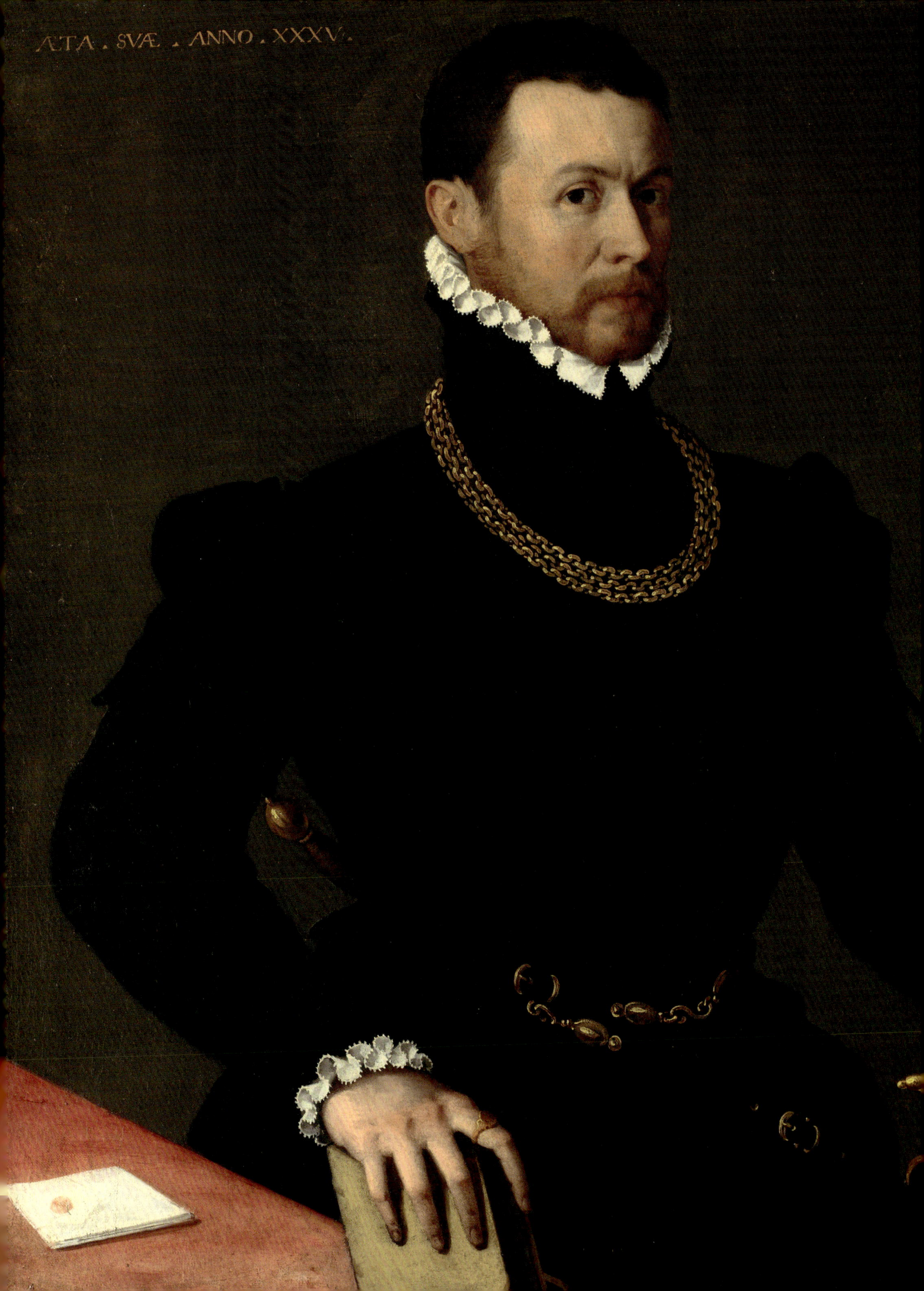

ÆTA . SVÆ . ANNO . XXXV .

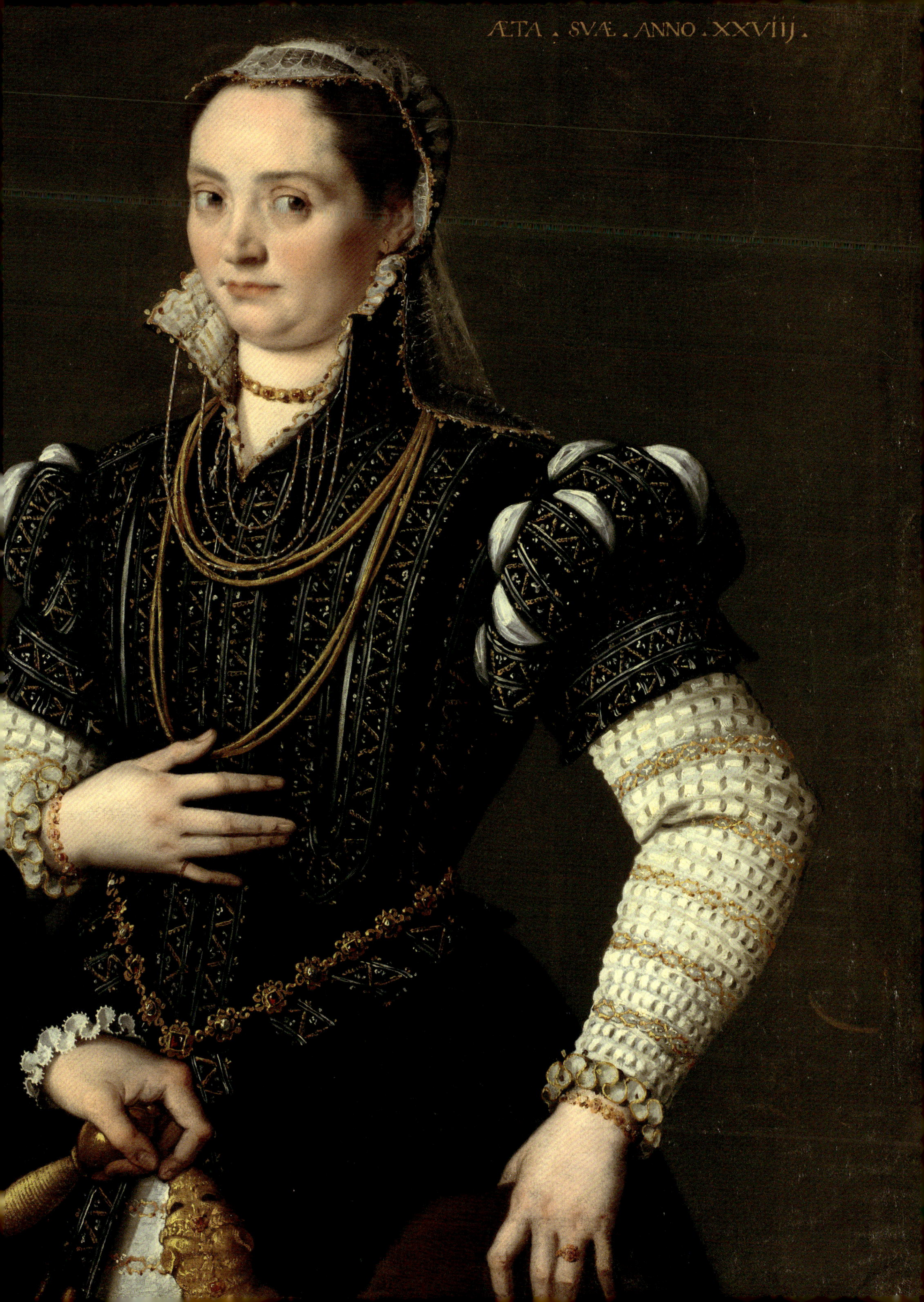
ÆTA . SVÆ . ANNO . XXVIIJ .

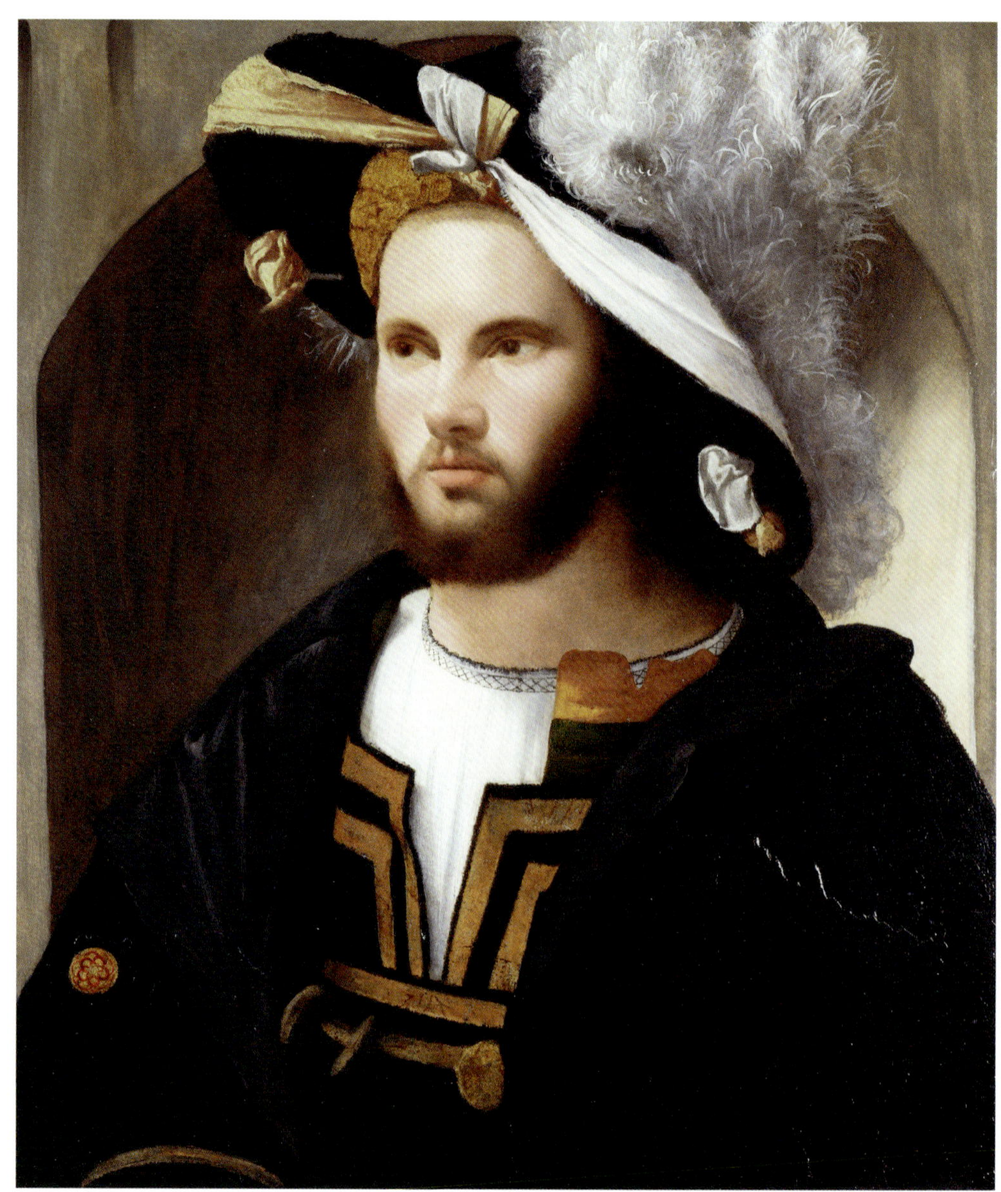

Plate 32: *Portrait of a Man*, c. 1515–17. Girolamo Romanino (Italian, c. 1485–c. 1566). Oil on panel; 58.2 x 47.4 cm. Royal Collection Trust, RCIN 406370. Photo: Royal Collection Trust / © His Majesty King Charles III, 2025 / Bridgeman Images

Plate 33: Evening Ensemble, Fall 2018 Privé. Giorgio Armani (Italian, 1934–2025) for Giorgio Armani (Italian, est. 1975). Lurex lace, crystals, sequins, and feathers. Courtesy of Armani / Silos

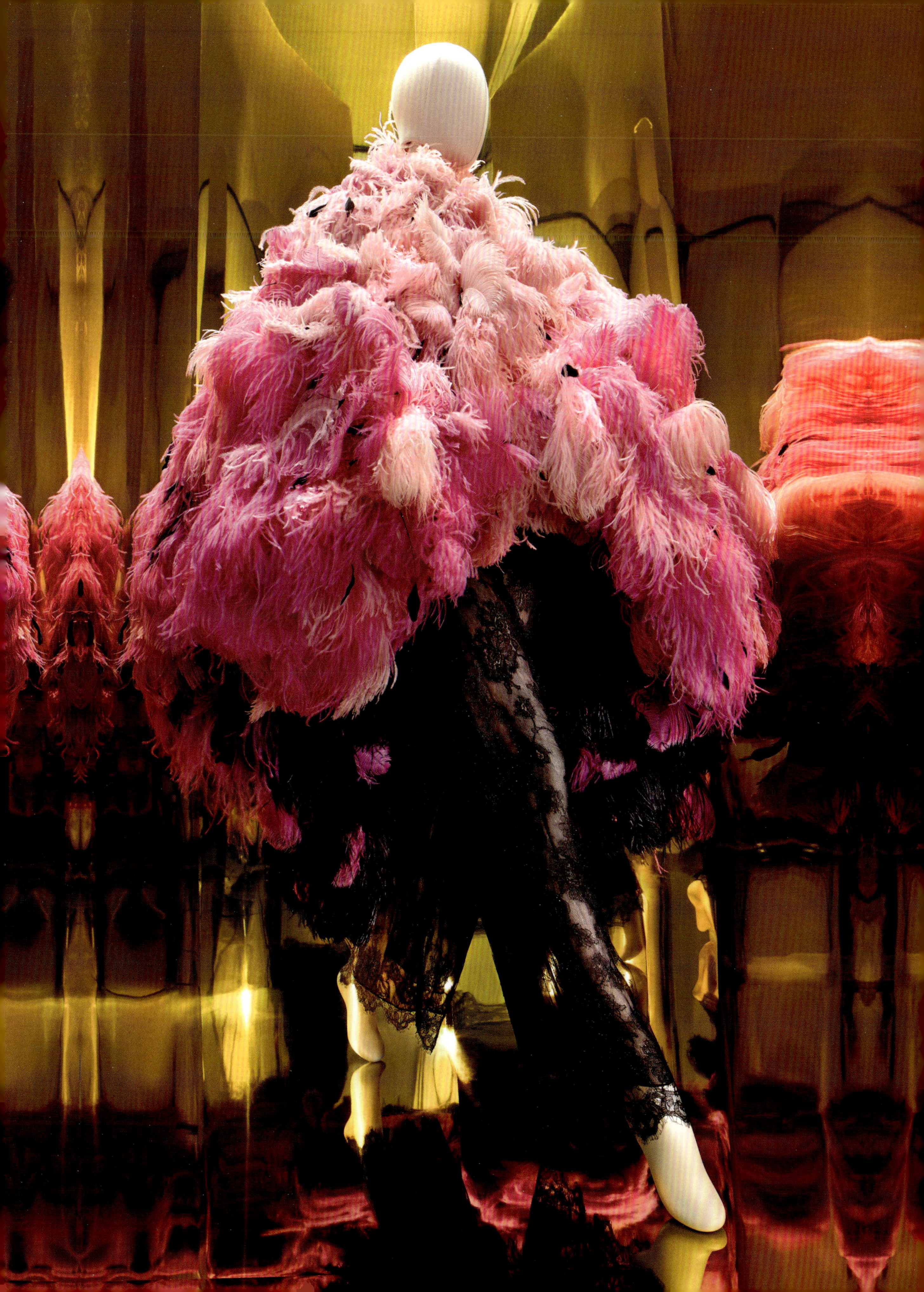

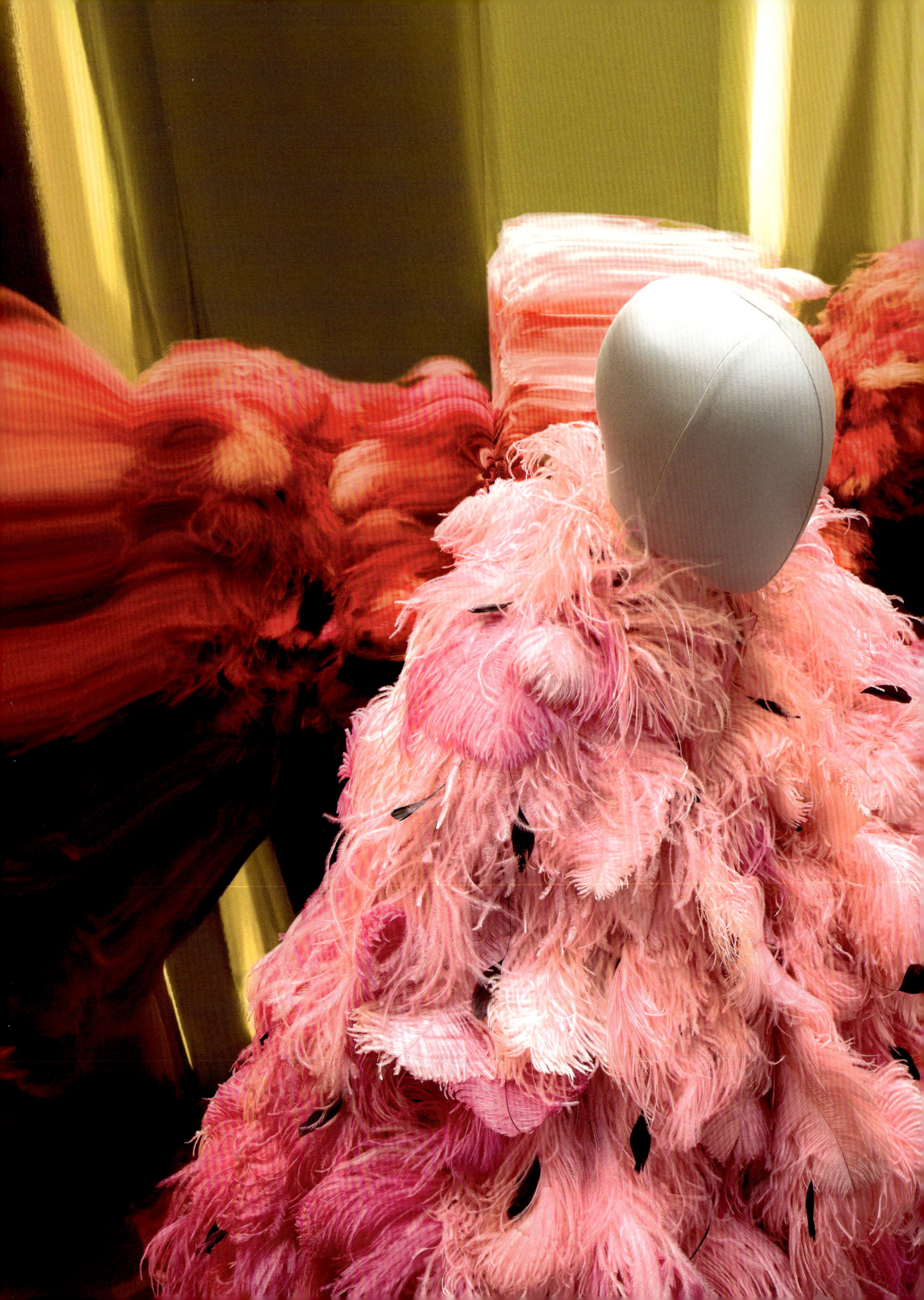

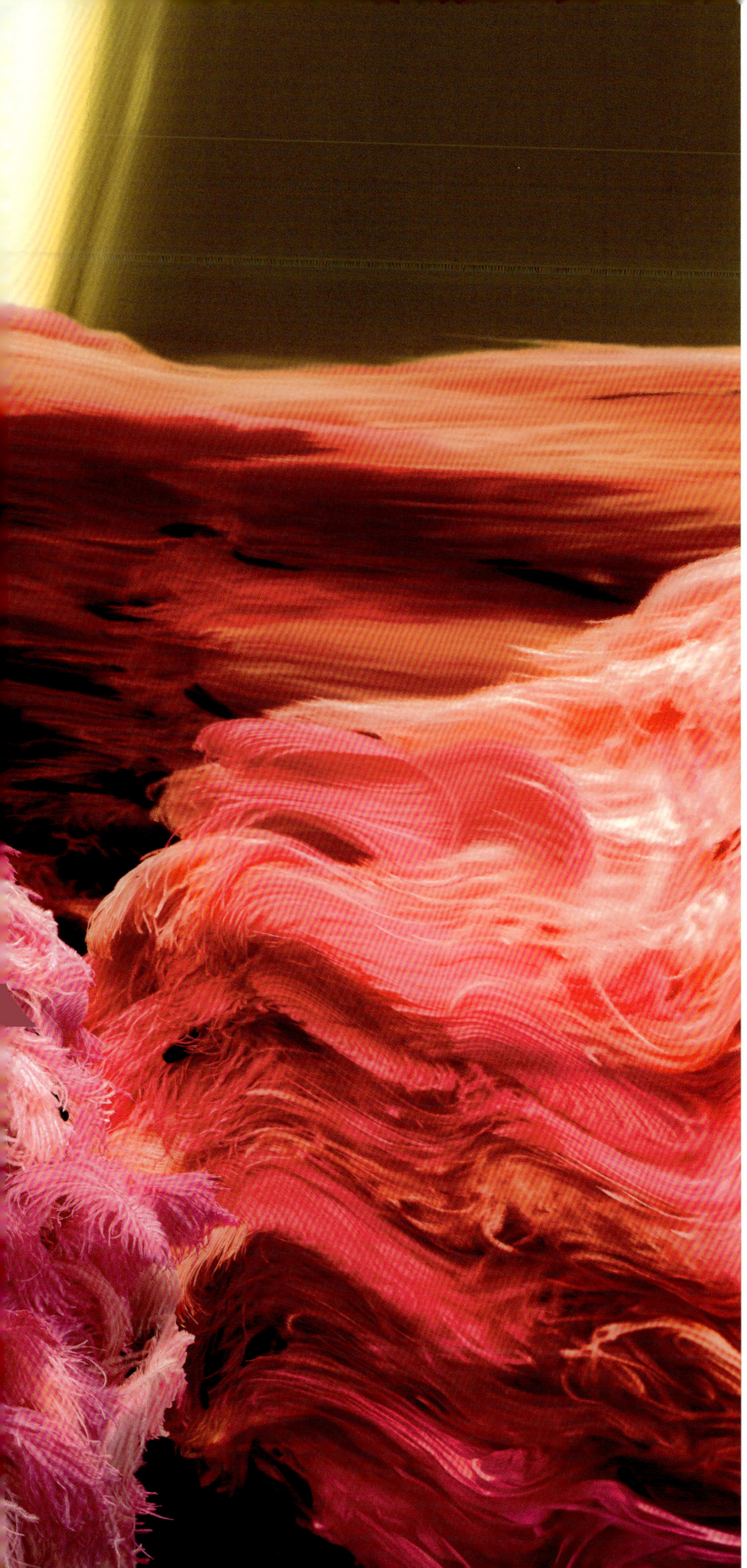

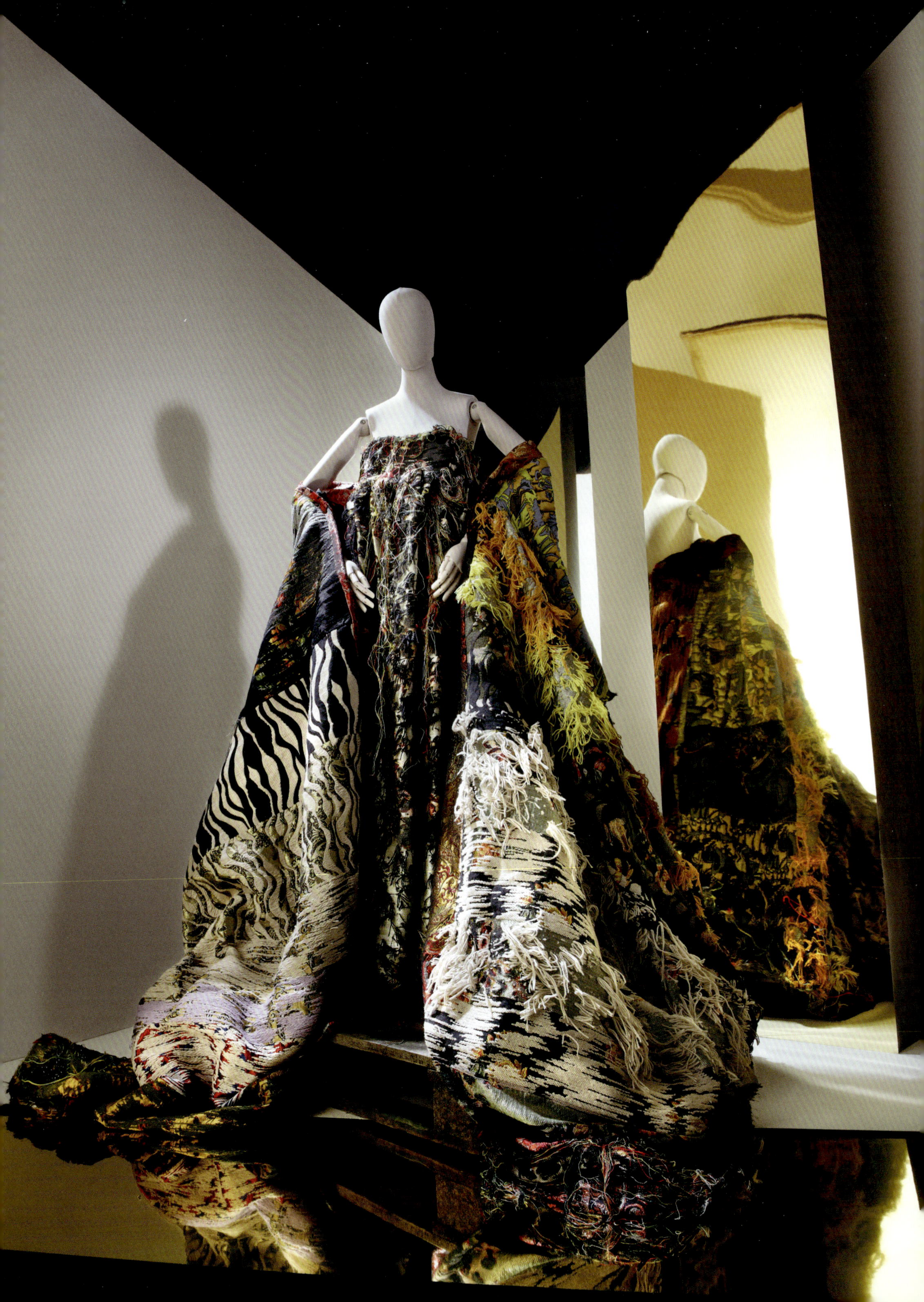

Plate 34: *"Eleanora d'Arborea"* Evening Ensemble, Fall 2024. Antonio Marras (Italian, b. 1961) for Antonio Marras (Italian, est. 1987). Wool jacquard fil coupé, viscose, cotton, polyester, and polyamide. Courtesy of Antonio Marras

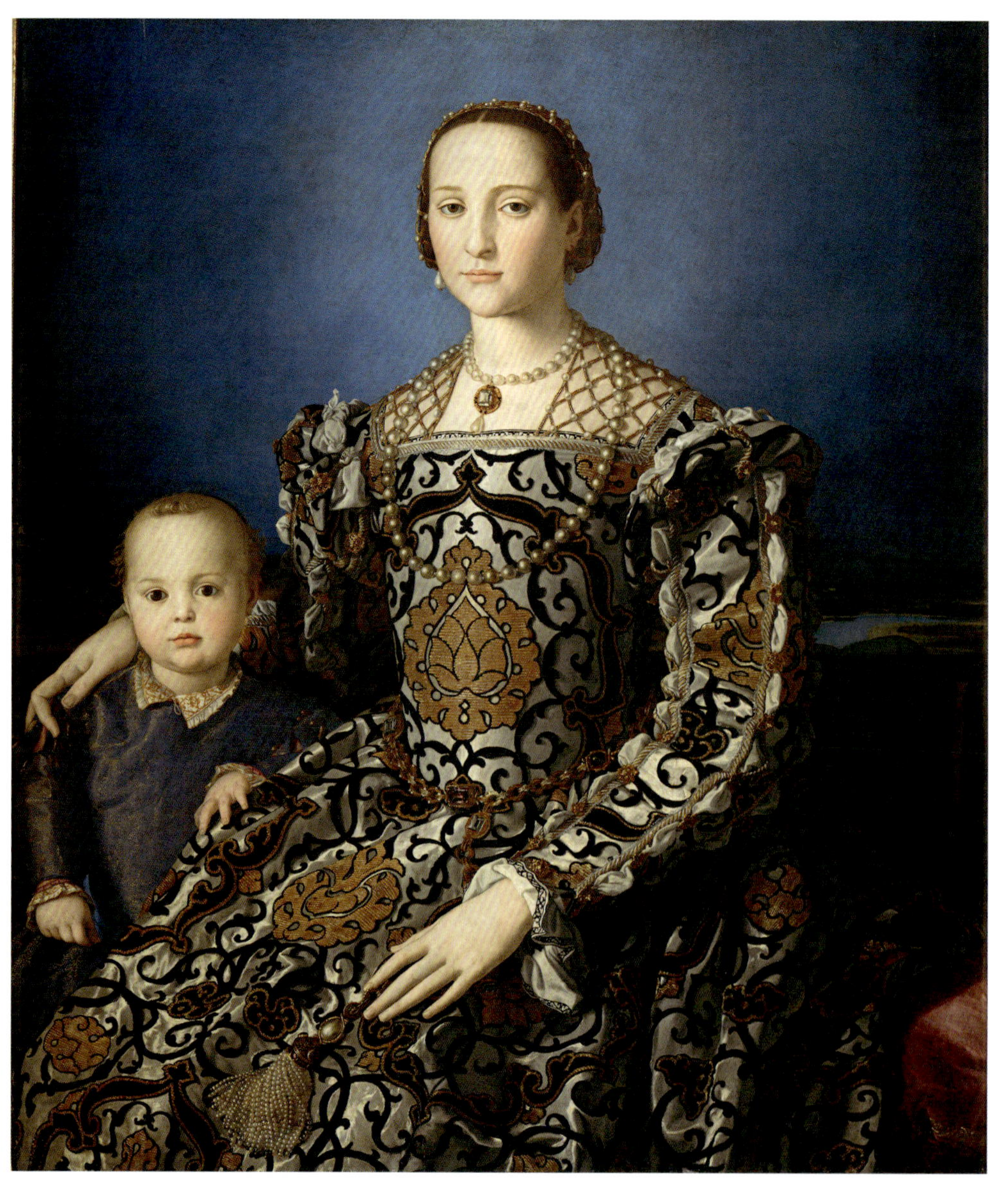

Plate 35: *Portrait of Eleonora di Toledo with Her Son Giovanni*, 1545. Agnolo Bronzino (Italian, 1503–1572). Oil on wood; 115 x 96 cm. Gallerie degli Uffizi, 1890 n. 748. Photo: © Gabinetto Fotografico delle Gallerie degli Uffizi

Plate 36: Gown, Spring 2018 Atelier. Donatella Versace (Italian, b. 1955) for Versace (Italian, est. 1978). Silk chiffon, polyester tulle, gemstones, and feathers. Courtesy of Versace

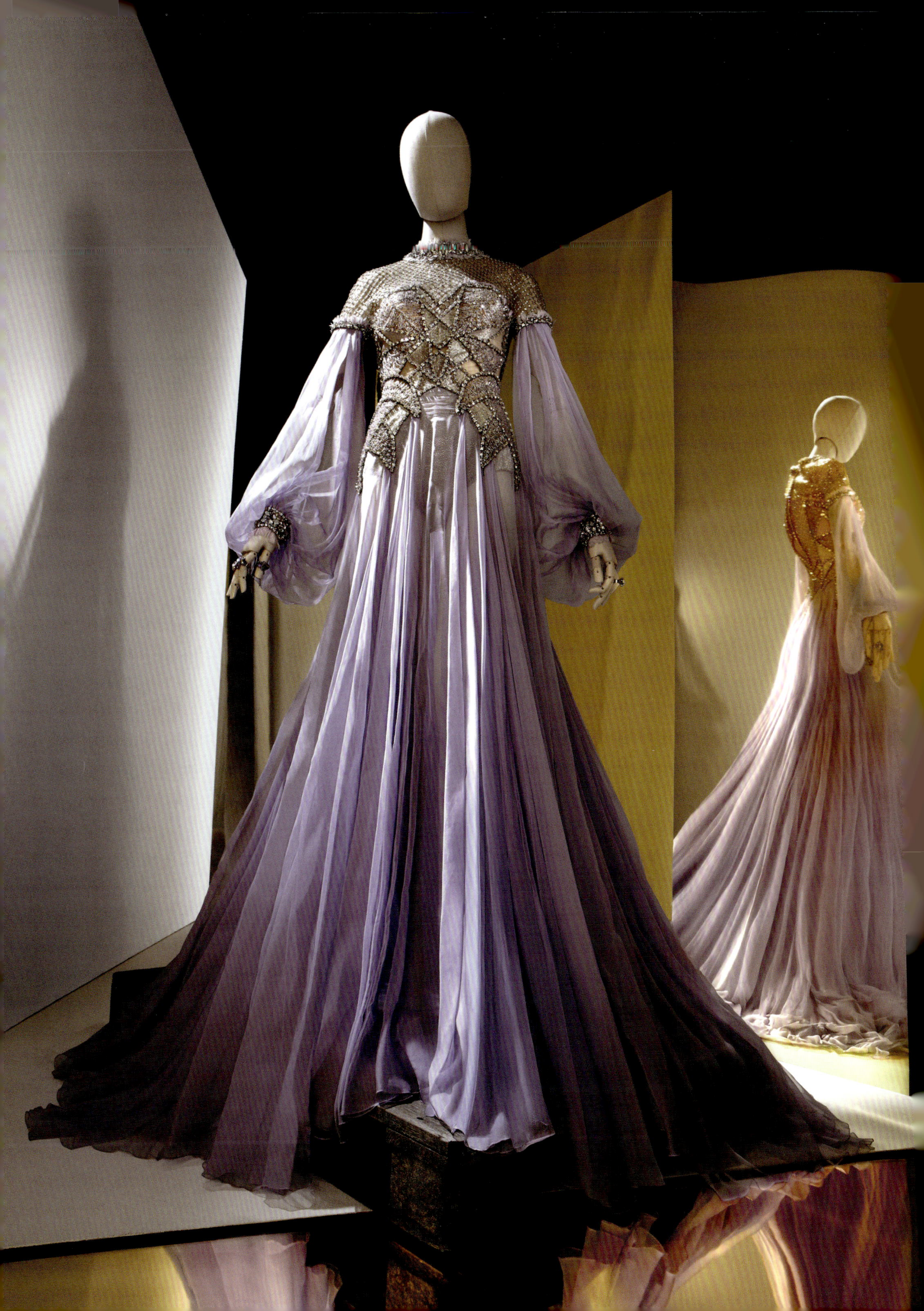

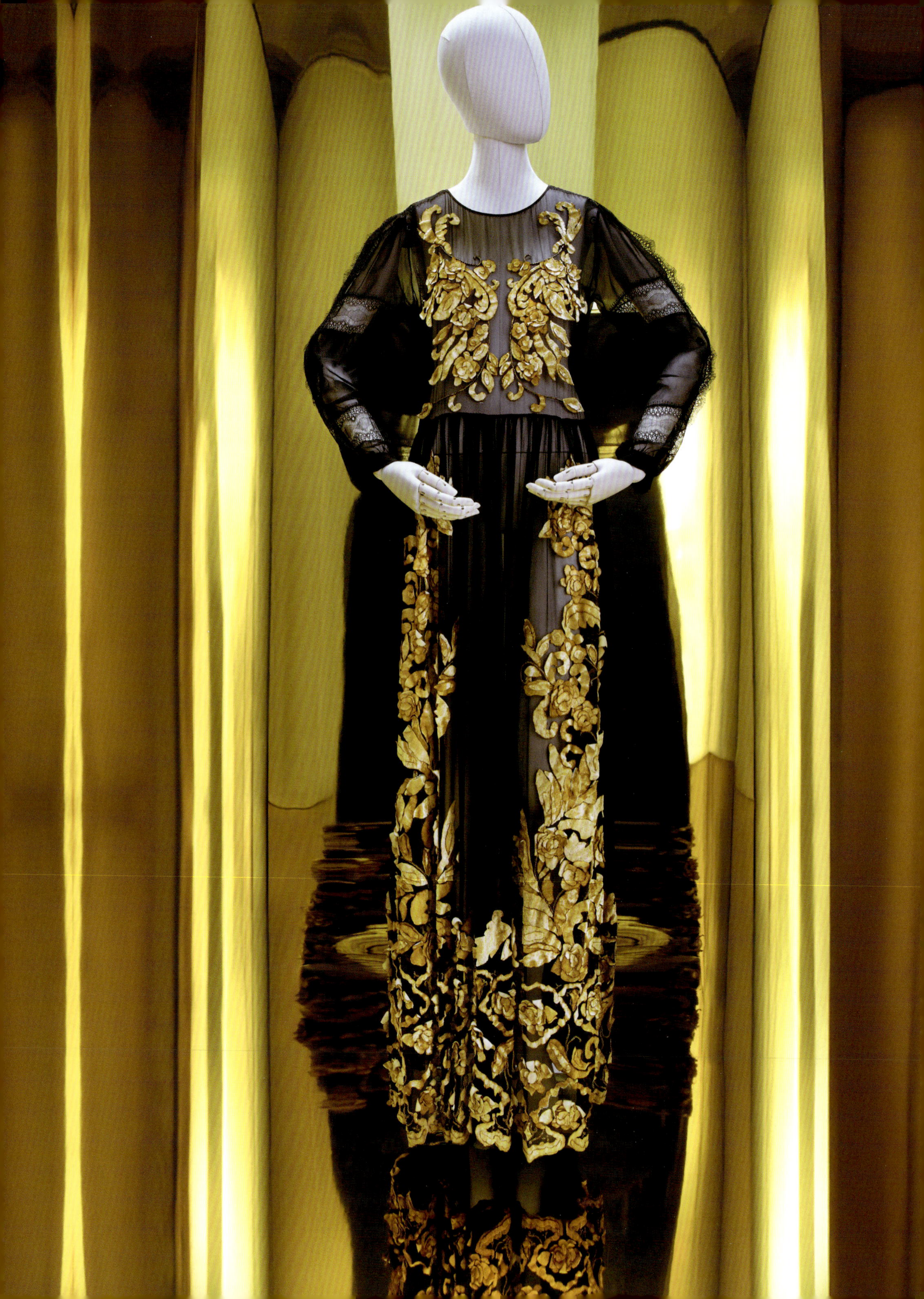

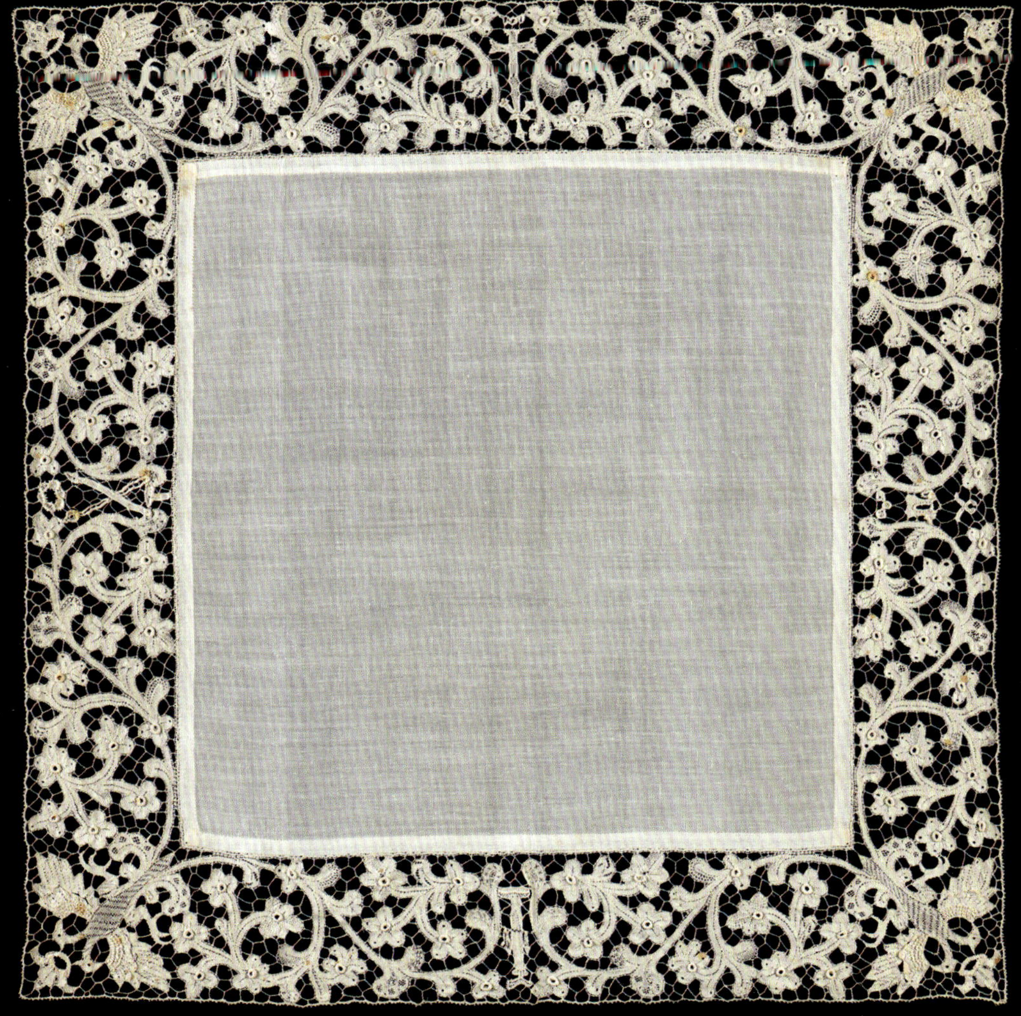

Plate 37: Evening Dress, Fall 2015. Alberta Ferretti (Italian b. 1950) for Alberta Ferretti (Italian, est. 1981). Silk chiffon and polyamide lace. Courtesy of Alberta Ferretti

Plate 38: Chalice Veil, 1600s. Italy, Milan. Lace, needlepoint, and bobbin (Punto di Milano); average: 51.2 x 52.4 cm. The Cleveland Museum of Art, Gift of Mrs. Edward B. Greene, G. G. Wade, and J. H. Wade Jr. for the Ellen Garretson Wade Memorial Collection, 1923.994

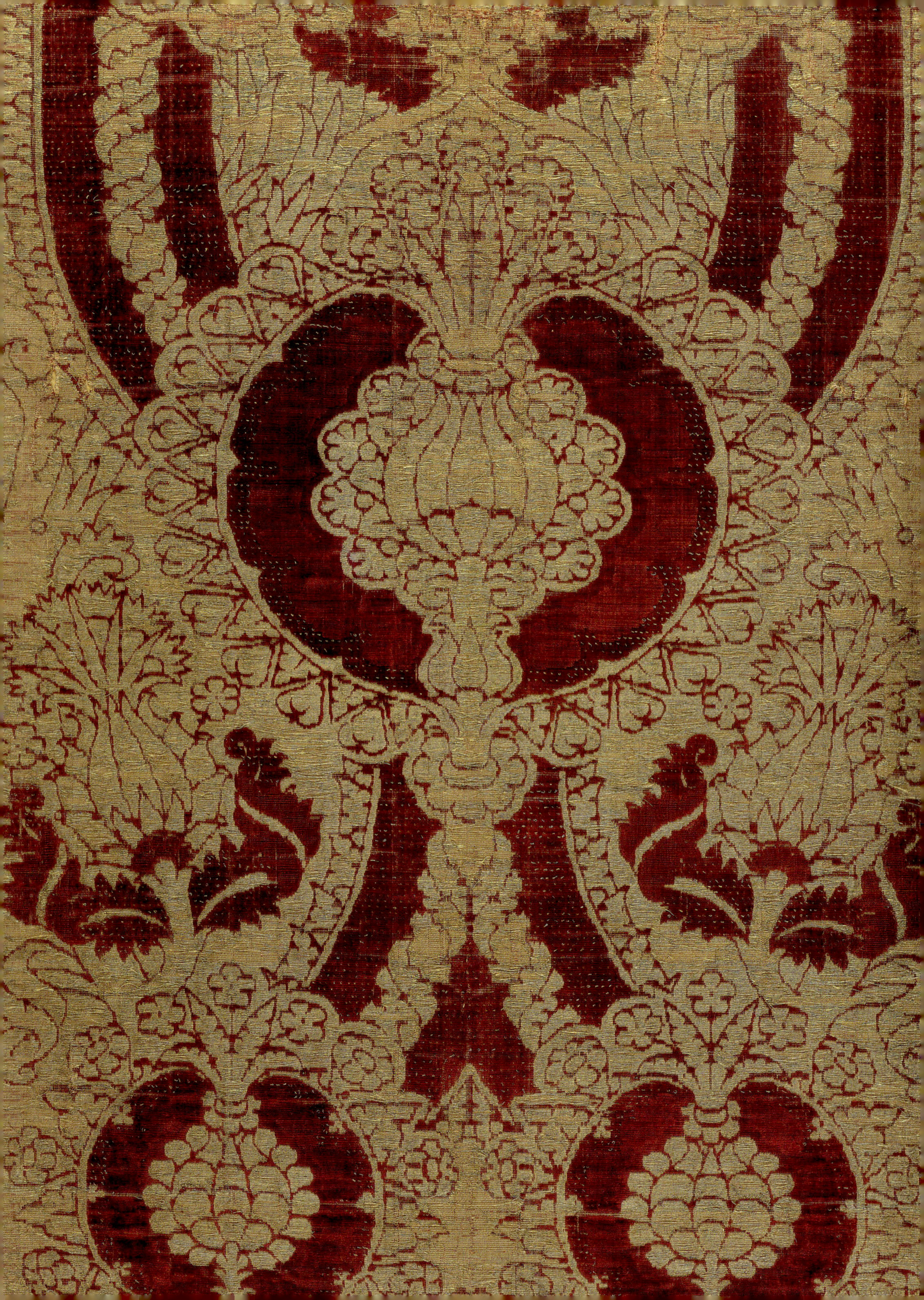

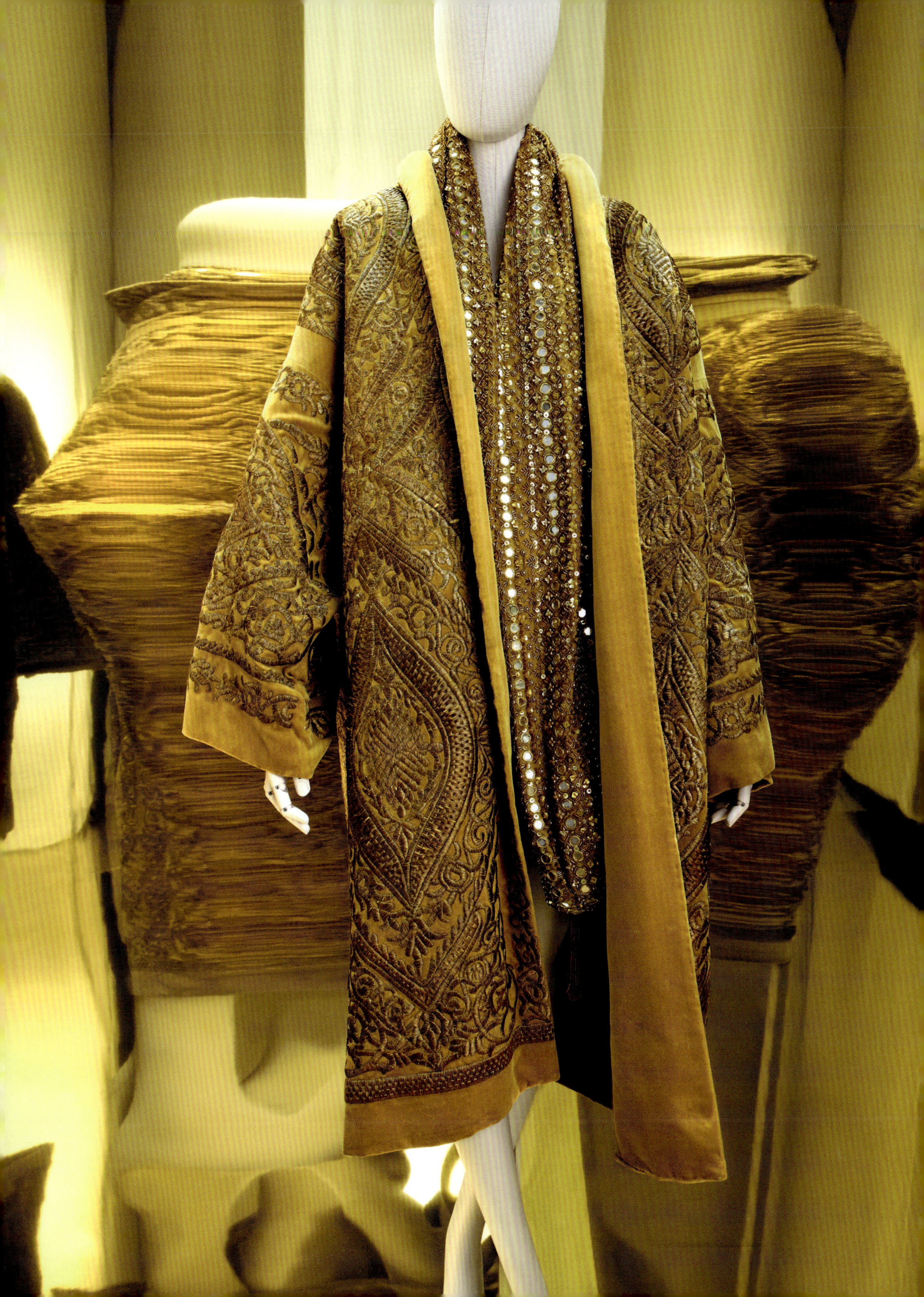

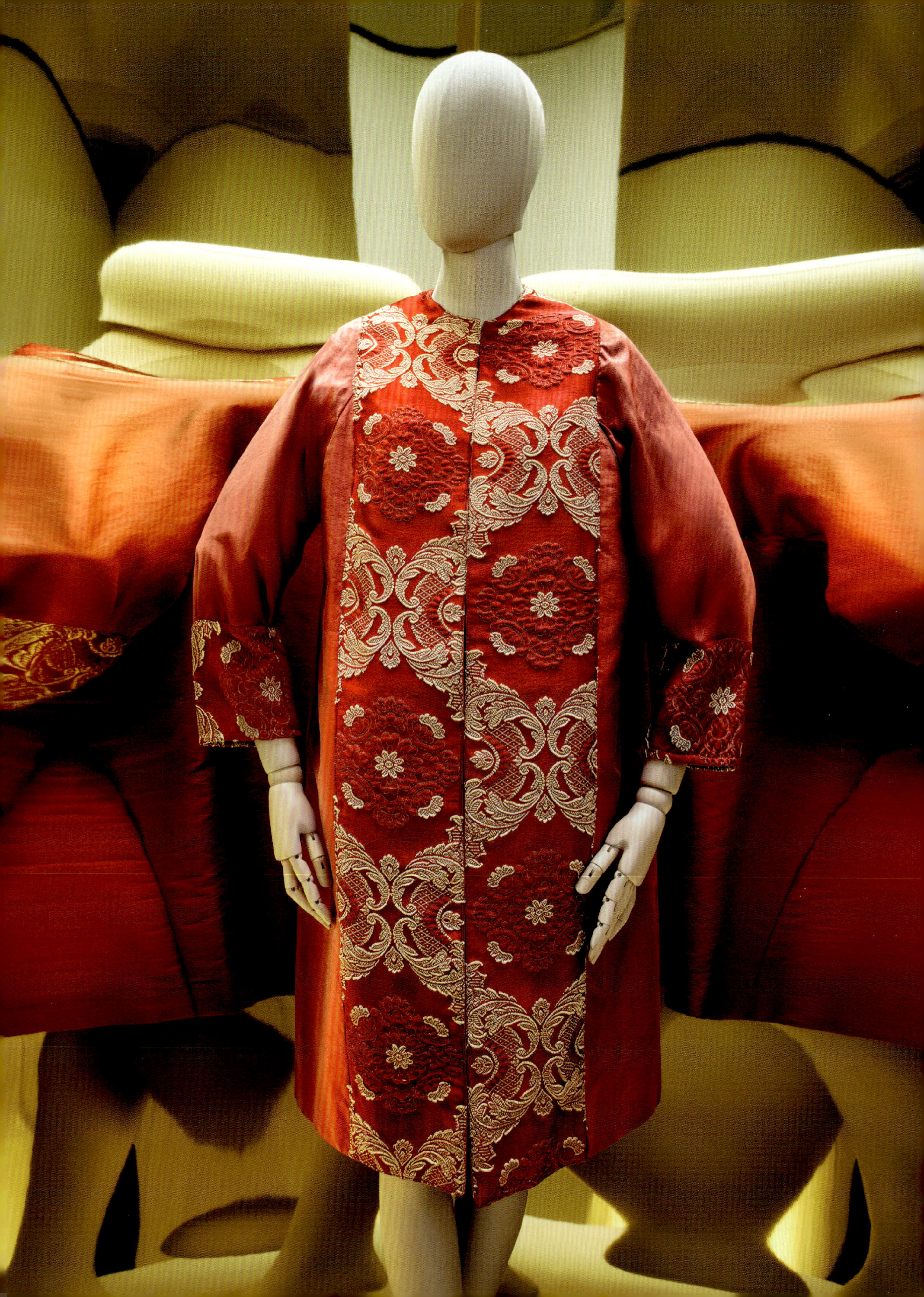

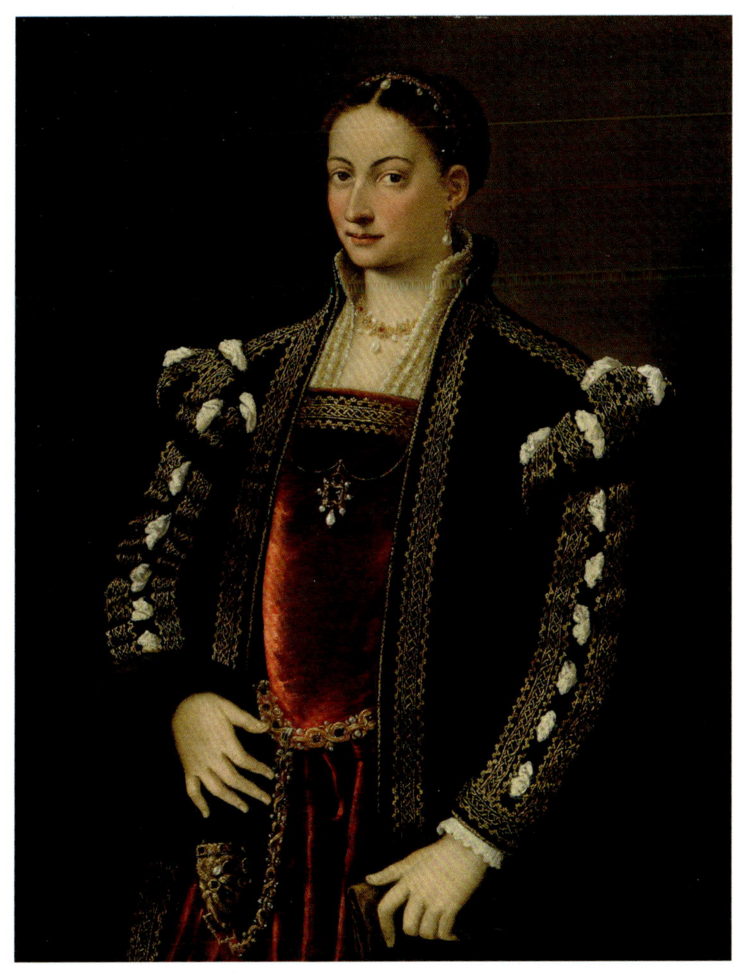

Page 158

Plate 39: Silk Velvet with Gold in Pomegranate Pattern, 1450–1500. Italy, possibly Florence. Silk, gold thread, and velvet: cut pile in two heights, uncut pile loops, gold-thread loops; overall: 118.7 x 60.6 cm. The Cleveland Museum of Art, Bequest of James Parmelee, 1940.596

Page 159

Plate 40: Coat and Scarf, Fall 1989. Romeo Gigli (Italian, b. 1949) for Romeo Gigli (Italian, est. 1981). Silk velvet, silk embroidery, and gold embroidery. Courtesy of the Sozzani Fondazione

Opposite

Plate 41: Coat, mid-20th century. Max Mara (Italian, est. 1951). Silk shantung and jacquard. Courtesy of Max Mara

Above

Plate 42: *Portrait of a Lady, Said to Be Ippolita Gonzaga*, c. 1553–54. Bernardino Campi (Italian, 1522–1591). Oil on canvas; 115.6 x 90.2 cm. Photo: Courtesy of Sotheby's, Inc., © 2025

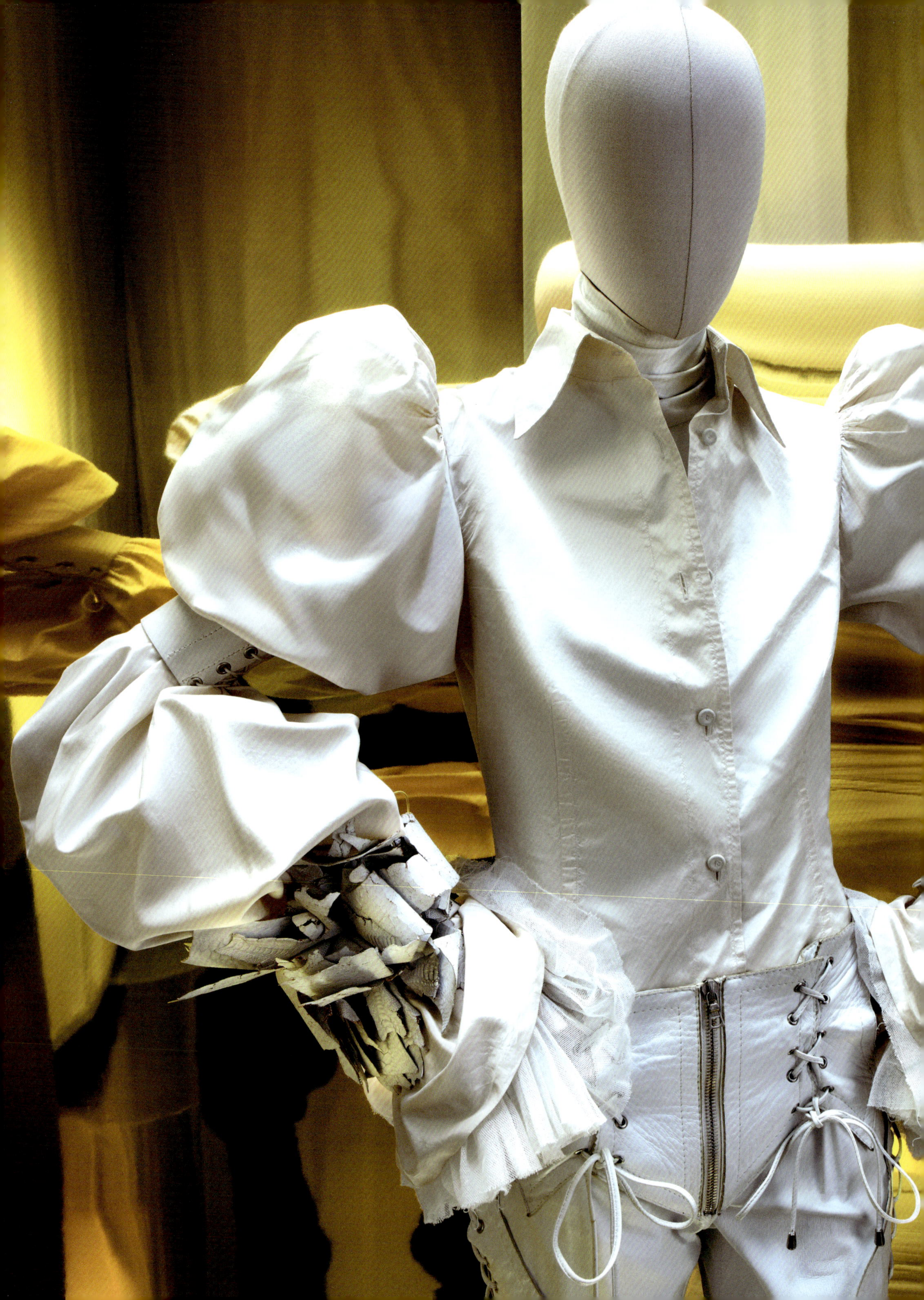

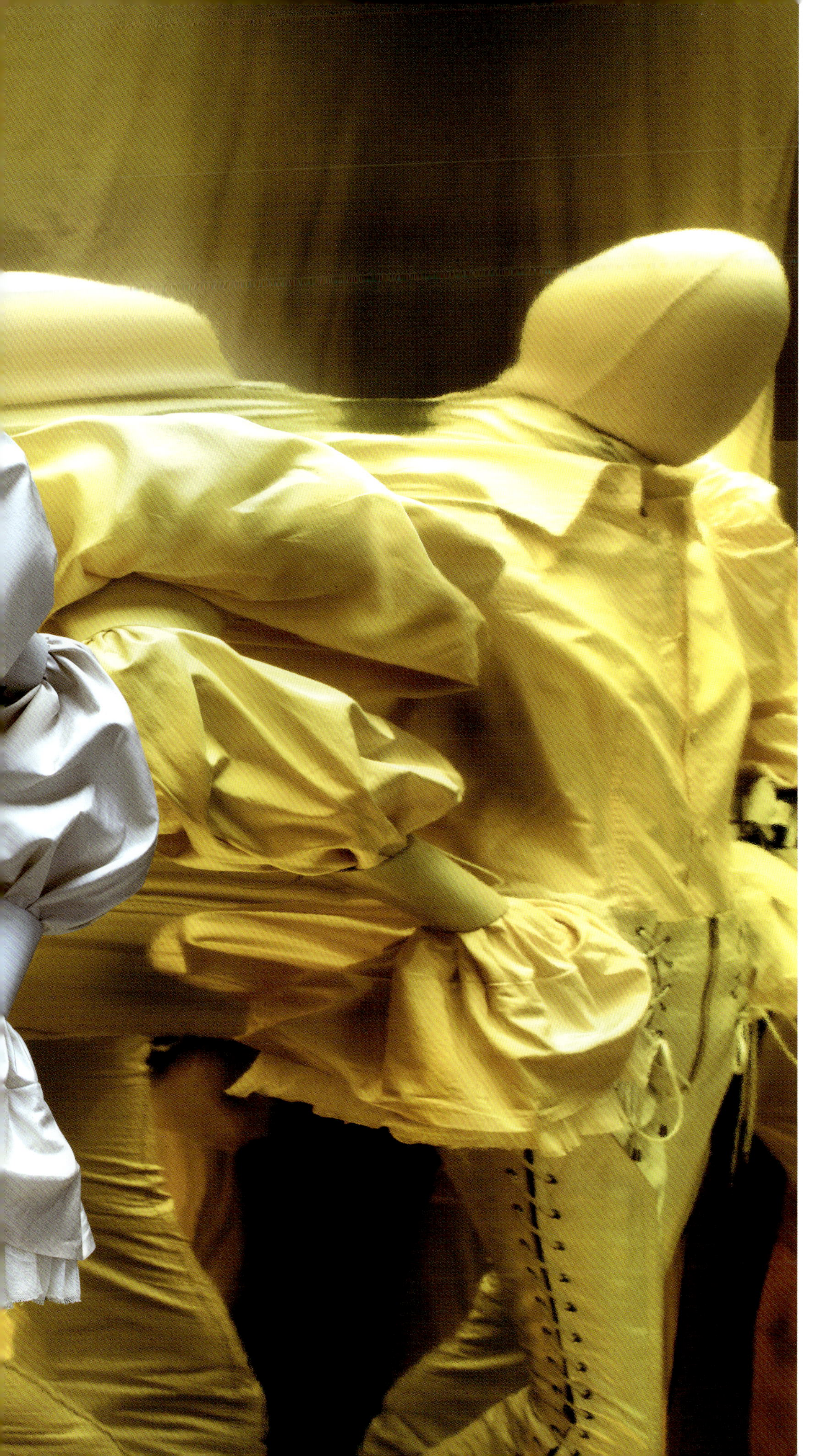

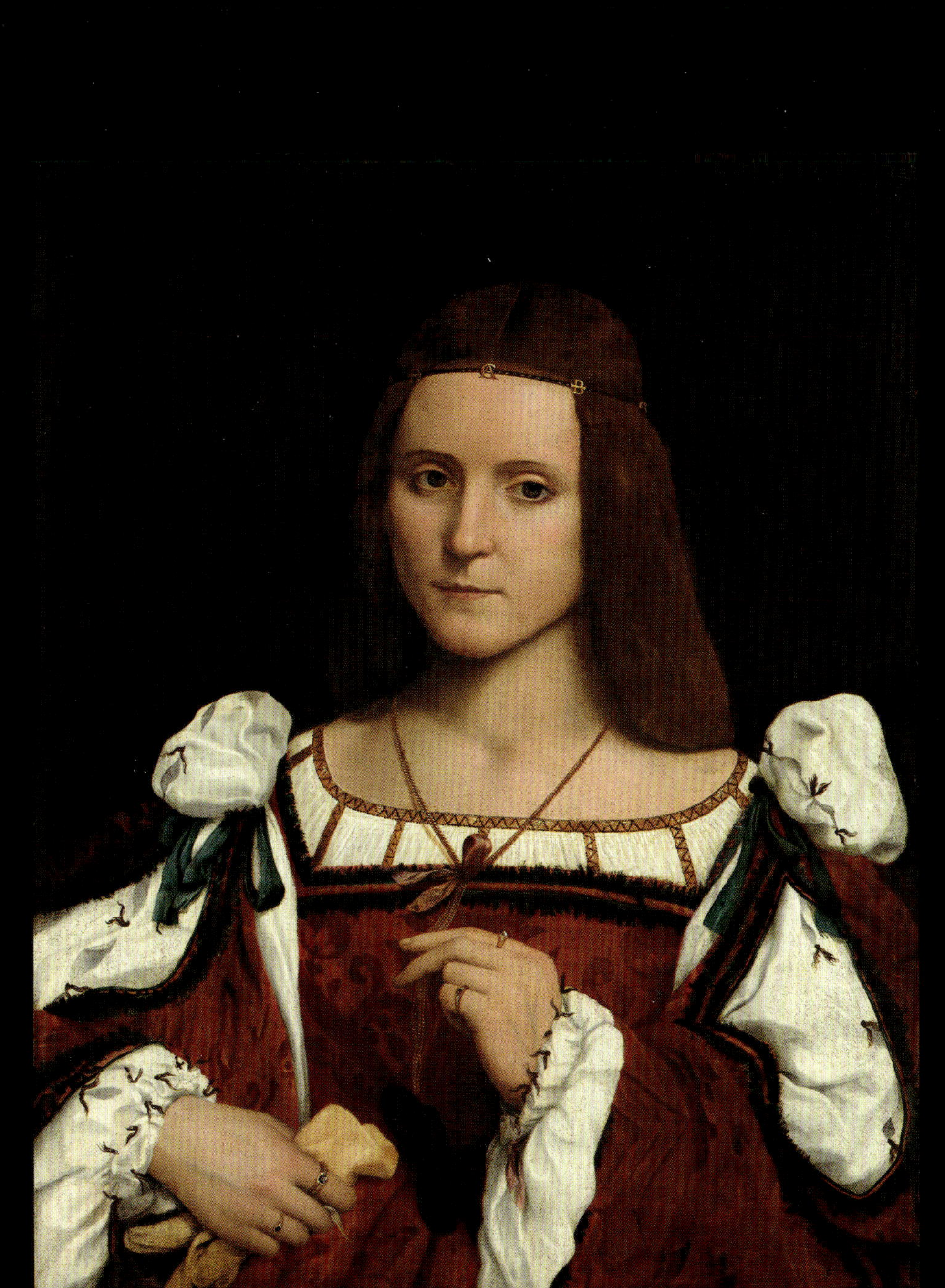

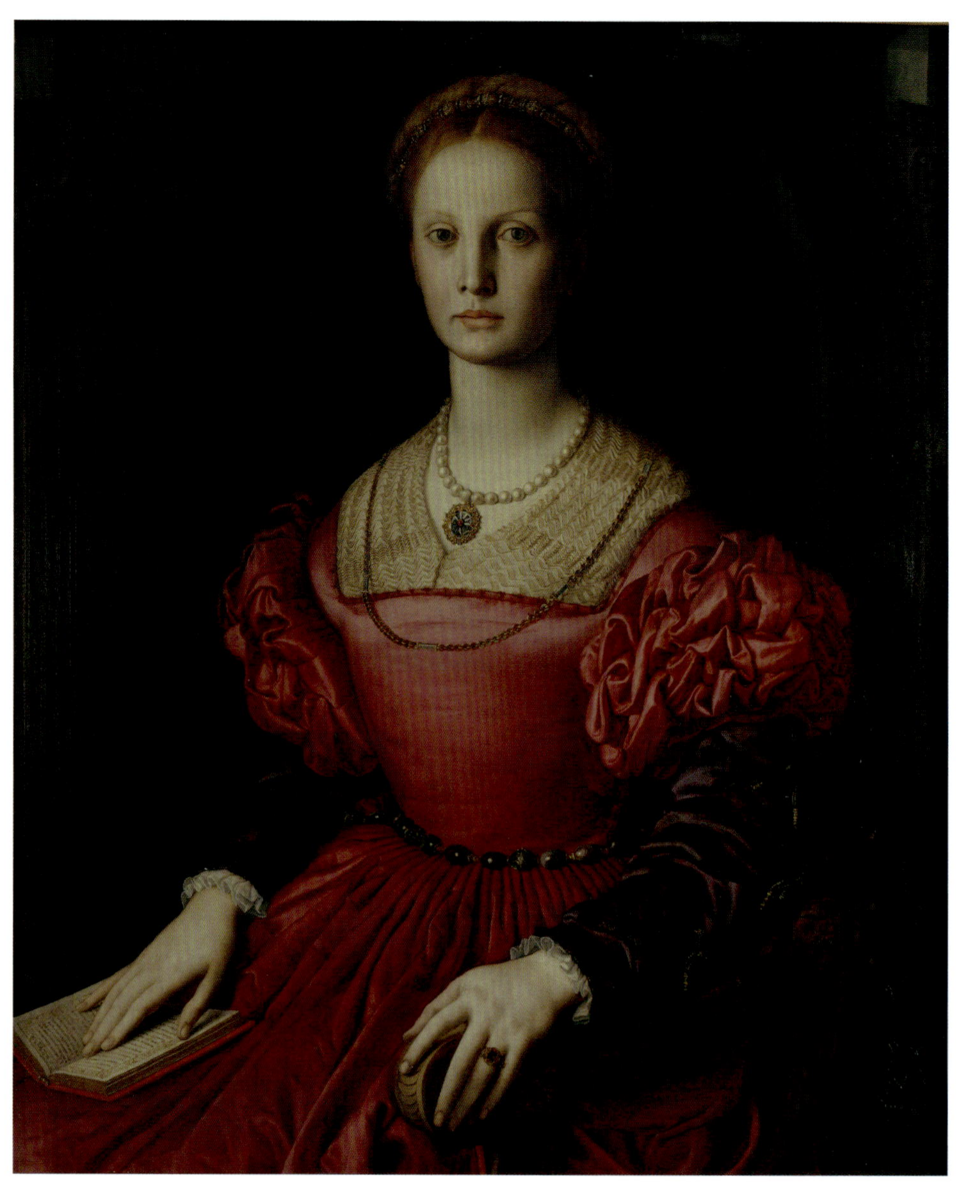

Plate 45: *Portrait of Lucrezia Panciatichi*, 1541–45. Agnolo Bronzino (Italian, 1503–1572). Oil on wood; 102 x 83.2 cm. Gallerie degli Uffizi, 1890 n. 736. Photo: © Gabinetto Fotografico delle Gallerie degli Uffizi

Plate 46: Gown, 1987. Roberto Capucci (Italian, b. 1930) for Roberto Capucci (Italian, est. 1950). Silk satin. Courtesy of the Fondazione Roberto Capucci

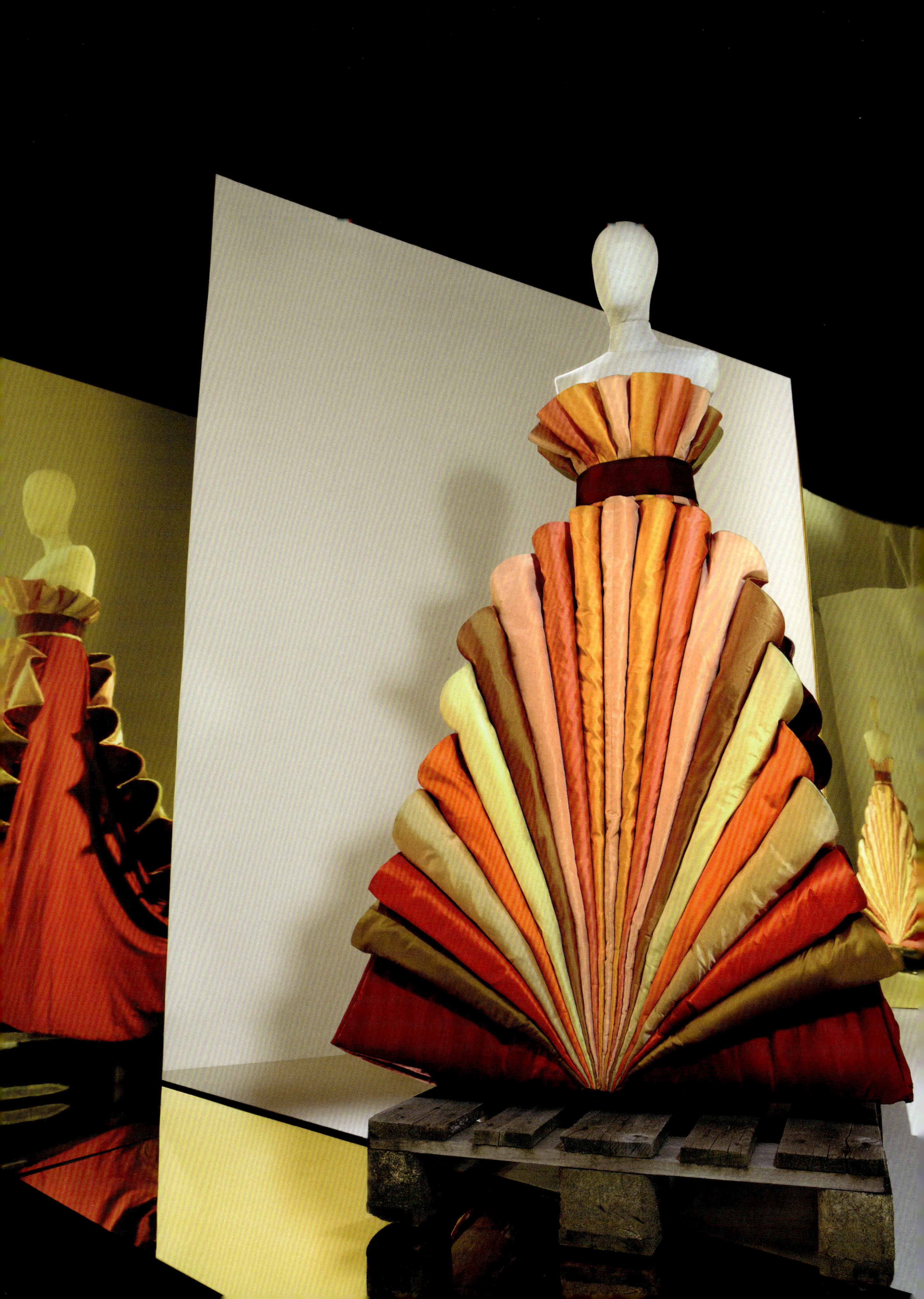

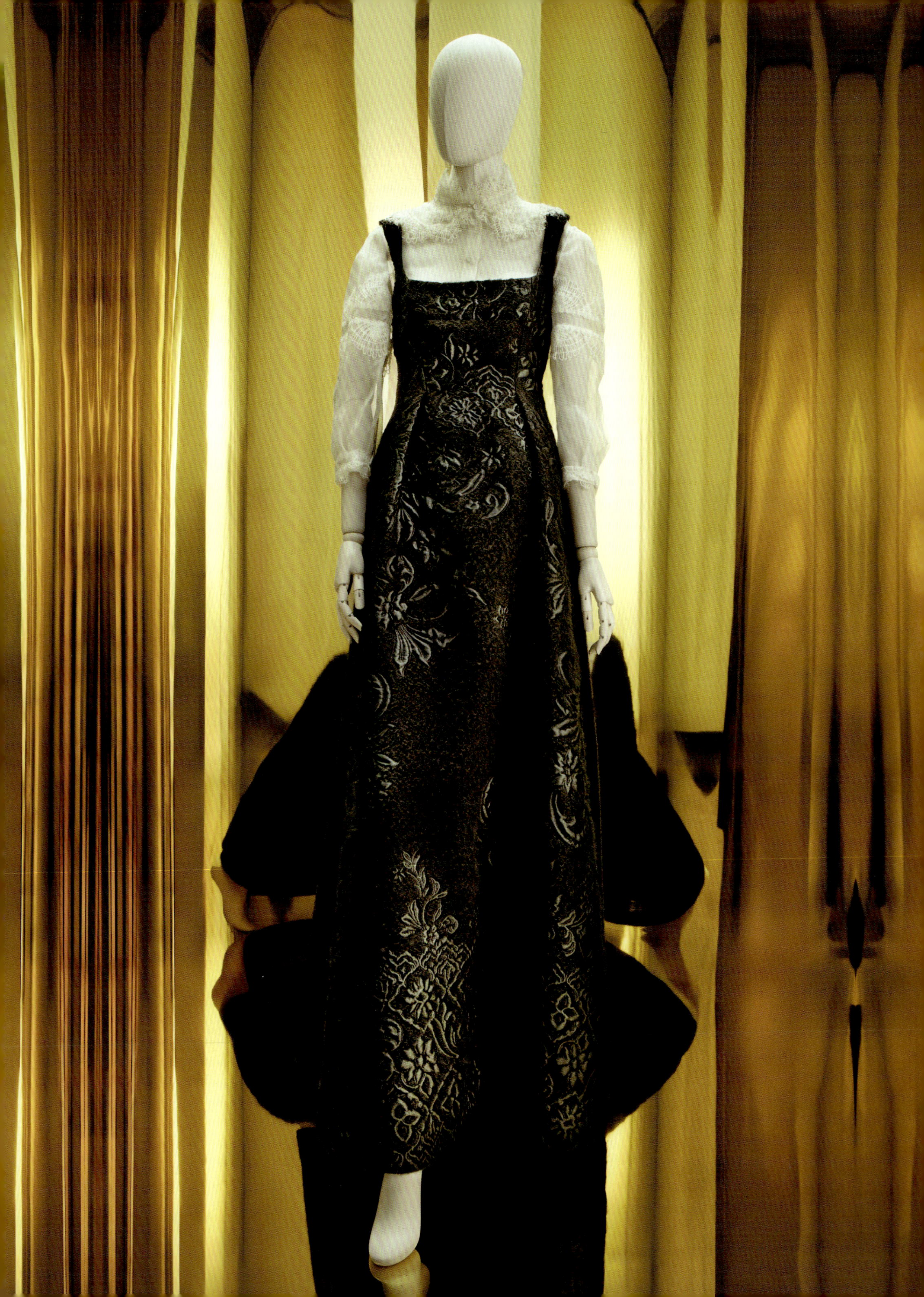

Plate 47: Ensemble, Fall 2015. Alberta Ferretti (Italian, b. 1950) for Alberta Ferretti (Italian, est. 1981). Silk, wool cotton, polyester, and nylon jacquard, silk chiffon, and nylon lace. Courtesy of Alberta Ferretti

Plate 48: *Portrait of a Woman*, 1550. Agnolo Bronzino (Italian, 1503–1572). Oil on wood; 60 x 48.8 cm. The Cleveland Museum of Art, Leonard C. Hanna Jr. Fund, 1972.121

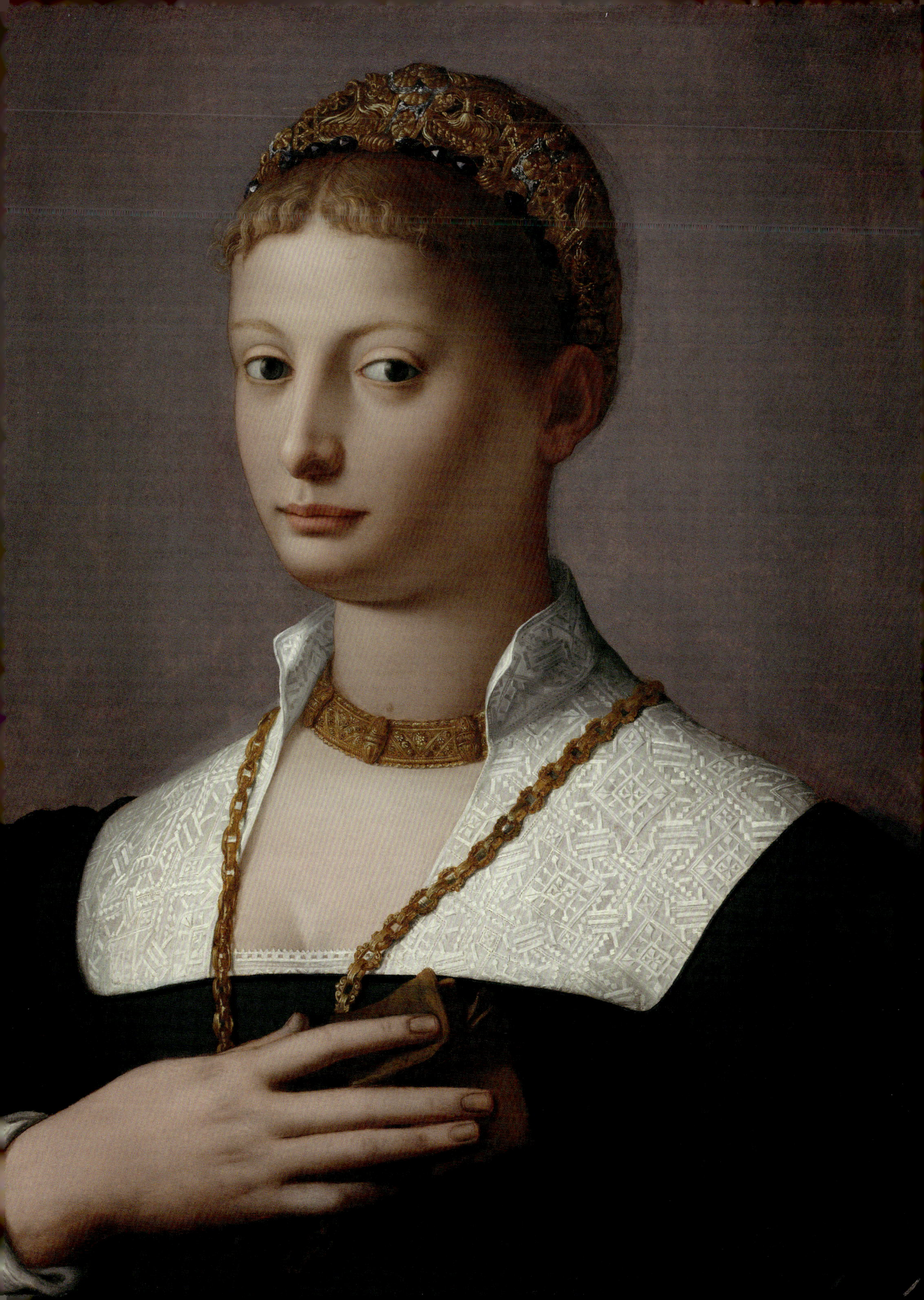

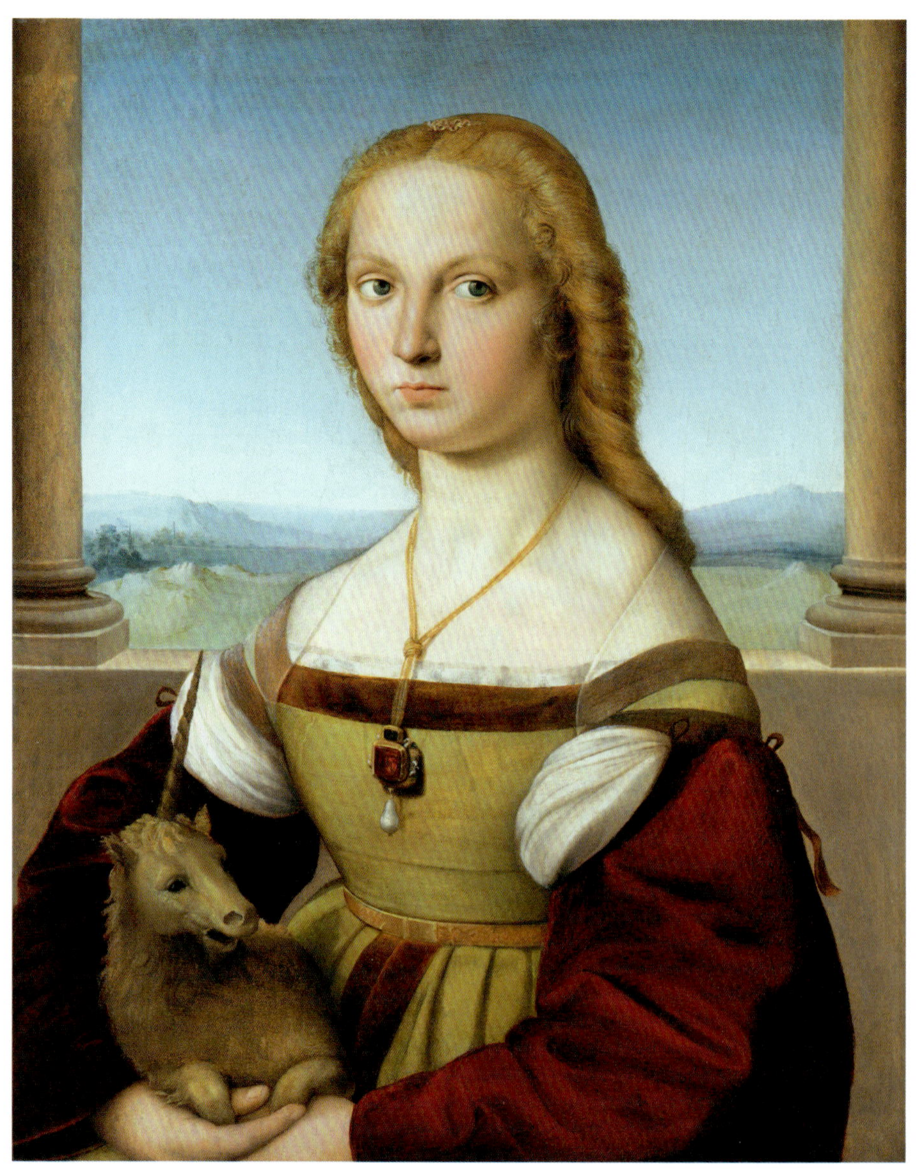

Plate 49: *Portrait of a Young Woman with Unicorn*, 1505. Raphael (Italian, 1483–1520). Oil on canvas laid down on wood; 67 x 56 cm. Galleria Borghese, Rome, 371. Photo: Scala / Ministero per i Beni e le Attività culturali / Art Resource, NY

Plate 50: Gown, 1961. Roberto Capucci (Italian, b. 1930) for Roberto Capucci (Italian, est. 1950). Silk taffeta. Courtesy of the Fondazione Roberto Capucci

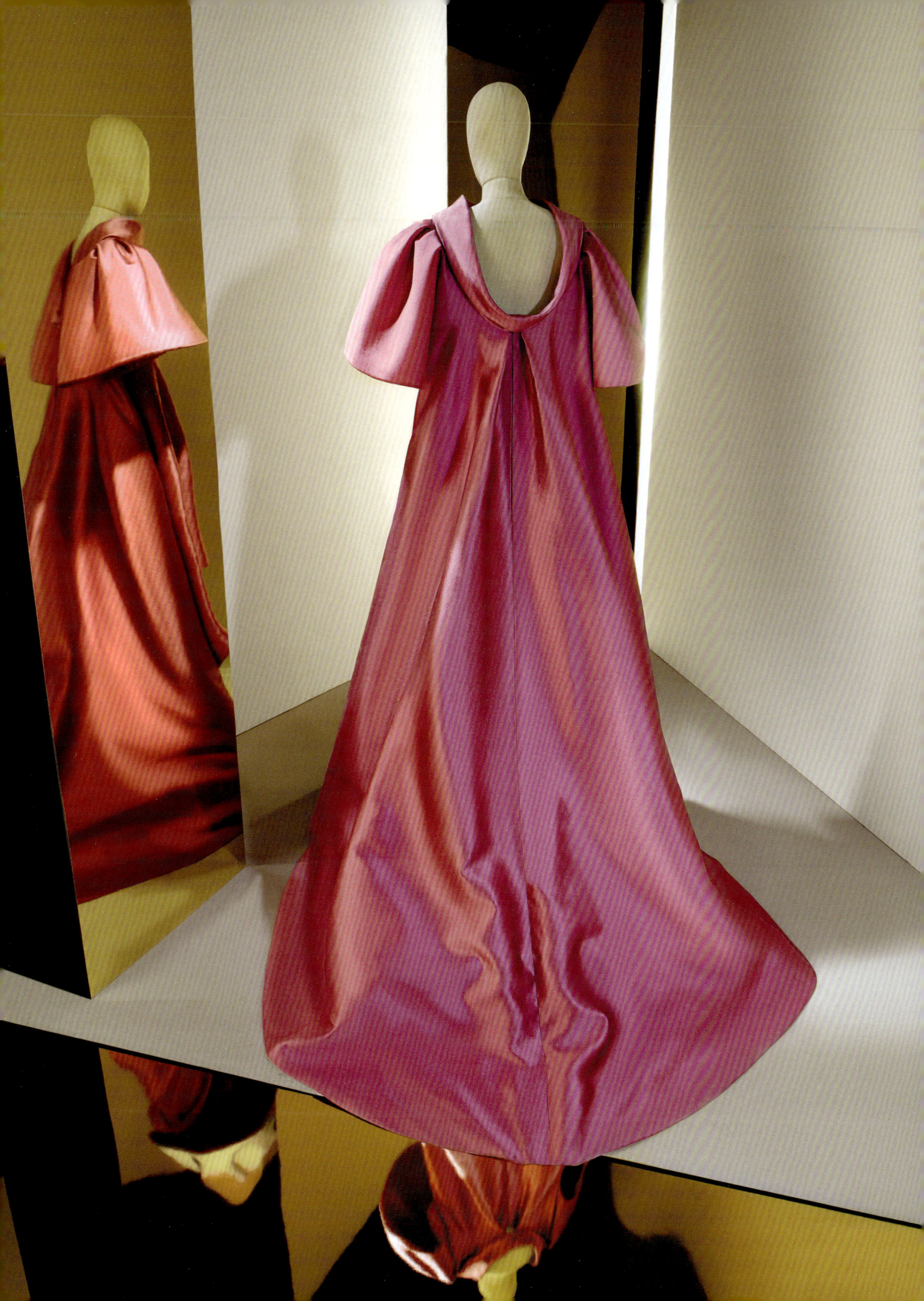

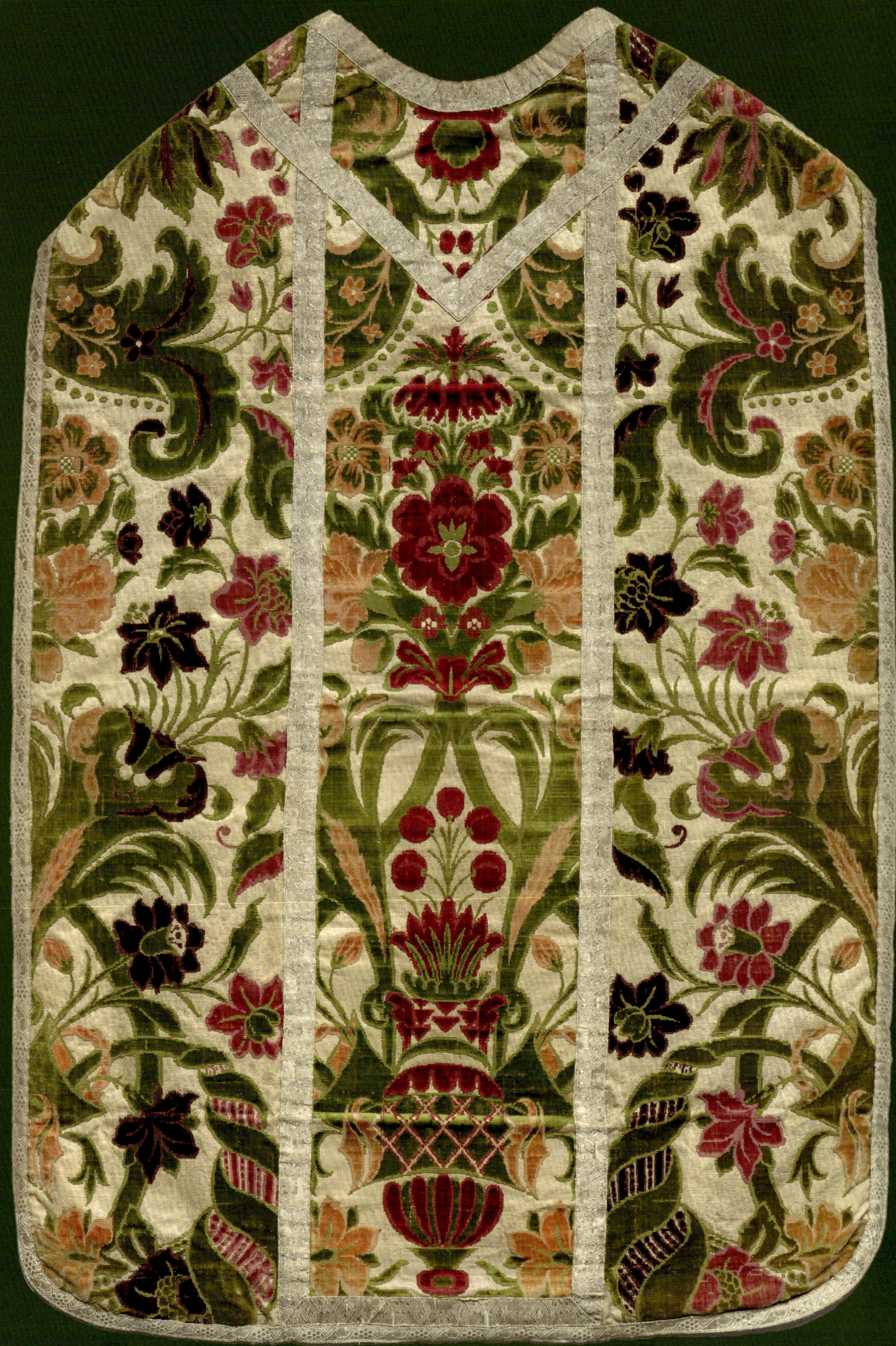

Opposite

Plate 51: Chasuble, Stole, Burse (Corporal Case), and Maniple, 1600s. Italy, Genoa. Woven polychrome silk and gilt metal threads, cut and uncut velvet; overall: 106 x 68.3 cm. The Cleveland Museum of Art, Gift of Mr. and Mrs. J. H. Wade, 1916.1443

Pages 176–77

Plate 52: Court Pump, Spring 2013. Peter Dundas (Norwegian, b. 1969) for Pucci (Italian, est. 1947). Silk velvet. Courtesy of the Villa Foscarini Rossi Shoe Museum

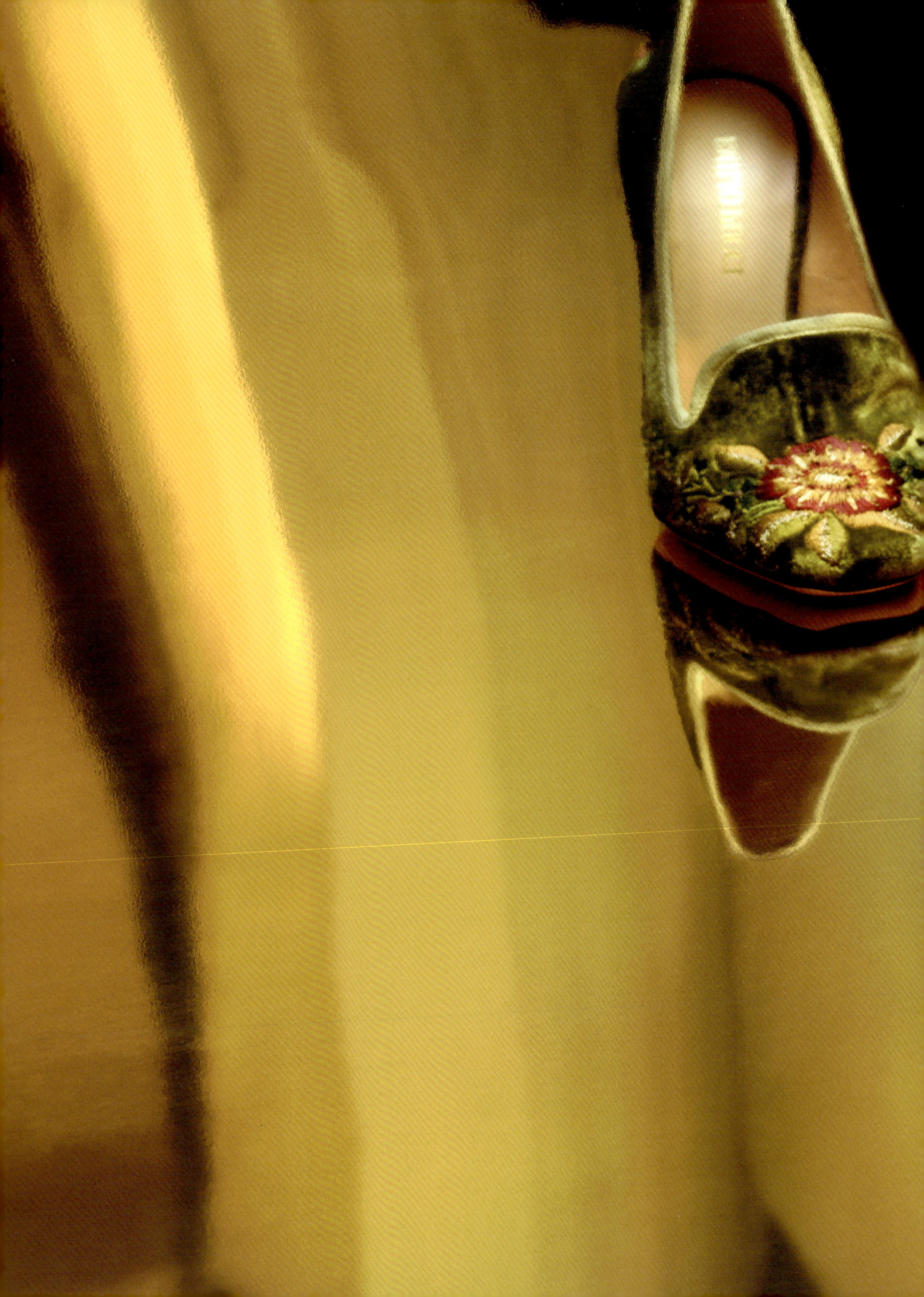

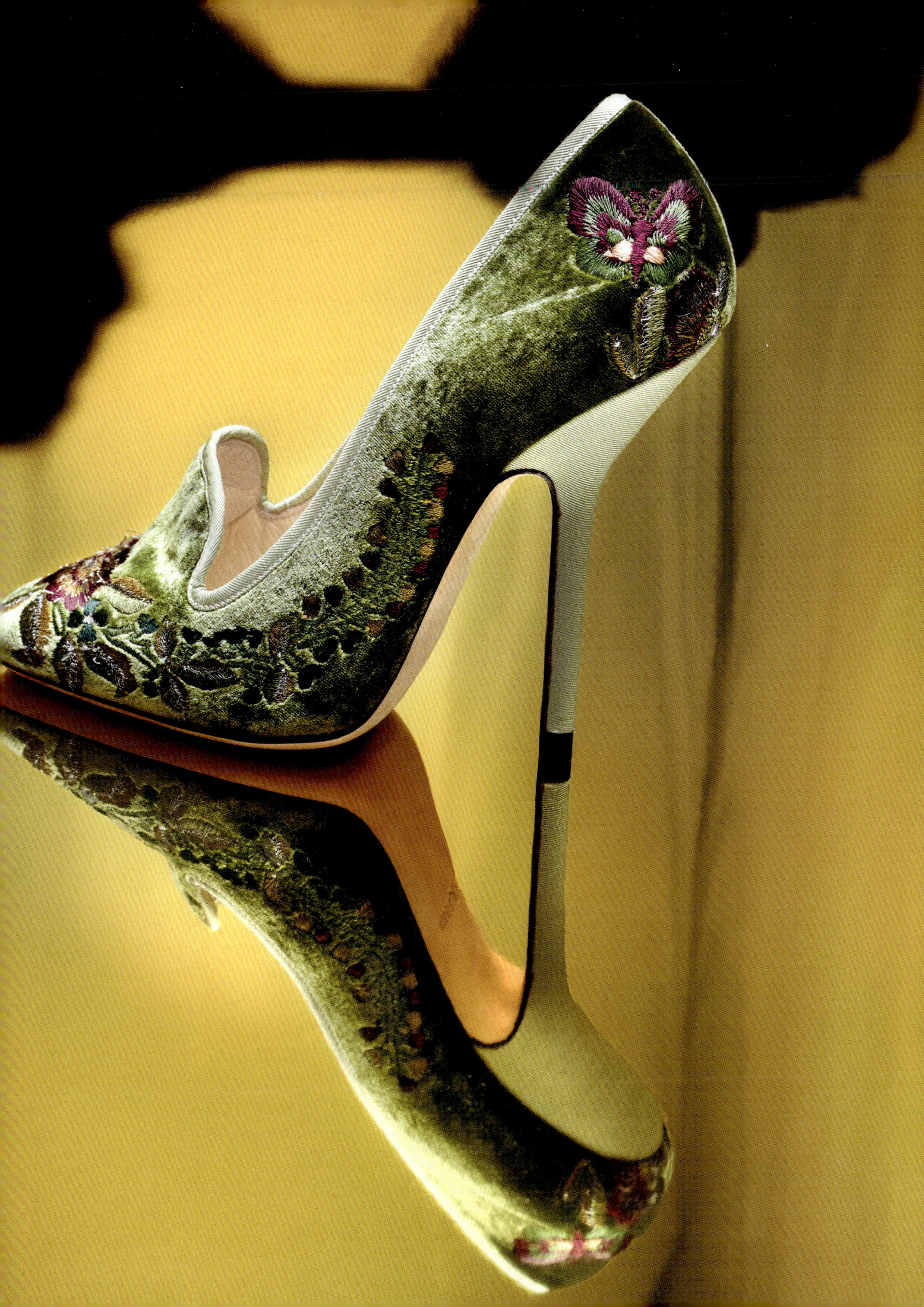

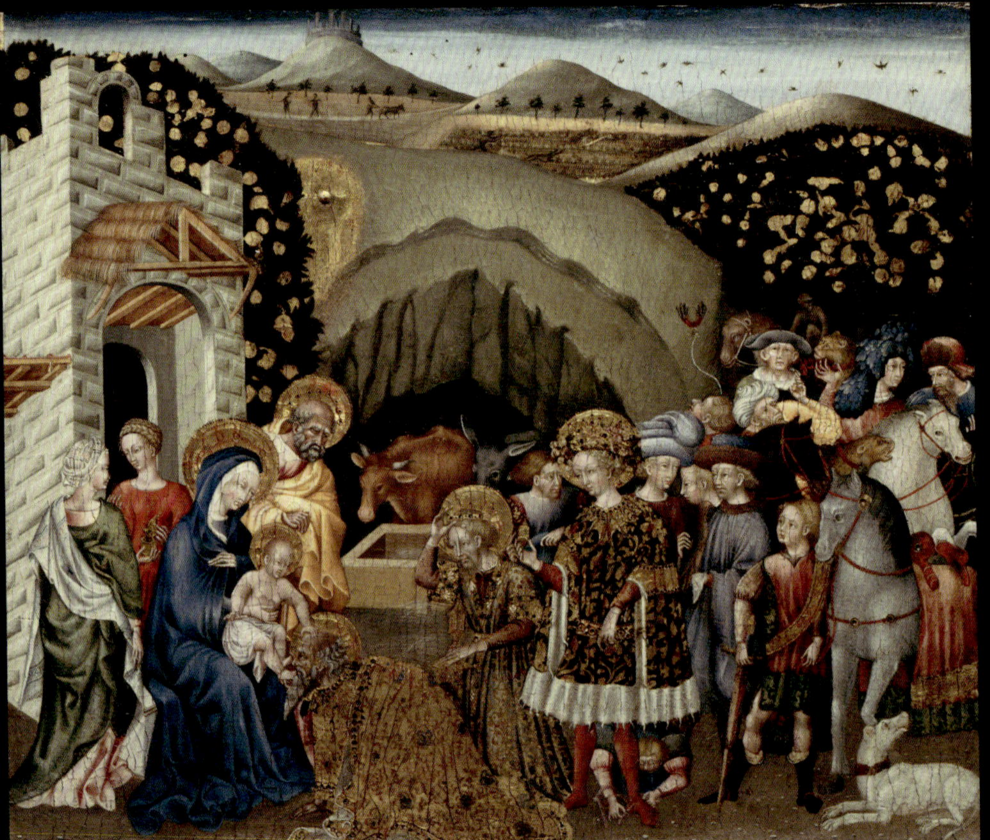

Plate 53: *The Adoration of the Magi*, 1440–45. Giovanni di Paolo (Italian, c. 1403–1482). Tempera and gold on wood panel; 38.4 x 44.3 cm. The Cleveland Museum of Art, Delia E. Holden and L. E. Holden Funds, 1942.536

Plate 54: Ensemble, Spring 2024. Marco De Vincenzo (Italian, b. 1978) for ETRO (Italian, est. 1968). Cotton, viscose chenille jacquard, and cotton twill. Courtesy of ETRO

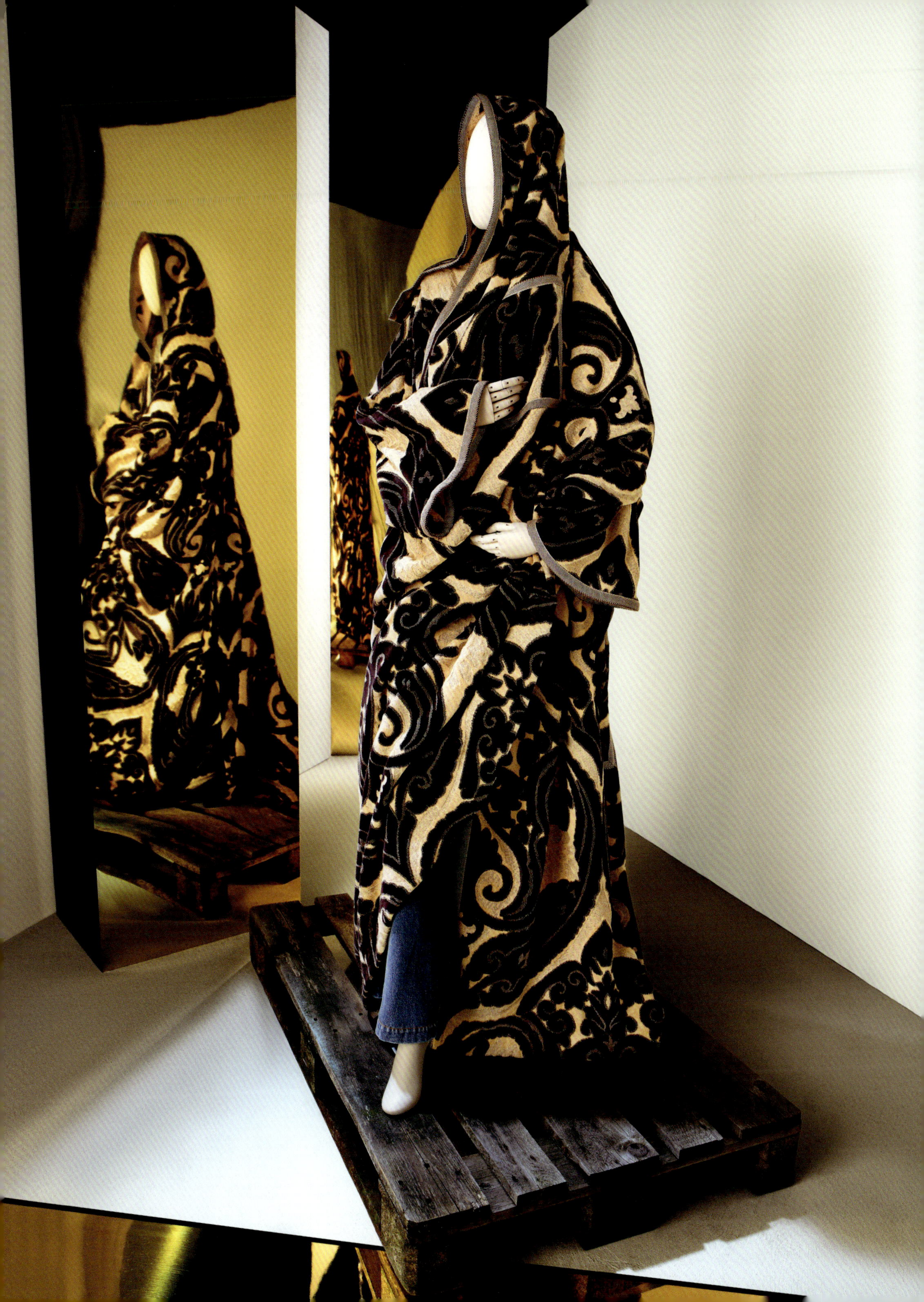

BIBLIOGRAPHY

Astor, William Waldorf. "Lucretia Borgia." *North American Review* 142, no. 350 (1886): 68–73. jstor.org /stable/25118572.

Augello, Matteo. *Curating Italian Fashion: Heritage, Industry, Institutions.* London: Bloomsbury, 2022.

Baudo, Giampietro. "Camille Miceli Talks Taking Over Pucci and Self-Confidence." *L'Officiel*, February 24, 2023. lofficielusa.com/fashion/camille-miceli-pucci-creative-director-fashion-designer.

Bew, Sophie. "When Mid-90s Prada Made Ugly Chic." *AnOther,* April 17, 2017. anothermag.com/fashion -beauty/9740/when-mid-90s-prada-made-ugly-chic.

Blanks, Tim. *Versace: The Complete Collections.* Catwalk. New Haven, CT: Yale University Press, 2021.

Borge, Jonathan. "11 Men's Fashion Trends to Watch for Fall 2025." *InStyle,* March 20, 2025. instyle.com/mens-fashion-trends-fall-winter-2025-11700048.

Boucher, François. *A History of Costume in the West.* London: Thames & Hudson, 1967.

Bowd, Stephen D. "The Republics of Ideas: Venice, Florence and the Defence of Liberty, 1525–1530." *History* 85, no. 279 (2000): 404–27. jstor.org/stable/24424949.

Brinkhof, Tim. "Art Bites: Who Was Simonetta Vespucci, Botticelli's Enduring Muse?" *Artnet*, August 17, 2024. news.artnet.com/art-world/art-bites-simonetta-vespucci-botticelli-2523589.

Buss, Chiara, ed. *Silk Gold Crimson: Secrets and Technology at the Visconti and Sforza Courts.* Milan: Silvana Editoriale, 2009.

Capella, Massimiliano. *Il Teatro alla moda: Theater in Fashion; Costumes for the Stage by Italy's Haute Couture Designers: Armani, Capucci, Coveri, Fendi, Ferretti, Gigli, Marras, Missoni, Ungaro, Valentino, Versace.* Beverly Hills, CA: Wallis Annenberg Center for the Performing Arts, 2011.

Capella, Massimiliano. *Missoni: The Great Italian Fashion.* New York: Rizzoli, 2019.

Capitani, Aurora Fiorentini, and Stefania Ricci. "The Winning Cards of Italian Fashion." In *The Sala Bianca: The Birth of Italian Fashion*, by Guido Vergani, ed. Giannino Malossi, trans. Antony Shugaar, 91–131. Exhibition catalogue. Milan: Electa, 1992.

Cappellieri, Alba. *Buccellati: A Century of Timeless Beauty.* New York: Assouline, 2021.

Caramel, Luciano, Luca Missoni, Emma Zanelli, and Ali Kazma. *Missoni: L'arte; Il colore.* Milan: Rizzoli, 2015.

Castiglione, Baldessare. *The Book of the Courtier.* Translated from the Italian and annotated by Leonard Eckstein Opdycke. London: Duckworth & Co.; New York: Charles Scribner's Sons, 1902. gutenberg.org/files /67799/67799-h/67799-h.htm#sec1.24. Originally published in 1528.

Colombo, Paolo. "Il mestiere dell'arte e il Made in Italy: Tra un passato lontano e un futuro assai prossimo." *Quaderni di ricerca sull'artigianato* 60 (2012): 41–61.

Costin, Glynis. "Gianni Versace: A Reflection on Pride, Honesty, and Women." *Women's Wear Daily*, March 1990. wwd.com/feature/article-1076461-1819641/.

Cox-Rearick, Janet. "Power-Dressing at the Courts of Cosimo de' Medici and François I: The 'Moda Alla Spagnola' of Spanish Consorts Eléonore d'Autriche and Eleonora di Toledo." *Artibus et Historiae* 30, no. 60 (2009): 39–69. jstor.org/stable/25702881.

Eagles, Lane. "'Beauty Adorns Virtue': Italian Renaissance Fashion." *Fashion History Timeline*, January 16, 2018, last updated March 5, 2019. fashionhistory.fitnyc.edu/beauty-adorns-virtue-italian -renaissance-fashion/.

Faggella, Chiara. "The New Renaissance in Italian Fashion: Ferragamo and the Post-War Era." In *Salvatore Ferragamo, 1898–1960*, edited by Stefania Ricci, 482–89. Exhibition catalogue. Milan: Electa, 2024.

The Fashion Book. London: Phaidon, 2013.

Gianfranco Ferré: Archivi del contemporaneo alla Galleria del costume di Palazzo Pitti a Firenze / Contemporary Archives at the Costume Gallery of Palazzo Pitti in Florence. I quaderni di Pitti. Florence: Giunti, 2000.

Fiore, Julia. "Why Jesus and Mary Always Wear Red and Blue in Art History." *Artsy*, December 19, 2018. artsy.net/article/artsy-editorial-jesus-mary-wear-red-blue-art-history.

Font, Lourdes. "1490–1499." *Fashion History Timeline*, published June 28, 2021, last updated June 30, 2021. fashionhistory.fitnyc.edu/1490-1499/.

Fornaciari, Federica. *Archiviare la moda: Evoluzioni di inizio millennio*. Milan: Pearson, 2022.

Frankel, David, dir. *The Devil Wears Prada*. 20th Century Fox, 2006. Streaming on Disney +.

Frick, Carole Collier. *Dressing Renaissance Florence: Families, Fortunes, and Fine Clothing*. Baltimore: Johns Hopkins University Press, 2005.

Frisa, Maria Luis, Anna Mattirolo, and Stefano Tonchi, eds. *Bellissima: Italy and High Fashion, 1945–1968*. Exhibition catalogue. Milan: Electa, 2014.

Goldthwaite, Richard A. "The Economy of Renaissance Italy: The Preconditions for Luxury Consumption." *I Tatti Studies in the Italian Renaissance* 2 (1987): 15–39. doi.org/10.2307/4603651.

Gregorovius, Ferdinand. *Lucrezia Borgia: Daughter of Pope Alexander VI*. Introduction by Samantha Morris. Las Vegas: Vita Histria, 2020.

Herald, Jacqueline. *Renaissance Dress in Italy 1450–1500*. London: Bell & Hyman; Atlantic Highlands, NJ: Humanities Press, 1981.

"History." Prada, last accessed February 1, 2025. pradagroup.com/en/group/history.html.

"The History of the It Girl." *Women's Wear Daily*, May 25, 2016. wwd.com/eye/people/gallery/the-history-of -the-it-girl-10437638/clara-bow-in-1927-bow-starredin-the-silent-film-it-after-which-she-was-nicknamed-the-it -girl-she-is-considered-hollywoods-first-sex-symbol/.

Hollander, Anne. *Seeing Through Clothes*. New York: Viking, 1978.

Jana, Rosalind. "A Brief History of Milan Fashion Week." *Vogue*, September 18, 2019. vogue.co.uk/fashion /article/history-of-milan-fashion-week.

La Galleria del naviglio presenta i nuovi arazzi di Missoni: Marzo–Aprile 1981. Exhibition catalogue. Milan: La Galleria del Naviglio, 1981.

Landini, Roberta Orsi. *Moda a Firenze, 1540–1580: Cosimo I de' Medici's Style / Lo stile di Cosimo I de' Medici*. Florence: Mauro Pagliai, 2011.

Landini, Roberta Orsi. *Moda a Firenze, 1540–1580: Lo stile di Eleonora di Toledo e la sua influenza*. Florence: Pagliai Polistampa, 2005.

Lugli, Emanuele. "The Hidden Meanings in Botticelli's Hair." Fine Arts Museums of San Francisco, January 11, 2024. famsf.org/stories/hidden-meanings-botticelli-hair.

Lunghi, Caterina. "The House of Mannequins." Bonaveri, last updated April 14, 2020. https://bonaveri.com /publications/the-house-of-mannequins/.

Lunghi, Caterina. "The Sculpting Atelier." Bonaveri, last updated April 21, 2020. https://bonaveri.com /publications/the-sculpting-atelier/.

Maisey, Sarah. "Paisley Patterns and Power Bags: Marco de Vincenzo's New Vision for Etro." *National*, April 18, 2024. thenationalnews.com/lifestyle/luxury/2024/04/19/etro-creative-director-marco -vincenzo/.

Marshall, Alexandra. "How an Italian Family Turned Paisley Prints and Haute-Hippe Garb into a 50-Year-Old Fashion Legacy." *W Magazine*, February 23, 2018. wmagazine.com/story/etro-family-50-year-anniversary-italy.

McCall, Timothy. "Materials for Renaissance Fashion." *Renaissance Quarterly* 70, no. 4 (2017): 1449–64. jstor.org/stable/26560612.

Meouchi, Lorena. "How Emilio Pucci Became the Prince of Prints." *L'Officiel*, April 15, 2021. lofficielusa.com /fashion/emilio-pucci-prints-history-book.

Missoni, Ottavio. *Una vita sul filo di lana*. Milan: Rizzoli, 2011.

Missoni, Ottavio, Mariuccia Casadio, Enzo Di Martino, Oscar Eleni, and Enrico Giustacchini. *Ottavio Missoni: Il genio del colore*. Ljubljana: Unione Italiana, 2012.

Molà, Luca. *The Silk Industry of Renaissance Venice*. Baltimore: Johns Hopkins University Press, 2000.

Monnas, Lisa. *Renaissance Velvets*. London: Victoria & Albert Museum, 2012.

O'Malley, Michelle, and Evelyn Welch. *The Material Renaissance*. Manchester: Manchester University Press, 2007.

Nardinocchi, Elisabetta. "From the Golden *Primavera* Footwear to Salvatore Ferragamo's Golden Sandals." In *Salvatore Ferragamo, 1898–1960*, edited by Stefania Ricci, 490–99. Exhibition catalogue. Milan: Electa, 2024.

Paulicelli, Eugenia. *Writing Fashion in Early Modern Italy: "Sprezzatura" to Satire*. Farnham, Surrey, UK: Ashgate, 2014.

Pezzi, Maria. "Sono pezzi da museo, ma indossateli pure." *Il Giorno*, March 26, 1979.

Phillips-Ewen, Isla. "3 Things You Might Not Know About Botticelli's Venus." *DailyArt Magazine*, May 2, 2023. dailyartmagazine.com/3-things-you-might-not-know-about-the-birth-of-venus/.

Piaggi, Anna. "Black Tie . . . White Shirt." *Vogue Italia*, September 2001. proquest.com/magazines
/black-tie-white-shirt/docview/1832516504/se-2.

Piaggi, Anna, and Gianni Brera. *Africa di Missoni per Italia 90*. Milan: Electa, 1990.

Pope, Miles. "How Wanda Ferragamo's Strength and Determination Built a Fashion Empire." *Vanity Fair,*
December 21, 2021. https://www.vanityfair.com/style/2021/12/how-wanda-ferragamos-strength-and
-determination-built-a-fashion-empire.

Ray, Meredith K. *Twenty-Five Women Who Shaped the Italian Renaissance*. Abingdon, Oxon, UK: Routledge,
2024.

Reynolds, Shola von. "Mastering Sprezzatura: The Fashionable Art of Nonchalance." *AnOther*, May 19, 2016.
anothermag.com/fashion-beauty/8699/sprezzatura-or-the-fashionable-art-of-nonchalance.

Rhodes, S. A. "Baudelaire's Philosophy of Dandyism." *Sewanee Review* 36, no. 4 (1928): 387–404.
jstor.org/stable/27534321.

Ricci, Stefania. "Florence Fascinates the World." In *Fashion in Florence: Through the Lens of Archivio Foto
Locchi, 1934–1970*, by Erika Ghilardi and Matteo Parigi Bini, 47–66. Prato: Gruppo Editoriale, 2017.

Ricci, Stefania. "L'artigianata della moda." In *La grande storia dell'artigianata*, vol. 6 of *Il Novecento*, edited by
Gloria Fossi, 229–95. Milan: Giunti, 2003.

Ricci, Stefania. "Salvatore Ferragamo, 1898–1960." In *Salvatore Ferragamo, 1898–1960*, edited by Stefania
Ricci, 416–81. Exhibition catalogue. Milan: Electa, 2024.

Ricci, Stefania. "Salvatore Ferragamo: Equilibrium and What It Means to Walk." Google Arts & Culture, last
accessed February 1, 2025. artsandculture.google.com/story/salvatore-ferragamo-equilibrium-and-what-it
-means-to-walk-museosalvatoreferragamo/oQXh4vrXcaLEIA?hl=en.

Ricci, Stefania, ed., *Ideas, Models, Inventions: The Patents and Company Trademarks of Salvatore Ferragamo
from 1929 to 1964*. Exhibition catalogue. Livorno: Sillabe, 2004.

Ricci, Stefania, ed. *Italy in Hollywood*. Exhibition catalogue. Milan: Skira, 2018.

Ricci, Stefania, and Carlo Sisi, eds. *1927: The Return to Italy; Salvatore Ferragamo and Twentieth-Century
Visual Culture*. Exhibition catalogue. Milan: Skira, 2017.

"Rome's New Day." *Interview Magazine,* August 1, 2011. interviewmagazine.com/fashion/alta-moda-rome
-summer-2011.

Roover, Raymond de. "The Medici Bank Organization and Management." *Journal of Economic History* 6,
no. 1 (1946): 24–52. jstor.org/stable/2112995.

Sabino, Catherine. "The Legendary Pitti Palace in Florence Offers a New Take on Fashion." *Forbes*, January
12, 2024. forbes.com/sites/catherinesabino/2024/01/12/the-legendary-pitti-palace-in-florence-offers-a-new
-take-on-fashion/.

Salibian, Sandra. "Ferragamo Stages Exhibition Celebrating the Brand's Founder." *Women's Wear Daily,*
October 27, 2023. wwd.com/fashion-news/fashion-features/ferragamo-stages-not-to-miss-exhibition-on-brands
-founder-life-shoes-florence-1235890869/.

Savi, Lucia. *A New History of "Made in Italy": Fashion and Textiles in Post-War Italy*. London: Bloomsbury, 2023.

Sgubin, Raffaella, and Mariuccia Casadio. *Caleidoscopio Missoni*. Gorizia: Musei Provinciali di Gorizia, 2006.

"1625–27—Anthony van Dyck, Genoese Noblewoman." *Fashion History Timeline*, May 29, 2019. fashionhistory.fitnyc.edu/1625-27-van-dyck-genoese/.

Stańska, Zuzanna. "Simonetta Vespucci: The Renaissance Top Model." *DailyArt Magazine*, March 6, 2025. dailyartmagazine.com/simonetta-vespucci-the-renaissance-top-model/.

Steele, Valerie. *The Corset: A Cultural History*. New Haven, CT: Yale University Press, 2001.

Thomas, Joe A. "Fabric and Dress in Bronzino's Portrait of Eleanor of Toledo and Son Giovanni." *Zeitschrift für Kunstgeschichte* 57, no. 2 (1994): 262–67. doi.org/10.2307/1482735.

"Timeline." Emilio Pucci Heritage Hub, last accessed January 1, 2025. emiliopucciheritage.com/timelinepucci/.

Townsend, Gertrude. "A Fifteenth Century Italian Velvet." *Bulletin of the Museum of Fine Arts* 29, no. 174 (1931): 63–65. jstor.org/stable/4170325.

"Velvet with Pomegranate Design." Walters Art Museum, last accessed January 1, 2025. art.thewalters.org/object/83.742/.

Vercelloni, Isa Tutino, ed. *Missonologia: Il mondo dei Missoni*. Milan: Electa, 1994.

Vergani, Guido. "Missoni." In *Dizionario della moda*, 796–800. Milan: Baldini Castoldi Dalai Editore, 2010. Originally published in 2003.

"Versace–Haute Couture–Runway Collection–Women." firstVIEW, last accessed January 1, 2025. firstview.com/collection_image_closeup.php?of=21&collection=656&image=260476.

Volli, Ugo. "Il faut être absolument maniéristes." *Vogue Italia*, May 1994, 136–37, 183. proquest.com/magazines/il-faut-être-absolument-maniéristes/docview/1824204554/se-2.

Watt, Melinda. "Renaissance Velvet Textiles." *Timeline of Art History*, Metropolitan Museum of Art, last modified August 1, 2011. metmuseum.org/essays/renaissance-velvet-textiles.

Yaeger, Lynn. "A History of Prada and Nylon—How the Textile Earned Its Fashionable Place." *Vogue*, September 24, 2021. vogue.com/article/prada-nylon-handbag-history.

Zargani, Luis. "Antonio Marras Fall 2024 Ready-to-Wear: A Master in Storytelling." *Women's Wear Daily*, February 21, 2024. wwd.com/runway/fall-2024/milan/antonio-marras/review/.

AUTHOR

DARNELL JAMAL-LISBY is the associate curator of fashion at
the Cleveland Museum of Art.

CONTRIBUTORS

DR. MATTEO AUGELLO is a curator, independent lecturer,
and cultural programmer in London, United Kingdom.

ALESSANDRA AREZZI BOZA is the founder of
AAB Studio in Milan, Italy.

MASSIMILIANO CAPELLA is the director of the
House Museum of the Paolo and Carolina Zani Foundation
for Art and Culture in Brescia, Italy.

LUKE MEAGHER is a fashion critic and influencer
(@HauteLeMode) in New York, NY.

STEFANIA RICCI is the director of the
Ferragamo Museum in Florence, Italy.

LUCA STOPPINI is the founder and creative director of
LucaStoppiniStudio in Milan, Italy.